Additional Praise for
The Investor's Dilemma Decoded

"This excellent book is a must-read for investors interested in acquiring a better understanding of the theory and practice of finance. It is exceptionally well-written. Complex ideas are explained thoroughly but in a simple and easy-to-understand and engaging fashion. Investors will find the numerous practical examples and advice invaluable in managing their portfolios."

—Professor Robert I. Webb, University of Virginia

"The Silks' book, The Investor's Dilemma Decoded, should be required reading for every American citizen, including college students of any background, who wants a better understanding of investments and the real-world economy. As a dually licensed attorney and CPA, the information contained in this book will help me to better communicate with my clients on the legal, tax, and business consequences associated with investments-related activities and issues which they confront on a regular basis. The book is also a good refresher for those of us who need to go back to basics to understand and address new problems and innovations on behalf of our clients."

—Clinton McGrath

"Roger has a gift of bringing clarity to virtually every item in the investor lexicon and makes it easy for the non-math layperson to understand while technical enough to challenge the most analytical professional investor's thinking. Armed with this book, any investor will be able to better able to understand, analyze and ask insightful questions about their portfolio and challenge their advisors. It is really a masterclass covering all of the important concepts and tools for analyzing asset classes, risk, returns and valuations that underly portfolio allocation and is a must read for serious investors, and a serious reference book that will still be relevant in 10 years."

—Reg Wilson, Pres EPIC Financial Consulting, Inc.

"I find the Intelligent Layman's Guide to Personal Investing to be very readable and surprisingly comprehensive given its length. I recommend it for a novice and for anyone looking to broaden their existing investment knowledge. The book discusses a number of different types of investment for someone who wants to shape their own investment strategy or who simply wants to understand what a given fund is trying to accomplish with a given investment strategy."

—**Tom Arnold, PhD., CFA, CIPM**
Joseph A. Jennings Chair in Business,
Robins School of Business, University of Richmond

"Roger and Katherine have taken a subject that can require years to master, and they have condensed the key areas into a single book that goes beyond the basics. With the information in this book, most people will be in a great position to work with their wealth manager much more effectively. For those without an advisor, this information will help them to make much better decisions."

—**Greg Freeman, Advisor Serve**

"With his latest publication of "The Investor's Dilemma Decoded" Roger Silk once again provides the reader with a timely, helpful & informative roadmap for individual investors across the wealth spectrum. Silk's detailed review and condensed reminder of investment fundamentals pairs well along with recently updated research on what specific value is attributed to receiving professional advice from reputable financial planners in today's often confusing marketplace. Whether you are already an informed investor or wish to become one, perhaps this book's most impactful and practical value is to help today's investor 'avoid making avoidable mistakes!'

—**Michael S. Millman, CFP®, ChFC®, CLU,**
AEP®, CASL, RICP, ChSNC
Independent Private Wealth Advisor

"Well-rounded and well-written book not only for the layman but a refresher for professional advisor alike. Asset classes, expected returns and risk, portfolio construction and even math! Yes, software is great but understanding the underlying math is essential and made accessible in The Investor's Dilemma Decoded. I found a gift for my team of CFPs."

—**Kevin Kroskey, CFP®, MBA, Managing Partner, True**
Wealth Design

The Investor's Dilemma Decoded

The Investor's Dilemma Decoded

Roger D. Silk, PhD
Katherine Silk, MA

WILEY

Library of Congress Cataloging-in-Publication Data is Available:

ISBN 9781394220359 (Cloth)
ISBN 9781394220373 (ePDF)
ISBN 9781394220366 (ePUb)

Cover Design: Wiley
Cover Image: © Vitalii Gulenok/Getty Images
Author Photos: Courtesy of the Authors

SKY10068021_022324

Contents

Contents

Synopsis of *The Investor's Dilemma Decoded*

The Investor's Dilemma Decoded provides readers with the background to make informed, effective decisions about their personal investing. The book explains, in a correct, thoroughly documented manner, the relevant economic and financial theory, as well as the historical performance of a wide variety of asset classes that an individual investor might consider.

The book offers some surprising insights, such as the idea that investing in 100% equities may well be the least risky option for young investors; that financial planners have been found in many studies to add significant value without "beating the market" and without exposing the client to excessive market risk; that a home is not a great investment; why Nobel Prize–winner Harry Markowitz did not use his own Nobel formula in his personal investing; and the truth about many supposed yields on futures contracts.

Chapter 1 explains the *Time Value of Money*. Everything else equal, a dollar today is worth more than a dollar tomorrow. Readers will learn how to compare the value of a dollar today to the value of a dollar in the future.

Chapter 2 models investments as a series of cash flows. The value of an investment is the present value of the sum of its future cash flows. Readers will learn how to value bonds using the present value of cash flows framework. We explain the difference between arithmetic and geometric returns, and the significance of the difference.

Chapter 3 focuses on bonds in more depth. Bonds generate returns primarily through their coupons. We review the risks to bonds, including credit risk, interest rate risk, inflation risk, and default risk. After explaining how bonds produce return, and examining how bonds have performed in the past, we show that a bond's current yield to maturity is the best predictor of its future return.

Chapter 4 focuses on equities. Many stock investors have no real understanding of how stocks generate returns. We explain that over the very long run, earnings are by far the dominant source of equities' returns. We review several useful measures for evaluating whether a market is cheap, expensive, or neither. Focusing on the Price-to-Earnings (P/E) ratio and Price-to-Book (P/B) ratio, we explain why, everything else being equal, expected returns are higher when a market has a lower valuation. Risks to equities include the risks of a decrease in valuation multiple or a decrease in earnings.

Chapter 5 examines real estate, the biggest asset class in the world (as measured by market value). We model the value of farmland as the value of a perpetual stream of cash flows. Farmland runs the risk of decreasing in value if its cash flow decreases or if interest rates rise. Homes, contrary to many perceptions, have not generally been a great investment. Over the past 120 years, the real compound annual growth rate of home prices is only about half a percent. The expected returns to apartment buildings are the net rents plus inflation. Overall, returns to income real estate are likely to equal the current yield plus some adjustment for inflation.

Chapter 6 explains that gold is not an investment, but is likely to hold its purchasing power over long periods of time. Over short periods, the price of gold is volatile. The returns to gold have been uncorrelated with the returns to equities, meaning that gold can play a diversifying role in portfolios.

Chapter 7 corrects some common misconceptions regarding futures contracts (sometimes referred to as "commodities"). We explain the arbitrage model of the pricing of futures contracts, and argue that the expected real return to commodity indices is negative. Furthermore, so-called "spot yields," "roll yields," and "collateral yields" are not true yields, and may not be positive.

Chapter 8 examines mutual funds, a vehicle used to invest in assets. We review the advantages of mutual funds, such as the fact that they allow for diversification and may offer reduced transactions costs, especially for bonds. We discuss the difference between open-ended funds, exchange-traded funds, hedge funds, and sector funds.

Chapter 9 discusses financial theories including the Markowitz Model, Capital Asset Pricing Model, Random Walk Theory, and Efficient Market Hypothesis. We examine the trade-off between risk and return in the Capital Asset Pricing Model and discuss that stock prices often follow (or seem to follow) a "random walk with drift" from day to day. We explain that while the Efficient Market Hypothesis is true in many cases, value (i.e. low market valuations) has historically outperformed the broad market over a wide range of markets and long time spans.

Chapter 10 explains the concept of financial leverage. Leveraging a portfolio can lead to greater returns and also carries greater risk. We argue that for the individual investor, investing in the already leveraged S&P 500 index or similar indices carries sufficient leverage.

Chapter 11 reevaluates the ideas of risk and uncertainty. We define *risk* as calculable statistical probabilities, whereas *uncertainty* refers to unknown possibilities. We review statistical approaches to calculating risk through traditional means, including standard deviation and variance. We revisit the importance of understanding the difference between the geometric and arithmetic mean when considering expected returns.

Chapter 12 evaluates portfolio allocation strategies, examining expected returns for equities, bonds, cash, gold, futures, and managed futures.

Chapter 13 reframes the idea of risk: Rather than focus on the risk of losing money, many investors may find that the most important risk they face is the risk of running out of money. We present 11 portfolio simulations in which investments are allocated between equities and cash. We find that for young investors, investing in 100% equities yields the *lowest* risk of running out of money, while the "riskless" alternative of 100% in cash (or equivalents) virtually guarantees disaster.

Chapter 14 explains the value of financial advisors. We report the results of a number of academic studies that find financial advisors add value in a number of ways, most of which don't involve "beating the market." Advisors help clients get appropriately invested, stay invested in the market during downturns, provide asset allocation strategies, help clients take advantage of opportunities to save taxes, and help clients rebalance their portfolios. Advisors can vastly increase a client's ability to earn the returns that are available to the informed investor who avoids avoidable mistakes. People with greater financial literacy tend to benefit more from professional advice.

Chapter 15 discusses the practical side of investing using the concepts we have introduced.

The appendix explains some of the math used in the book. You should feel absolutely free to skip it. If you took a statistics course, or if you have read finance texts, and not fully understood some of the concepts, this appendix will, we hope, help. We try to clarify some of the concepts that are often seen (or hidden) in investment contexts. In our experience, in classes and in books, the professor or author often maddeningly skips steps, so that it is a great struggle for people who don't already understand to follow. If we've done that here, please email Roger at Roger.Silk@SterlingFoundations.com and let us know. We'll try to fix it in the next edition.

Acknowledgments

W e would like to thank everyone who has contributed to the creation of this book. Writing a book is a collaborative effort, and we are fortunate to have received support from many people. Unfortunately, space doesn't allow us to name everyone who has, in one way or another, contributed to this book. Among those we can thank are the following.

We wish to thank particularly Professor Tom Arnold, of the Robins School of Business, and Jade Lintott, PhD candidate at Georgie Institute of Technology, for generously reviewing the math in this book. Of course, any errors that remain (which, please point out to us if you find them – we'll give you gift card as a thank-you) remain solely our responsibility.

In addition, we thank Shannon Swery of Sterling Foundation Management for her careful review of the final manuscript. Again, any errors that remain are our responsibility, and if you spot them and point them out to us, we'll send you a gift card as a thank-you.

For Roger, some of the ideas and understandings presented in this book represent the evolution of ideas and concepts I learned

decades ago from teachers. Among them are many of my professors at Stanford, including Anne Peck, Roger Gray, Jeffrey Williams
(now at UC Davis), Walter P. Falcon, V. "Seenu" Srinivasan, Bruce
Grundy, Scott Pearson, Harry Paarsh, and Carl Gotsch.

In addition, we thank all the readers who read our book and
gave us comments that helped us improve the book. Tyler Cowen's
feedback and comments were very valuable, and we are grateful for
his insights. We also thank Kevin Kroskey, Clinton McGrath, Jimmy
Jacobs, Tom Myers, Bruce Popper, Reg Wilson, Michael Millman,
Robert Webb, and Tom Arnold for their review of the draft.

Again, we thank everyone who contributed to the writing and
publication of this book.

Introduction

Successful investing is hard, even for professionals. As Warren Buffet's partner, Charlie Munger (himself a billionaire investor) told Howard Marks (another billionaire investor), investing is "not supposed to be easy. Anyone who finds it is easy is stupid."[1] Nevertheless, according to Buffet, "You don't need to be a rocket scientist,"[2] either.

The purpose of this book is to help you learn *how to think* about investing. Then, if you choose not to do all your investing yourself (few non-professionals do, or should), you will be able to be an informed, careful consumer of professional investment services. And evidence shows (see chapter 14) that the more you know, the more value you are likely to gain from professional advice.

---

[1] Oaktree Capital Management, 2021, "It's Not Supposed to Be Easy: How Oaktree Strives to Add Value in Uncertain Times," https://www.oaktreecapital.com/insights/oaktree-insights/special-editions/it-s-not-supposed-to-be-easy-how-oaktree-strives-to-add-value-in-uncertain-times
[2] Carol J. Loomis, "The Wit and Wisdom of Warren Buffett," *Fortune* (November 19, 2012), https://fortune.com/2012/11/19/the-wit-and-wisdom-of-warren-buffett/

We provide a framework for thinking about investing in a consistent, careful way. If you develop a thoughtful approach to your personal investing, and implement it consistently, you'll be ahead of most people, and well on your way to investment success.

This is not a get-rich-quick book. But if you want a get-rich-quick scheme, you need look no farther than Will Rogers's advice from almost a hundred years ago. "Take all your savings and buy some good stock, and hold it till it goes up, then sell it. If it don't go up, don't buy it."[3] Most get-rich-quick schemes are scams, and we won't have any more to say about them.

Instead, we will explain the basics, and build up to a systematic approach to personal investing that, while not guaranteed, should give you about the best odds that are available.

We begin with the "time value of money," and explain how that concept is used in investment analysis. We then devote chapters to bonds, stocks, real estate, gold, and commodity futures, explaining how each of these types of assets generates returns (or doesn't), and we look at long-run historical performances.

In short, we try to explain in theoretical terms how each asset produces returns, and in historical terms what those returns have been. These discussions are intended to help you understand what future returns might reasonably be. We also discuss historical volatility of returns.

We then turn to a discussion of funds as useful vehicles through which to invest, followed by four chapters that focus on portfolio theory. Portfolio theory is mainly about how to get as much return as possible for each "unit" of risk that you accept. We discuss risk in some depth, and also leverage, which can affect risk greatly.

The next two chapters discuss how to assemble a portfolio, and what you might reasonably expect from a variety of different portfolios.

---

[3] Will Rogers, "Thoughts of Will Rogers on the Late Slump in Stocks," *New York Times* (November 1, 1929), https://www.nytimes.com/1929/11/01/archives/thoughts-of-will-rogers-on-the-late-slump-in-stocks.html

We devote a chapter to the role of professional financial advisors, and conclude that for many people, the right professional financial advisor offers a sound value proposition.

We have tried to present the material as clearly as possible, without dumbing it down. There are zillions of dumbed-down books out there promising that it's easy. If it were that easy, you would probably already know it, and wouldn't have picked up this book.

However, if you're willing to put in a bit of effort to learn the basics, we believe that the concepts and tools provided here will give you an excellent shot at building real, life-changing wealth over time.

You may notice that there are footnotes in this book. If you don't like footnotes, please feel free to ignore them. They are there to offer additional detail that didn't quite fit into the text and to show the source of quotations or other claims.

There is some math in this book. You don't necessarily need to know the math, but we've found that there are too many people out there giving advice, including some recognized "experts" whose failure to understand the math leads them into errors that could be very costly to people who rely on their advice. So we've included the math for the people who want it.

Even if you don't understand everything, you'll still be able to gain valuable ways of thinking about different asset classes, about risk, and about where returns come from and what might be expected in the future.

We've included a mathematical appendix for those who want a refresher on the math.

Chapter 1

Time Value of Money

Which is worth more: one dollar today, or one dollar tomorrow?

The Standard Theory

The standard theory of the time value of money states that a dollar in your hand today is worth more than the same dollar in your hand in the future. This is true even if there is no inflation.

Here's one example. Would you rather have $100 today, or $100,000,000 in a million years? Even if you were absolutely certain that the $100,000,000 would be "yours" in a million years, it would be worth nothing to you, because you would not expect to be around to enjoy it. Further, even if your great, great, great, etc., grandchildren could be assured of receiving it, it would probably mean little to you.

But what about more realistic waiting periods? For example, suppose you have the choice between $100 now, and $100 in a year from now. The standard theory says that the rational person will always choose the $100 now, because you could do everything with $100 now that you could do with it in a year from now, and you could invest it to earn interest between now and then.

This standard theory is right, but it has a few important assumptions buried in it. The most important of these assumptions is that you can save money at no cost and at no risk between now and the future. In thinking about the standard theory, or any economic theory, it is important to remember the assumption of "all other things equal" (from the Latin, ceteris paribus).

Assumption: You Can Save Money at No Cost

The assumption that you can save money at no cost means that if you have a certain amount of money today, you can save that money for any period at no cost. No cost means that you don't have to pay any storage charges, or insurance charges, or handling charges, or taxes, or charges of any kind.

In the last hundred years or so, citizens in developed economies have gotten used to the idea that they can save money, in a bank for example, and not have to pay for the service. We will not be surprised if financial historians of the future look back and see this as a sort of financial magical thinking, which has indirectly had catastrophic costs by making the entire banking system unstable.

In general, if you want to store any valuable commodity, you would have to do it yourself – perhaps in your home, in a rented vault, or perhaps even burying it in the ground. You would not expect that you can store it securely for free.

In principle, money is no different. But the way banking has developed over the past several hundred years, bankers, with the willing cooperation of their depositors, have purported to "save" money for free for their depositors. Of course, nothing is free. The bankers have been willing to offer this service for free so that they could get their hands on the money. Do they "save" it for you? Absolutely not. They lend it out. This lending puts your money at risk, and generates income for the bank, provided that the bank doesn't suffer too many loan losses. If the bank suffers too many loan losses, they may not even be able to pay you back the money that you deposited.[1]

Despite the inherent instability of this practice, it has become so entrenched in the modern banking system that it seems like a permanent feature. We don't think history will prove it so, but for the time being (and perhaps for the foreseeable future), it is.

Assumption: You Can Save Money at No Risk

The assumption that you can save money at no risk of not getting it back (in other words, that you can save money with the guarantee that you'll receive 100% of it back) is easy to understand in principle. It is a bit surprising that so many people believe it to be literally true. There is no truly riskless proposition in the material world. It may be the case that some things carry extremely low risk, but in our world, that risk is never actually zero.

Nevertheless, most people in the developed world behave as though they can put money in the bank, and have no risk of not getting it back in the future.

As long as you can put money in the bank and expect to receive it back in the future, and the bank doesn't charge you for the service, a dollar now is worth more than a dollar in the future, because you can turn it into a dollar in the future by storing it. Anything you can do with a dollar in a year, you could do with a dollar now because you could just wait. But you can do things with the dollar now, such as spend it now, that you cannot do with a dollar in a year. So the dollar now is worth at least as much as the dollar in the future.[2]

---

[1] In the current system, deposits may be "insured" by government guarantees. These are not true insurance, because it is not optional, it is not truly risk-based, and it is ultimately backed by taxpayer funds. Furthermore, it is very likely the case that deposit insurance results in bankers taking greater risks with depositors' funds than they would without it, and thereby make the entire system less stable. The financial crisis of 2008 was a case in point, and ended up costing taxpayers at least half a trillion dollars. (See Deborah Lucas, 2019, "Measuring the Costs of Bailouts," *Annual Review of Financial Economics* 11: 85–100.) For a discussion of how deposit insurance causes instability, see Asli Demirgüc-Kunt and Enrica Detragiache, 2002, "Does Deposit Insurance Increase Banking System Stability? An Empirical Investigation," *Journal of Monetary Economics* 49: 1373–1406.

[2] The pure time value of money analysis does not depend on the assumption of there being no risk of not getting your money back, but the assumption simplifies the analysis.

Time Value of Money and Compound Growth

Economists, financial professionals, and talking heads often conflate the time value of money with the phenomenon of compound growth. You don't need to worry about the finer points of theory as discussed earlier, but you do need to understand the math of exponential or compound growth.

Perhaps the easiest way to understand compound growth is to think in terms of "interest on interest." Suppose you have $100 and you can earn 10% per year. (For the purpose of illustration, we assume that the 10% earnings are risk-free, but remember the real world is never risk-free.) Table 1.1 shows how your money would grow if you get paid interest at the end of every year, and reinvest the interest.

Table 1.1   Compound Growth Assuming Interest Payments Are Reinvested

Year	Beginning Principal	Interest	Ending Principal
1	100.00	10.00	110.00
2	110.00	11.00	121.00
3	121.00	12.10	133.10
4	133.10	13.31	146.41
5	146.41	14.64	161.05
6	161.05	16.11	177.16
7	177.16	17.72	194.87
8	194.87	19.49	214.36
9	214.36	21.44	235.79
10	235.79	23.58	259.37
11	259.37	25.94	285.31
12	285.31	28.53	313.84
13	313.84	31.38	345.23
14	345.23	34.52	379.75
15	379.75	37.97	417.72
16	417.72	41.77	459.50
17	459.50	45.95	505.45
18	505.45	50.54	555.99
19	555.99	55.60	611.59
20	611.59	61.16	672.75

In the first year, you earn $10 of interest, which is 10% of your $100. But in the second year, you earn $11, because you earned your 10% on your original $100, but you also earned 10% on your $10 of interest. That "interest on interest" earned you $1 in year two. You earned a total of $11, which could be thought of as $10 on your original $100, plus $1 on the interest you earned the first year.

Each year, you still earn the $10 on your original $100, but the "interest on interest" gets bigger every year. By the ninth year, you are earning more "interest on interest" than on your original $100!

This compound growth is the phenomenon that people get so excited about. Almost everyone who has ever amassed significant wealth legitimately (i.e. other than by stealing it) has done it, at least in part, by putting compound interest, or exponential growth (another term for the same phenomenon), to work. Just in case you're not convinced, here is a bit of *argumentum ad verecundiam* (just a fancy sounding way of saying *argument from authority*).

"Compounding is the magic of investing."

—Jim Rogers

"The effects of compounding even moderate returns over many years are compelling, if not downright mind boggling."

—Seth Klarman

"Understanding both the power of compound interest and the difficulty of getting it is the heart and soul of understanding a lot of things."

—Charlie Munger

"The sooner you start, the more compounding can do for you. If, beginning at the age of twenty, you sock away just $100 a month in stocks, and your portfolio compounds at 10%, which is what stocks have provided historically, you will be a millionaire when you retire at sixty-five."

—Ralph Wanger[3]

---

[3] All these quotations were sourced from http://www.valuewalk.com/2016/10/compounding-quotes/. We have not independently verified them.

Comparing Values Across Time

The ability to compare values across time, a process called *present value analysis*, is useful to understand the process of building wealth.

Suppose I told you that a gallon of regular gas is $3.50 at the Exxon station and $3.65 at the Chevron station down the block. Assuming both stations are equally convenient, safe, busy, etc., you would have no difficulty telling me that the Exxon station was a better deal.

But what if I told you I was going to buy an item you're selling, and I'll pay you either $65 for it now, or $68 in a year. Now how easy it is for you to say which is a better deal? As we explained in the previous section, you know that a dollar today is worth more than a dollar in a year. But is $65 today worth more than $68 in a year?

For most people, thinking about money across time does not come naturally. You have to work at it, just as you do for most skills. It's not hard, but you do have to practice.

It's great to have the tools of present value in your toolbox, but it's even better if you know how to use them. You learn by practice. You might keep your eye out for retail offers such as per month pricing versus subscription discounts for longer terms, for investment advertisements, and for claims made by politicians, and apply the tools of present value analysis where you can.

Real-World Compounding Versus "Pure" Theory of Time Value of Money

In the basic models discussed in this chapter, we always assumed a known and constant rate of return. However, in the real world, there is always risk, and rates of return are rarely, if ever, stable over time. Even so, these models can give you a rough idea of what something is worth now compared to some time in the future. As long as you don't believe that your models represent reality, you will be well served by being as comfortable as possible with making present value calculations, future value calculations, and in general using the concepts of compounding in a wide variety of situations.

In order to compare the value of $65 today to $68 in a year, you may use the following formula:

$$FV = PV(1 + r)^t \tag{1}$$

In this formula, *FV* represents the *future value* of your investment in the future, while *PV* represents the *present value*, or value today, of your investment. The length of time, in years, is represented by *t* while the rate of return is represented by *r*. (This formula is explained in the Appendix to this chapter.)

For the purposes of the above example, $65 is the *present value*, $68 is the *future value*, and *t* is one year.

Whether $65 now is worth more than $68 in a year, depends on your own personal *discount rate*. A rate of 4.6% per year makes $65 now equal to $68 in a year. There are several ways to think about this, but the most useful one for investing is that if the market rate of interest (e.g. the rate on one-year loans of the same risk category as the loan in question) is 4.6%, then the market value of $65 now is the same as the market value of $68 in a year.

Appendix

The Math of Compounding

In the example in this chapter, interest was compounded each year. It is possible to compound more often, for example monthly, weekly, or daily. It turns out that you can even compound continuously and still get a meaningful answer. If you can use a calculator, you can make all the time value of money calculations you will need. It is often easier, however, to use a computer spreadsheet. You can also do the calculations using natural logs and the exponential function, but in my experience the need or usefulness of those in the real world has been limited.

There is one equation that you really should know your way around backwards and forwards, because that equation is at the heart of the miracle of compounding. Here it is:

$$FV = PV(1 + r)^t \qquad (1)$$

Where *FV* is the Future Value (the value you'll have in the future), *PV* is the Present Value (the value you have now), *r* is the growth rate (or interest rate) per period, and *t* is the number of periods. Often, *r* is expressed as an annual interest rate, and *t* is measured in years. So, for example, if the *PV* is $100, *r* is 10%, and *t* is 7, the future value will be $194.87.

Here is the calculation:

$$FV = 100 \times (1 + 0.1)^7 = 100 \times 1.1^7 = 100 \times 1.9487 = 194.87 \quad (2)$$

You might have noticed that you could have looked this up in Table 1, because that table used $100 as the beginning value, 10% annual interest, and compounded annually.

More Frequent Compounding

What if we used the same 10% annual interest rate, but compounded twice a year? The formula is equation (1), but now *r* is 5% because interest is paid twice, so we divide 10% by 2 and t is 14, because there are now twice as many periods. So the calculation is:

$$FV = 100 \times (1 + 0.05)^{14} = 100 \times 1.05^{14} = 100 \times 1.9799 = 197.99 \tag{3}$$

We can generalize the compounding formula to

$$FV = PV\left(1 + \frac{r}{n}\right)^{nt} \tag{4}$$

where r is the annual interest rate, t is the number of years, and n is the number of times we're compounding during the year.

As we make n larger and larger, we are compounding over shorter and shorter periods of time. We can use calculus to show that as n goes to infinity, the limit of the function becomes:

$$FV = PVe^{rt} \tag{5}$$

where e is the base of the natural log function, approximately 2.71828.

You don't have to understand where equation (4) or (5) comes from to use it. For most purposes, either one is fine.

A Little Algebra

Equations (1), (2), and (3) are good if we know the value now, the interest rate, and the number of years. But what if we know how much we're going to get in the future, when we're going to get it, and the interest rate, and we want to calculate what that is worth today? We want the present value, and we can get it by just rearranging one of our equations. Let's take equation (1) and solve it for PV. We get:

$$PV = \frac{FV}{(1 + r)^t} \tag{6}$$

Rearranging equation (5) gives us

$$PV = \frac{FV}{e^{rt}} = FVe^{-rt} \tag{7}$$

Given any three of PV, FV, r and t, it is possible to solve for the fourth one. Above we gave equations solving for FV and PV. As an exercise, you can try solving for r, and then for t. Following are the answers.

$$r = \sqrt[t]{\frac{FV}{PV}} - 1 = \left(\frac{FV}{PV}\right)^{\left(\frac{1}{t}\right)} - 1 \tag{8}$$

For example, 55 years ago a man bought a building for $200,000. Now the building is worth $10 million. His annual rate of return is:

$$.0737 = \left(\frac{10,000,000}{200,000}\right)^{\left(\frac{1}{55}\right)} - 1 \tag{9}$$

The man earned a 7.37% compound annual rate of return.

Fortunately, calculators and computers make it simple to perform these calculations.

Now we will solve for t. The equation is:

$$t = \frac{ln\left(\frac{FV}{PV}\right)}{ln(1 + r)}, \tag{10}$$

where ln is the natural logarithm function.

Again, it is easy to perform these calculations with a calculator or computer. For example, suppose you put $1,000 into an investment that you expect will earn 5% each year indefinitely. How long would it take to grow to $10,000?

$$t = \frac{ln\left(\frac{10,000}{1000}\right)}{ln(1 + .05)} = 47.19 \tag{11}$$

Exercises

Here are 40 sample problems, consisting of 10 each where you are to solve for *PV, FV, r,* and *t*. The answers are on the following page.

Table 1.2   Chapter 1 Exercises

Exercise #	FV	r	t	PV
1	795		14	76.51
2	734	0.068		210.30
3	17	0.094		7.57
4	246	0.122	7	
5		0.018	14	303.03
6	752		19	59.34
7		0.023	15	396.02
8	875		2	685.25
9		0.168	15	6.91
10	972	0.09		206.06
11	723	0.147	19	
12	56	0.055		47.69
13	542	0.175	10	
14		0.082	4	227.64
15	412	0.05		338.95
16	669	0.086	15	
17		0.076	19	98.71
18	325	0.178	16	
19	438	0.009		372.76
20	417		9	171.16
21	848	0.049	20	
22	490		18	282.84
23	704		18	329.96
24		0.012	5	77.25
25		0.159	0	321.00
26	505	0.084	18	
27	592	0.042		319.38
28	754		13	95.79
29	422		20	25.78
30	933	0.04		498.14
31	667	0.127	19	
32	91		10	16.95
33	166	0.179	2	
34	875	0.046		426.09
35	293	0.017		278.55
36		0.033	13	9.84
37		0.167	1	419.88
38	530		12	61.26
39	391	0.07	5	
40		0.117	9	237.17

Answers

Table 1.2   Chapter 1 Answers

Exercise #	FV	r	t	PV
1	795	0.182	14	76.5107
2	734	0.068	19	210.3014
3	17	0.094	9	7.5734
4	246	0.122	7	109.8968
5	389	0.018	14	303.0266
6	752	0.143	19	59.3389
7	557	0.023	15	396.0233
8	875	0.13	2	685.2533
9	71	0.168	15	6.9122
10	972	0.09	18	206.0579
11	723	0.147	19	53.3867
12	56	0.055	3	47.6904
13	542	0.175	10	108.0490
14	312	0.082	4	227.6384
15	412	0.05	4	338.9534
16	669	0.086	15	194.0791
17	397	0.076	19	98.7091
18	325	0.178	16	23.6352
19	438	0.009	18	372.7633
20	417	0.104	9	171.1648
21	848	0.049	20	325.7512
22	490	0.031	18	282.8395
23	704	0.043	18	329.9553
24	82	0.012	5	77.2523
25	321	0.159	0	321.0000
26	505	0.084	18	118.2400
27	592	0.042	15	319.3787
28	754	0.172	13	95.7883
29	422	0.15	20	25.7843
30	933	0.04	16	498.1363
31	667	0.127	19	68.7973
32	91	0.183	10	16.9509
33	166	0.179	2	119.4209
34	875	0.046	16	426.0898
35	293	0.017	3	278.5510
36	15	0.033	13	9.8353
37	490	0.167	1	419.8800
38	530	0.197	12	61.2556
39	391	0.07	5	278.7776
40	642	0.117	9	237.1682

Chapter 2

Basic Investment Analysis

F rom a financial point of view, all investments may be viewed in terms of cash flows. When you make an investment, cash goes out. Some time (or times) in the future (we hope) cash flows back in. In this chapter, we look at some of the basic ways of analyzing such cash flows.

Basic Terminology

In financial terms, an investment is the exchange of cash for some other asset (which could be a business, a share in a business, or a loan) with the expectation of receiving a greater value of cash in return at some future date.

Many sophisticated investors think about investment returns almost exclusively in terms of cash flows. A cash flow is money going out or money coming in. The *return* is then calculated from the cash flows, using the time value of money concepts. In everyday language, people tend to use a few different terms when speaking of cash flows. Common terms include *interest*, *principal*, *dividends*, and *capital gains*. A few examples will help illustrate these terms.

A simple investment might consist of you depositing $100 into a bank account, and receiving back $101 after one year. In this case, the $100 you deposit, and the $100 you get back, are the *principal*. The additional $1 cash flow you receive is referred to as *interest*.

A stock purchase is another example of an investment. An investor might purchase a share of stock for $100, and receive a payment each quarter, called a *dividend*, of $.50, for a total of $2 in a year. If the investment were then sold for $103 after a year, the $3, the difference between the selling price and the purchase price, would be a *capital gain*. The investor's *total return* in this case would be the sum of all the dividends received, $2, plus the capital gain of $3, for a total of $5. Again, the $100 in this example is the *principal*.

Modeling an Investment as a Series of Cash Flows

Bonds are a common form of investment, in which you invest a certain amount, such as $1,000, for a certain period, such as five years. Most bonds pay interest on a regular basis. In the United States, most bonds pay a *coupon* every six months. For example, if the bond mentioned earlier in this paragraph (which we'll call *bond 1*, and refer to later) has a 5% coupon, then you'd receive payments corresponding to 5% of $1,000 every year.

Suppose you paid $1,000 for the bond now. If you held the bond to maturity (meaning that you held it for the entire length of the period the bond was supposed to last; in this case, five years), you would receive $50 of interest in a year ($25 twice a year), another $50 in two years, and so on, until at the end of the fifth year you receive the final $25 interest payment, as well as your $1,000 principal.

The heart of all investment analysis involves the projection of the cash flows involved, and then the adjustment of the expected cash flows for the time value of money. You can make allowances for risk in the way you adjust the expected cash flows for time value. You might also build more complicated models (which we don't do here) by explicitly applying a probability to the future receipt of any specific cash flow.

Net Present Value

In the previous chapter, we explained how to calculate the present value of an amount of money at one future period. When there are multiple future periods, we can apply the same tools multiple times.

In theory, and in practice, you can calculate the present value of a stream of cash flows by applying the present value formula to each cash flow individually, and then summing them all up. This is easy to do with a spreadsheet. For example, the bond discussed earlier would be analyzed as follows, assuming that the *discount rate*, which we called *r* in the previous chapter, was 5% per year. When people refer to a model similar to this model, they may refer to *r* as the *discount rate*, the *interest rate*, or the *rate of return*.

First, we map out the cash flows in Table 2.1 as follows:

Table 2.1   Cash Flows from Bond

Time 0	Time 1	Time 2	Time 3	Time	Time 5
−$1,000	+$50	+$50	+$50	+$50	+$1,050

We now calculate the present value of each cash flow, using the present value formula. We show the calculation in Table 2.2 below.

Table 2.2   Present Value of Cash Flows from Bond with Discount Rate of 5%

	Time 0	Time 1	Time 2	Time 3	Time	Time 5
Cash Flow	−$1,000	+$50	+$50	+$50	+$50	+$1,050
PV Formula	$\frac{-1000}{(1+.05)^0}$	$\frac{50}{(1+.05)^1}$	$\frac{50}{(1+.05)^2}$	$\frac{50}{(1+.05)^3}$	$\frac{50}{(1+.05)^4}$	$\frac{1050}{(1+.05)^5}$
PV	−1,000	47.62	45.35	43.19	41.14	822.70

Summing up all the numbers in the bottom row, we get a number called the *net present value* ("NPV") of the stream of cash flows. It is zero. Why? Because the present values of all the cash flows, calculated at 5%, exactly equals the amount we invested at time zero.

That is not coincidence. It is a direct result of the fact that we set the cash flows on the basis of a 5% annual return.

The net present value of a stream of cash flows does not have to be zero. In fact, it will only be zero when the discount rate and the original rate of return are exactly equal.

Let us take again the example of the bond with $50 coupon payments. Suppose that the day after the bond was issued at a price of $1,000, interest rates (by which we mean r in the model) immediately fell to 4%. We'll now calculate the net present value of the stream of cash flows. For convenience, we'll ignore the passing of one day. Notice that the cash flows themselves are exactly the same. The only thing that is changing is the discount rate we're using to calculate the NPV. We demonstrate this in Table 2.3 below.

Table 2.3   Present Value of Cash Flows from Bond with Discount Rate of 4%

	Time 0	Time 1	Time 2	Time 3	Time	Time 5
Cash Flow	−$1,000	+$50	+$50	+$50	+$50	+$1,050
PV Formula	$\frac{-1000}{(1+.04)^0}$	$\frac{50}{(1+.04)^1}$	$\frac{50}{(1+.04)^2}$	$\frac{50}{(1+.04)^3}$	$\frac{50}{(1+.04)^4}$	$\frac{1050}{(1+.04)^5}$
PV	−1,000	44.08	46.23	44.45	42.74	863.02

Now, when we sum up the individual present values, we get $44.52. If we owned the bond that we paid $1,000 for, we would find that it was now worth $1,044.42. Because the discount rate is now lower, the value of each future payment is higher. If the discount rate were 6% instead of 5%, what do you think would happen to the NPV of the cash flows? Or, put differently, what would happen to the price of the bond that started at $1,000? Let's look. Again, notice that the cash flows are exactly the same. All that's changing is the discount rate.

With the higher discount rate, the present value of the future payments is lower. Now the future payments sum to only $957.88. This example, in Table 2.4 below, illustrates that bond prices fall when interest rates rise.

Table 2.4   Present Value of Cash Flows from Bond with Discount Rate of 6%

	Time 0	Time 1	Time 2	Time 3	Time	Time 5
Cash Flow	−1,000	+$50	+$50	+$50	+$50	+$1,050
PV Formula	$\dfrac{-1000}{(1+.06)^0}$	$\dfrac{50}{(1+.06)^1}$	$\dfrac{50}{(1+.06)^2}$	$\dfrac{50}{(1+.06)^3}$	$\dfrac{50}{(1+.06)^4}$	$\dfrac{1050}{(1+.06)^5}$
PV	−1,000	47.17	44.50	41.98	39.61	784.62

The inverse relationship between bond prices and interest rates seems counterintuitive for some people. The following explanation is meant to grant you some intuition. Say you have $1,000 today and you have a choice: You can invest in a bond that pays out coupons of 5% per year, or $50, OR you can invest in something else which pays you an interest rate of 6%. Clearly, you would rather invest in that "something else" which gives you a higher rate of interest. In other words, if the prevailing interest rate is higher, your opportunity cost of investing in a particular bond that pays less than the prevailing interest rate is higher. In these examples, you had already bought the bond before the interest rate changed, but the changing interest rate still influences how other potential buyers of bonds value the bonds. So the interest rate influences the market price of the bond, which in turn influences the value of the bond.

Valuing a Stream of Cash Flows

What if you had a stream of cash flows that would continue "forever"? What would it be worth?

When we first came across this question, our initial thought was that a stream of cash flows lasting forever, that is an infinite stream, should have infinite value. But it doesn't.

There's an easy way to think about this, and a harder way. Let's look at the easy way first.

Easy Way

Assume, for the sake of discussion, that you, and anyone else who wants to, were able to earn 5% annual interest, every year with no uncertainty and no risk. If you invested $100 now, and did not reinvest the interest, each year you would have a cash flow of $5. Assuming that the interest rate is 5%, that cash flow of $5 a year, forever, is worth $100. Why?

Because if I have $100, I can turn it into $5 a year by investing the $100 at 5% per year, forever, as we assumed was possible, given that the interest rate is 5%. By the same logic (we're assuming away here all the complexities – including transaction costs, uncertainties, taxes, liquidity constraints, and information costs – of real markets), if I have a perpetual stream of $5 a year, I can turn it into $100 now by selling it. If the interest rate changes, this will change the value of the perpetual, as we will discuss in the following section about duration.

Using the same logic, we might ask what is it worth if I have a perpetual stream of $10,000 a year, and the interest rate is 10%? In other words, how much would you pay today in order to guarantee that you will receive payments of $10,000 per year forever? Remember that the prevailing interest rate is 10%. One way to answer the question is to ask, "How much would I have to invest at a rate of 10% to generate $10,000 a year?" The answer is $100,000, because $10,000 is 10% of 100,000. What if the interest rate were 8% a year? To find the answer, we use a bit of simple algebra.

We know that the annual cash flow, C, equals the interest rate, r, times the principal invested, P. So we can write $C = rP$. We can solve for P by dividing both sides by r. We get $P = C/r$.

If we know that C is $10,000 and r is 8%, we calculate $C = $10,000/.08$, which gives us $125,000.

Harder Way

There is nothing wrong with the preceding easier (for most people other than John von Neumann[1]) approach. Nevertheless, there is

---

[1] The present value of an infinite series of cash flows is a special case of the mathematics of infinite series. Paul Halmos, a mathematician who worked under von Neumann at Princeton's Institute

some understanding to be gained from seeing how an infinite series of cash flows can have a finite value.

We can use the logic of present valuation to find an answer.

Let r = the required rate of return
Let n = the number of years
Let V = the value of the infinite stream

Then we can state the present value of the sum of each year's cash flow as follows in equation (1):

$$V = \frac{1}{(1+r)^1} + \frac{1}{(1+r)^2} + \frac{1}{(1+r)^3} + \dots \frac{1}{(1+r)^n} \qquad (1)$$

This equation (1) will hold for any value of n, even as n goes to infinity. But, as we will see, we can vastly simplify the equation with a little algebra.

Multiplying both sides of equation (1) by $(1 + r)$ gives us equation (2):

$$V(1+r) = 1 + \frac{1}{(1+r)^1} + \frac{1}{(1+r)^2} + \frac{1}{(1+r)^3} + \dots \frac{1}{(1+r)^n} \qquad (2)$$

Note that everything to the right of the 1 on the right side of the equals sign is itself equal to V. Therefore, the right hand side of equation (2) above equals $1+V$. We rewrite thus:

$$V(1+r) = 1 + V \qquad (3)$$

---

for Advanced Studies and was later a professor at Indiana University, wrote in "The Legend of John von Neumann" in the *American Mathematical Monthly* (April 1973), about "the famous fly puzzle," a story that has been repeated many times since. "Two bicyclists start twenty miles apart and head toward each other, each going at a steady rate of 10 m.p.h. At the same time a fly that travels at a steady 15 m.p.h. starts from the front wheel of the southbound bicycle and flies to the front wheel of the northbound one, then turns around and flies to the front wheel of the southbound one again, and continues in this manner till he is crushed between the two front wheels. Question: what total distance did the fly cover? The slow way to find the answer is to calculate what distance the fly covers on the first, northbound, leg of the trip, then on the second, southbound, leg, then on the third, etc., etc., and, finally, to sum the infinite series so obtained. The quick way is to observe that the bicycles meet exactly one hour after their start, so that the fly had just an hour for his travels; the answer must therefore be 15 miles. When the question was put to von Neumann, he solved it in an instant, and thereby disappointed the questioner: "Oh, you must have heard the trick before!" "What trick?" asked von Neumann; "All I did was sum the infinite series."

Expand the left side:

$$V + Vr = 1 + V \qquad (4)$$

Subtract V from both sides to get:

$$Vr = 1 \qquad (5)$$

Finally, divide both sides by r:

$$V = \frac{1}{r} \qquad (6)$$

Remarkably, the infinite series of cash flows not only has a finite value, but we have a very simple formula to find that value.

For example, if the required rate of return is 5%, and we have a perpetual cash flow stream of $5, the present value of that stream is $100. (This is because $100 = 5/.05$, the annual cash flow stream divided by the required rate of return.)

In the above example, we assumed that the cash flow in each period was 1. If we were to substitute a variable C for the cash flow, then the value would be $V = C/r$, where C is the cash flow per period, and r is the rate of return.

Present Value of a Growing Perpetual Stream of Cash Flows

If the cash flow is growing at a known rate, g, and we expect it to grow at that rate "forever," the present value of the perpetual stream is:

$$V = \frac{1}{r - g} \qquad (7)$$

where r is the required rate of return.

For example, if we have a dollar per year cash flow, growing at 2% and the required return is 10%, the present value of the stream is $12.50. If the stream were not growing, the value would be $10. Because the stream is growing, we think it should be worth more than a stream that is not growing. It is, and the formula tells us it is worth $12.50. If the cash flow stream is more than a dollar, we just put in the annual amount instead of a dollar. For example, if the cash flow stream is $8,000 a year, and the required rate of return, r, is 5%, we find the value (the present value) by dividing 8,000 by .05, to get a result of $160,000.

Duration: A Measure of Interest Rate Sensitivity

In our example about bonds at the beginning of this chapter, we saw that the present value of the stream of bond cash flows changed depending on the prevailing interest rate. The term *duration* is used to describe the sensitivity of the present value of a stream of cash flows to a change in the interest rate, r. Thus duration is commonly considered to be a measure of interest rate risk. We illustrate the concept with reference to a perpetual bond, because the math is easier to follow (just in case you are interested in the math).

There are few perpetual bonds today, although Britain famously had "consols" outstanding for about 250 years. However, many equity-type assets, such as real estate or stocks, can be thought of as perpetuals, because they have no maturity and no scheduled redemption date.

One definition of duration[2] is the sensitivity of a bond or stream of cash flows to a change in the required rate of return (i.e. the relevant discount rate). We called this r previously when we said the that value today (the present value) of a perpetual stream of cash flows[3] is:

$$V = \frac{1}{r} \tag{8}$$

Or, if the cash flow is C, instead of 1, then

$$V = \frac{C}{r} \tag{9}$$

By using this theoretical value of a perpetual, we can also develop a simple estimate of the perpetual's price sensitivity to

---

[2] Another very similar measure, also called duration, measures the weighted average present value of the cash flows where the time until the cash is received is the weight. This results in a duration measured in years. It is called *Macauly Duration* after the economist Frederick Macauly.

[3] In general, if your cash flow is C instead of 1, then $V = \frac{C}{r}$.

a change in the required rate of return, r. It turns out that that sensitivity is simply:

$$-\frac{1}{r} \tag{10}$$

That is, if r (which might be called the *required rate of return*, or the *interest rate*, or the *discount rate*) is 5%, (same as .05), the price will change by a factor of 20, because $1/.05 = 20$. If the rate rises, the price will go down, which is why we have the minus sign to the left.[4]

For example, if we return to our perpetual stream of cash flows that provides $5 per year forever, when the interest rate is .05, that stream of cash flows is worth $100. (Remember you can figure this out by asking, "How much would I have to pay to receive $5 per year forever?" You'd pay $100, because 5 is 5% of 100.) But if the prevailing interest rate increases to 10%, the stream of $5 per year forever suddenly becomes worth less. If the interest rate is 10%, you would now pay only $50 to receive $5 per year, because $5 is 10% of $50.

The important part of this to remember is that if you know the yield of an asset, and the asset is some kind of perpetual or quasi-perpetual (such as the stock market), you can calculate a very rough estimate of its theoretical exposure to interest rates by simply dividing 1 by the yield. For example, if the yield (say, the net rental yield) on a piece of real estate is 4%, everything else equal, a 1% increase in the interest rate will reduce the value of the real estate by roughly 25%. The calculation is that $1/.04 = 25$.

Keep in mind that this is a very rough estimate. A number of empirical studies of stock markets have found that factors other than interest rates are also important to explain the apparent sensitivity of stocks (and real estate) to changes in interest rates.[5]

---

[4] This duration is called *modified duration*. It is the sensitivity (economists call it *elasticity*) of the value of the perpetual with respect to a change in r. In mathematical symbols, duration is $\frac{\left(\frac{dV}{dr}\right)}{V} = \frac{\left(-\frac{1}{r^2}\right)}{\frac{1}{r}} = -\frac{1}{r}$.

[5] For example, see David Hartzell et al., "A Look at Real Estate Duration," *Journal of Portfolio Management* 15, no. 1 (1988), or Lewin and Satchell, "The Derivation of a New Model of Equity Duration," Cambridge Working Papers in Economics (June 16, 2004).

How Is Rate of Return Calculated?

People often talk about the "rate of return" on an investment. They may be talking about the past, as for example, "the Dow Jones Industrial Average has returned 7.95% annually over the last 10 years." Or they may be making a projection about the future, as in, "Large company stocks should return an average of 6.5 to 7% over the long run," as Wharton professor Jeremy Siegel says.[6]

Simple Annual Rate of Return Versus Compound Rate of Return

It is important to understand that "average rate of return" can have significantly different meanings. For example, suppose that you bought 1,000 shares of Dot Hill Systems on December 19, 2008, at $0.50 per share, and held it until October 8, 2015, when the company was bought for $9.75 per share in cash. The stock never paid a dividend[7] during that time, so the only cash flows you have to consider are the cash you paid out for the purchase and the cash you got back when the stock was converted into cash. The time period was 2,484 days, or 6.805 years (both of which are easily calculated using a spreadsheet program).

To find the simple return, you divide the cash you got back by the price you paid for the stock, then subtract $1. (We subtracted 1 because it represents getting your money back. For example, if you invest $100 and get back $102, you made $2, so your return is 2%, not 102%.)

The simple return was 9.75/.5 = 18.5, which is the same number as 1,850%. The 1,850% return is correct, but you might want to know what it comes to as an annual return. One way to do the calculation is simply to divide by the number of years, which would give an

---

[6] The fact that Siegel is well known and well respected does not imply that he is right. As of this date, early January 2023, we think that US stocks are unlikely to produce after-inflation-adjustment compound yields as high as 6.5% over the next 10 years, because the valuation levels today seem too high. We return to this theme later.

[7] A dividend is a periodic payment sometimes paid out to shareholders, as we discussed briefly above.

annual return of 271.86%. That number is not strictly wrong, but it is deceptive. Why? Because it is not compounded.

You know how to find the compounded rate of return, using the formula from the previous chapter. The PV is the original price paid, $0.50, the FV is $9.75, and t is 6.805. Plugging into the formula (see chapter 1) and solving for r, we calculate a compound annual rate of 54.7%. When measured over multiple years, the simple annual rate will always be larger than the compound rate for positive returns, but the larger the returns the bigger the difference will be.

This difference between simple annual rate and compound annual rate can cause errors if you don't know which you're dealing with. If you mistake a simple annual return for a compound return, you may significantly overestimate the return over multiple years. Here is a particularly stark example.

Consider a two-year period. In the first year, your investment doubles, a 100% rate of return. Since this is only one year, the compound return is the same as the simple return. Both are 100%. In the second year, the investment loses half its value. If you started with $100, at the end of the first year you had $200, then at the end of the second year you were back to $100. The simple and compound return for the year are again the same, negative 50%. But the two-year returns are very different.

Arithmetic Versus Geometric Mean

The arithmetic[8] average of the two-year simple returns is:

$$\frac{100\% - 50\%}{2} = 25\%$$

But if you look at the entire period, you started with $100 and ended with $100. Your *compound average growth rate* (also called the *geometric mean*) was 0%. There is nothing wrong with the mathematics of the arithmetic returns. The problem is that arithmetic (sometimes

---

[8] Here *arithmetic* is an adjective, and is pronounced with the accent on the third syllable: ar-ith-MET-ic.

called *simple*) return is a poor fit with what you as an investor really care about.

Now, suppose that an investment advisor presented you with a (true) claim that over the past two years the advisor's client accounts earned an average annual return of 25% a year. That sounds pretty darn good. Only if you know to ask about the compound return will you get the information you need.

Compound return goes by a number of names. You might see *CAGR*, which stands for *compound annual growth rate*, or *geometric mean* or *time-weighted rate of return*. If there is any doubt, ask how the return is calculated.[9]

Compound return is easy to calculate with a calculator or computer. Assuming there is one beginning amount of money, one ending amount, and no additions or subtractions, the compound return is calculated as follows: first, divide the ending number by the beginning number, then take the nth root[10] of the quotient, where n equals the number of periods. Then subtract 1. For example, if we invest $100 in a stock for five years, and the stock is worth $110 at the end of those five years, the geometric return is $= .019$.

Here is the formula:

$$r_g = \left(\frac{EndVal}{BegVal}\right)^{\left(\frac{1}{n}\right)} - 1 = \sqrt[n]{\frac{EndVal}{BegVal}} - 1. \qquad (11)$$

And here we plug in the numbers from the above example:

$$r_g = \left(\frac{110}{100}\right)^{\left(\frac{1}{5}\right)} - 1 = \sqrt[5]{\frac{110}{100}} - 1 = 0.019 = 1.9\% \qquad (12)$$

In the investing world, there is another return calculation in common use. It is the *internal rate of return*, or *IRR*, and is described in the appendix to this chapter.

---

[9] The geometric average of the positive returns will always be less than or equal to the arithmetic average. This is an application of a well-known mathematical fact called the *AM-GM Inequality*.
[10] An nth root can be found by raising the number to the power of $1/n$.

Appendix

Internal Rate of Return

Compound return is easy to understand, and it is a reasonable way to calculate the return on an investment when there is a one-time investment of cash, and later a one-time return of cash. A real-world example is a zero-coupon bond. A zero-coupon bond, sometimes simply called a *zero*, is a bond that does not pay any interest until it matures. (In the example of *bond 1,* at the beginning of this chapter, which had $1,000 of principal and annual payments of $50, the $50 coupon payments were payments of interest. A zero-coupon bond would not make these payments.)

For example, as of this writing, you could buy a zero-coupon US Treasury bond for $410 which promises to pay $1,000 in 29 years and 7 months, for a CAGR of about 3.3%. (If you use a bond return calculator to calculate the bond's yield to maturity, you will get an answer of about 3.1%, because in the US, yield-to-maturity is not quite the same calculation as compound return. Bond math is a specialized subfield involving a number of conventional assumptions. It is beyond the scope of this book.)

Internal rate of return, *IRR*, is straightforward, and not misleading when there are only two cash flows, in which case the IRR equals the CAGR. But when there are multiple investments going in, or multiple payments coming back out, IRR can be quite misleading.

IRR Defined

IRR is defined as the interest rate that will make the NPV of a stream of cash flows equal zero. For example, *bond 1* at the beginning of this chapter, if it sells for $1,000, has an IRR of 5%, because 5% is exactly the discount rate that will make the NPV zero.

However, the same bond, if it sells for $957.88, will have a positive NPV if discounted at 5%. The value of the cash flows after the initial investment, discounted at 5%, is $1,000. Therefore, at a 5% discount rate, if the bond sells for 957.88, it has an NPV of $42.12

($1,000 – $957.88). What discount rate makes that NPV zero? We know it is 6%, because we already calculated it. We used a discount rate of 6% to arrive at $957.88. So, if the bond is selling at $957.88, and it pays all its payments on time, the IRR will be 6%.

Internal rate of return is easy to calculate, once you know the cash flows and the timings, using a spreadsheet.[11]

Some Limitations of IRR

IRR can be a useful measure, but it is not perfect, and doesn't always fit. A set of cash flows doesn't always have a unique IRR. This can be true when the cash flows change sign more than once during the period. That is, for example, you make an investment, it pays out some, you make another investment, and then it pays out more.

Table 2.5 shows a simple example of a set of cash flows that do not have a unique IRR:

Table 2.5   Cash Flows Without Unique IRR

Year	Cash Flow	PV at 0%	PV at 10%
1	−10	−10	−9.09
2	21	21	17.36
3	−11	−11	−8.26

Here's what Table 2.5 says. Suppose that you start with $10 and invest it in year 1. Your cash flows are minus $10 for year 1; plus $21 for year 2; minus $11 for year 3. At the end of year 3, you have the same $10 you started with (because you've had outflow of 10 + 11, and inflow of 21). Most people would say that if we invest $10 and three years later still have $10, the rate of return was zero. But in this example, the sum of the present values of the cash flows is zero for discount rates of both 0% and 10%.

---

[11] When we say "easily," we mean that the spreadsheet, or other computer program, does the hard work. In general, there is not a closed-form solution for most IRR problems. A closed-form solution means that you could write down an equation and solve it directly. IRR generally is solved for by a process of successive approximation.

Internal rate of return is defined as the discount rate that makes the net present value (i.e. the sum of the individual year present values) equal to zero. If the discount rate is zero, the present value of each cash flow is simply its face value. It is easy to see that $-10 + 21 - 11 =$ zero, so 0% is a valid solution to the IRR calculation.

But at the end of year 3 you could also claim that the IRR of these cash flows was 10%, and you would not be lying. That seems strange. Let's see how the math works. The right-most column in Figure 2.5 shows the present value of each cash-flow using an annual discount rate of 10%. The sum of $-9.09 + 17.36 - 8.26$ (except for rounding) is also zero, meaning that a 10% annual discount rate is also a valid solution to the IRR calculation.

So, which is the correct IRR? Both. And that's the problem.

Sometimes actual investments are really like this. For example, so-called private equity funds may require you to put in cash at the beginning, then they'll pay some out, then they'll have you put more in, and so on. If those same private equity funds then report to you an IRR, unless you do the calculations yourself (impossible given the information they disclose, based on my experience), you really have no idea if they have cherry-picked a high number when a low number might also suffice.

Here is another example, based on the preceding example. Suppose the first three years are the same, and in year 4, the investment pays you $3 and then you're done. A common sense way of evaluating the return would be to look at the ending value, $13 (i.e. the original $10 investment plus $3 of net gain), and compare it against the original investment of $10. If we use the standard present value formula and solve for r, we find that the compound return works out to 6.78% per year. Not bad, but also nothing to get overly excited about.

However, if we take these same cash flows and calculate the IRR, we find that the return was 50%! Table 2.6 shows that a 50% discount rate does indeed equate to a zero NPV for the example cash flows.

A second possible problem with IRR is that it implicitly assumes that the cash flows will be reinvested at the IRR rate. However, that is unlikely to be true in the real world. There is a modified version of

Table 2.6 IRR for Discount Rate of 50%

Year	Cash Flow	PV of Cash Flow at IRR Rate (50%)
1	−10	−6.666666667
2	21	9.333333333
3	−11	−3.259259259
4	3	0.592592593
Sum		*0*

IRR called Modified IRR, or *MIRR*, which takes into account likely future reinvestment return rates, and likely future cost of capital.

The main point in this section on IRR is that IRR can be a fickle number, and depending on the configuration of the cash flows, might be misleading.

Chapter 3
Bonds/Fixed Income/Loans

Bonds

Bonds are loans. Bonds, and similar loans, are also known as "fixed income" investments. The main asset classes in this category are government bonds, "investment grade" corporate bonds, non-investment-grade or "junk" bonds, foreign (from the point of view of a US investor) bonds, emerging market bonds, mortgage-backed bonds, tax-exempt municipal bonds, various forms of bank deposits, and certain fixed annuities.

What Are Bonds?

When a bond is originally issued, the borrower (the bond issuer) is borrowing money from the original buyer of the bond. Most bonds are tradeable, so that the original buyer may sell the bond before the bond matures.

When an investor buys a bond, it generally makes little difference whether the bond is bought at the original issuance, or later, in the *secondary* market. From an economic point of view, buying a bond means that the bond investor is making a loan to the government, a corporation, or whoever issued the bond. The investor purchases a bond that will mature in a certain number of years, and often receives interest payments along the way. (If the bond does not specify periodic interest payments, the bond is called a *zero coupon bond* or just a *zero*.) In the final period, the bond-holder receives both the interest and the payment of principal.

Bond Terms

Bonds are loan contracts. In a tradeable bond, the key terms are expressed in the bond *indenture*. The key terms will generally include all of the following: *redemption price*, *coupon rate*, *payment schedule*, and *maturity date*. In addition, some bonds will include terms regarding convertibility, collateral, covenants, and/or restrictions on transferability. Bond law is a technical area, and generally need not concern the retail bond investor provided that the investor uses the intermediary services of a professional, such as a mutual fund manager.

For the remainder of this chapter, we will focus on the economics of bonds as they concern investors.

What Determines Bond Returns?

As with any investment, when an investor buys a bond and holds it for some period, the investor's *nominal*[1] return is a function of the cash flows to the investor. The real return is the nominal return adjusted for inflation. In the case of a bond, the cash flows are the coupon payments, and any gain or loss on the price of the bond. If you buy a bond at par (i.e. 100% of its face value or redemption value), and hold it to maturity, assuming the bond does not default,

---

[1] *Nominal* means returns not adjusted for inflation. For example, if the nominal return were 4% and inflation were 3%, the *real* return would be 1%.

the nominal return you earn will simply be the coupon on the bond. This should sound simple, because it is.

For example, if you pay $1,000 for a 10-year bond that pays a $60 coupon once a year, and hold the bond for the full 10 years, you will receive 10 payments of $60 and your original principal investment back at the end of 10 years. Your return will be 6%.

But in the real world, things are rarely this simple. If you reinvest the interest payments (assuming no tax), your compound return over the 10-year period will be 6% *only* if interest rates do not change at all during that period. But rates do change, pretty much every day. Changes in interest rates cause changes in bond prices. Changes in bond prices cause changes in returns to owning bonds, everything else equal, because as the price of bonds rises, your return rises, and as the price falls, your return falls.

Return Versus Yield

In the preceding example, it was easy to calculate returns. In general, returns equal the ending value of the bond plus coupon interest, minus the starting value of the bond. (In the preceding example, the coupon return was 6%, and the starting value of the bond was $1,000. The ending value of the bond, as noted, depends on interest rates.)

The term *yield* can be confusing, because, as we'll discuss later in this chapter, there are different kinds of yields. For now, when we say *yield*, we mean *yield-to-maturity*, which is the rate of return such that the present value of the sum of the cash flows equals the price of the bond. If you buy a bond at the market price and hold it to maturity, the rate that you will earn is, by definition, the yield-to-maturity when you bought it.

If interest rates remain constant, then the yield-to-maturity is the same as the return. However, if the interest rate rises or falls, and you sell before the bond matures, the change in interest rates may change the price of the bond, which influences the return. In such a case, returns and yields will not be exactly the same.

Even if you hold a bond to maturity, if interest rates change during your holding period (which they probably will), and you reinvest the coupon payments, your *ex-post* (i.e. after-the-fact) return will, in general, not equal the yield-to-maturity at which you purchased the bond. The reason is that the two numbers, while related, are not measuring exactly the same thing. If it helps, you might want to think about the *yield-to-maturity* as the *expected* return, and the after-the-fact return as the *actual* return. Actual returns are expressed as a percentage per unit of time, for example: "5% per year."

A simple example demonstrates why the yield-to-maturity can deviate from the coupon payment. Suppose you purchase a bond above par, at $102, with coupon payments of 5% annually, which is $5. (*Par* for a bond almost always means $100.) Over the lifetime of the bond, you will receive coupons, and when the bond reaches maturity, you will receive a coupon payment plus a principal payment of $100. Note that you will receive $100, NOT $102. This means that everything else equal, you will lose $2 during the time you hold the bond. If you had purchased the bond at par, at $100, your yield-to-maturity would have been 5%. But now that you lose $2, your yield-to-maturity is less than 5%. Similarly, if you bought the bond below par – say, for example, at $98 – and redeemed it at par, your yield-to-maturity would be greater than the coupon payment.

Short to Medium Term

Over periods shorter than the maturity of the bond, returns can be higher or lower than the coupon payment, because of changes in the value of the bond. If we ignore changes in the credit quality of the bond, the changes in the bond's market price will be a function of changes in interest rates.[2]

---

[2] Credit quality and the market level of interest rates are by far the most important factors in pricing most bonds most of the time. Some economists distinguish between the "real" component of interest rates and the "inflationary" component. This distinction does not affect our analysis here.

Remember that, as we saw in chapter 2, when interest rates rise, everything else equal, bond prices fall, and vice versa. Also, everything else equal, the longer the maturity of the bond, the greater the sensitivity to changes in interest rates. As a result, in the short run and medium run (i.e. from intraday to many years), much of the return from holding a bond can come from changes in interest rates, and therefore in changes in bond prices, and possibly from changes in the interest rate at which coupons can be reinvested.

Over the past century or so, the annual returns from owning the US Treasury 10-year note have been anything but stable. If the past is any guide, it is all but impossible to predict the return for the following year for the US Treasury 10-year note. And because the yields and returns on most similar maturity US dollar bonds, including corporate bonds and municipal bonds, are highly correlated with the returns to the US 10-year note, we can be confident that the one year returns on other bonds returns are just as unpredictable, as is shown in Figure 3.1 below.[3]

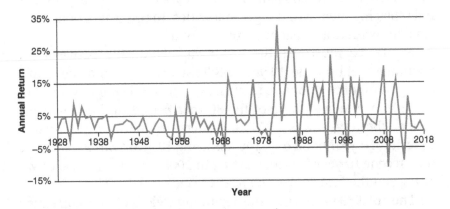

Figure 3.1   Annual Returns from US Treasury 10-Year Notes

But all is not lost. As long-term investors, we care more about the long-term returns than the short-term returns. And those long-term

---

[3] If an investor could reliably predict changes in interest rates, he could earn a fortune by trading on those predictions. While there have been arbitrage opportunities in the bond markets over the years, we are not aware of convincing evidence that interest rates can be consistently and profitably predicted.

returns are considerably more predictable. And it turns out there's a very simple way to make the prediction, too. You don't have to be an expert, and you don't even have to know any bond math. Over the long run, you can make an excellent prediction of the long-run return to bonds simply by observing the yield at the beginning of the period.

To explain how today's yield can predict the return to owning a bond, we introduce the concept of a *constant maturity* bond. If you bought and held a 10-year bond today, then in one year, you would no longer own a 10-year bond: you'd own a 9-year bond. Bonds of different maturities have different sensitivities to interest rates. While a 9-year bond will behave very similarly to a 10-year bond, the difference between a 10-year and 5-year might be significant enough that they constitute a different asset class. An individual bond (whose time to maturity decreases every year), is effectively becoming a different type of asset every year.

For this reason, a bond mutual fund manager will usually try to maintain a relatively constant maturity, by selling bonds as they age, and replacing them with longer maturities. In this way, a bond fund can approximate a constant maturity bond.

Figure 3.2 illustrates the historical relationship between the beginning yield on the 10-year US Treasury bond and the actual average annual compounded return over the following 10 years. For example, at the beginning of the 80-year period in the graph, the yield on the 10-year was 3.17%, and the return to owning a constant maturity[4] 10-year bond over the following 10 years was 3.6%. In the most recent 10-year period, starting in 2008, the starting yield was 2.21%, and the return over the next 10 years was 1.97%.

The *r* of .953 means that the beginning yield is closely correlated with the annualized 10-year return. Here, "*r*" means a statistic called the *Pearson correlation coefficient*. If the *r* were 1, that would mean that the beginning yield and the annualized 10-year return were perfectly correlated. We can see this relationship in Figure 3.2, which follows.

---

[4] This approximates what a mutual fund that targeted a 10-year maturity would do. It is different from buying the bond and holding it to maturity. If you did that, after a year, you'd have a 9-year bond, after two years, you'd have an 8-year bond, etc.

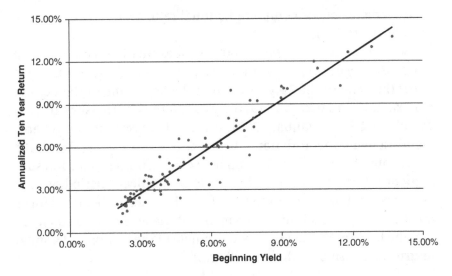

Figure 3.2   Ten Year Treasuries Beginning Yield vs. Subsequent 10 Yr Total Return 1928–2018

We might ask why does the return follow so closely the initial yield? Is that merely the product of chance, or is there something more fundamental going on?

There is something fundamental going on. Namely, over the life of a bond issued at par, the entire return to owning the bond must come from the coupons. Almost all bonds are issued at or near par, so the coupon rate is an excellent predictor (not counting default, and in our sample of Treasury notes, there were no nominal defaults[5]) of the nominal return that will be earned by holding the bond.

The historical evidence from the past 80 years suggests that even if we were to maintain a constant maturity of 10 years (e.g. buy the 10-year bond, hold it for one year, then sell it and use the interest and principal proceeds to buy a new 10-year bond every year, or every time a new 10-year bond was issued), the beginning yield is still a

---

[5] That is, if a bond was supposed to pay a certain number of dollars on a certain date, it did. However, we are ignoring the value of those dollars, whose real value may have decreased due to factors such as inflation.

good predictor of the compound annual return we'll earn over the subsequent 10 years.

So now we have a pretty good way of estimating what nominal return to expect over 10 years from 10-year bonds, given that we know the yield of the 10-year bond at the beginning of the period. For example, in January 2019, the yield on the US Treasury 10-year was about 2.7%. In January 2021, it was 1.1%, less than the government's stated target inflation rate of 2%.

Because historical correlation between beginning yield and subsequent returns has been so high over a significant period of time (80 years) and because of the logic that ultimately, a bond's returns must come from its interest payments, it makes sense to conclude that the beginning yield is a good estimate of the compound annual return we'll earn over the next 10 years.

Inflation Adjusted or "Real" Returns

The bond yield at the beginning of the period is a pretty good predictor of the nominal (i.e. not adjusted for inflation) return to expect. It is a less good predictor of the "real" or inflation-adjusted return, but in the past it has been a decent predictor.

Using the same data for yields and returns on the US Treasury 10-year over the past 80 years, and also using CPI[6] data, we can calculate the inflation-adjusted returns. The following chart shows that relationship.

On its face, this looks like a pretty good fit. The correlation coefficient r[7] is .65. But if we look a little closer, we see that perhaps most of that correlation is mostly determined by the neatly ordered points representing starting yields of over 8%. (Figure 3.3 below shows this relationship).

---

[6] Consumer Price Index, compiled by the US Dept. of Labor, Bureau of Labor Statistics, CPI-U, data from https://www.minneapolisfed.org/community/financial-and-economic-education/cpi-calculator-information/consumer-price-index-and-inflation-rates-1913

[7] This is a statistic whose full name is the Pearson Correlation Coefficient. Its value can be anywhere from 1 to –1. An r of 1 indicates perfect correlation; an r of –1 indicates perfect negative correlation, and an r of 0 indicates no correlation. There is no precise science of how "good" a fit is indicated by correlations with absolute value between 0 and 1. In the social sciences and economics, an r of .65 is generally considered a fairly good fit.

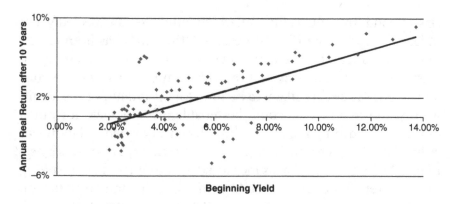

Figure 3.3   Beginning Yield vs. Subsequent 10 Year Real Return 1928–2018

We can also look at the data against time, as shown in Figure 3.4. When we do, it looks like this:

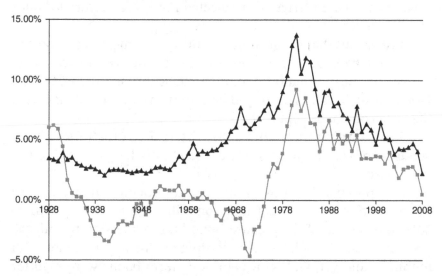

Figure 3.4   Starting Yield on US Ten Year and Subsequent 10 Year Real Return, 1928 to 2008

Here, it looks like there is no relationship before about the 1970s. And indeed the correlation between the two before 1971 is just about zero.

We wrote this paragraph in 2021, and the inflation risk we highlighted turned out to be quite prescient. "In 2021, the big inflation risk to bond investors is that inflation would rise unexpectedly. For at least a decade, the Federal Reserve ("the Fed") has been targeting CPI inflation of 2%, and has been close to that target. If inflation averages 2%, or more, the real returns from bonds, given the 2021 low interest rates, are likely to be low. And if inflation rises significantly, the real returns could be terrible, as they were for much of the period during the mid-twentieth century when inflation was rising." In 2021, the annual return on US Treasury bonds was a *negative* 4.42%,[8] and inflation as measured by the CPI was 7%, resulting in a real return of *negative* 11.42%. In 2022, the annual return on US Treasury bonds was a negative 17.83%, and inflation was 6.5%, resulting in a real return of *negative* 24.33%.

If we were to assume long-run inflation of 3%, and the early 2021 10-year bond yield of 1.1% as our 10-year expectation for the return to bonds, we would arrive at an expected 10-year real return to bonds of −1.9% a year.

It turns out that in the almost-century that most of the world's currencies have been cut loose from gold, the key to real bond returns has been inflation. From the 1950s through the end of the 1970s, rising inflation destroyed bond returns, despite the fact that the yields on bonds kept rising.

Then, starting in around 1981, the real returns to long-term bonds were very high by historical standards for most of the last four decades.

That presents bond investors with a difficult conundrum. It's not enough to "know" that inflation will continue. From 1981 to 2018, during one of the greatest bond bull markets on record, the US dollar lost 64% of its value according to official government CPI numbers; and yet, real returns on long-term bonds were high for most of that time.

Back in the early 1980s, almost no one was expecting that bonds would do well. The very widespread expectation was that inflation would continue in double-digits, and investors continued to demand high coupons for many years until they came to believe that inflation would stay low.

[8] Stern/NYU, January 2023, Historical Returns on Stocks, Bonds and Bills: 1928–2022, https://pages.stern.nyu.edu/~adamodar/New_Home_Page/datafile/histretSP.html

We find no evidence of anyone with a consistent ability to predict future inflation with enough accuracy to make it a useful guide to expected real returns on bonds.[9]

By definition, we cannot say before the fact which is the best prediction of future inflation. But at least, now, instead of having to (blindly?) choose from among various expert opinions, we can have a basis, grounded in history and theory, for forming our own expectation, even if, as in the case of inflation, it's just a long-term average number.

Risks to Bonds

Investing in bonds involves three main types of risk: credit risk, interest rate risk, and inflation risk. In the case of foreign bonds, there may also be currency risk. Credit risk is the risk that the borrower will not repay the bond in full, not repay it on time, or some combination of the two. Interest rate risk stems from the mathematical and empirical fact that as interest rates rise, everything else equal, the value of a bond falls (chapter 2). A third risk is that inflation will erode the value of the dollars you receive when the bond pays interest and principal as scheduled. Currency risk is the risk that the value of your foreign currency bonds will drop because the dollar rises relative to the foreign currency.

Credit Risk

Credit risk is the risk that a borrower fails to live up to the terms under which the money was borrowed. Failure to live up to any of the terms is called a *default*. A missed or delayed payment is a *money default*.[10] Credit risk is difficult to assess, even for professionals.

---

[9] Harvard's James Stock and Princeton's Mark Watson begin their paper *Phillips Curve Inflation Forecasts*, (NBER working paper #14322) with the laconic observation: "Inflation is hard to forecast." Eighty-two pages, and more econometrics than you can shake a stick at later, they have demonstrated that thesis.

[10] Certain bonds can have nonmoney defaults. For example, many corporate bonds require that the borrower maintain certain financial ratios, such as levels of collateral or interest coverage. If a company fails to maintain one of these *covenant* terms, it may be in default, even if it has never been late or missed a bond payment.

To avoid credit risk, most experts advise investing in the bonds of governments that have the ability to print the money required to pay back the bonds. For this reason, and this reason only, US government bonds are considered by many people to be "risk free" in the sense that, they believe, there is no chance that the US government will fail to meet its nominal obligations under the terms of the bond.[11]

While as of this writing, in 2023, there seems to be no obvious reason that the US government cannot continue to create the fiat dollars required to service its debt, it is good to keep in mind that there have been many, many instances of sovereign governments unexpectedly defaulting on debt. If you want to read more about this, we recommend Reinhart and Rogoff's book, *This Time Is Different*.[12] The authors point out that in addition to explicit default, bondholders run the risk of being subject to *financial repression*.

> Financial repression includes directed lending to government by captive domestic audiences (such as pension funds), explicit or implicit caps on interest rates, regulation of cross-border capital movements, and (generally) a tighter connection between government and banks.[13]

In her study of the United States and the United Kingdom between 1945 and 1980 (both countries had very large debts in the wake of World War II), Reinhart observes that both countries liquidated debt via negative real interest rates, which the governments of those countries caused by printing lots of money. A real interest rate is the rate of interest minus the rate of inflation. When inflation is higher than the interest rate, lenders lose purchasing power even

---

[11] The United States has failed to live up to the terms of its borrowings at least twice since the country was founded. In the 1790s, Alexander Hamilton restructured the US debt. Brown University economist Peter Garber, in his 1991 NBER Working Paper #3597 argues that this amounted to default, as "a large part of the face value of the debt was effectively written off." Similarly, in 1933, the US government unilaterally redefined the dollar. Prior to 1933, the dollar was defined as 1/20.67 of an ounce of gold. In 1933, the government redefined it to 1/35 of an ounce of gold. The government had borrowed expensive dollars, and paid off with cheap ones.

[12] Carmen Reinhart and Kenneth Rogoff, *This Time Is Different: Eight Centuries of Financial Folly* (Princeton University Press, 2011).

[13] Carmen Reinhart and M. Belen Sbrancia, *The Liquidation of Government Debt*, NBER Working Paper # 16893 (March, 2011): 2.

though they earn interest, because the interest they earn is not enough to keep up with inflation. This is a real-world example of *inflation risk*. Borrowers who cannot print the currency necessary to repay their debt are at greater risk of default than those who can. Similarly, borrowers that must rely on voluntary transactions, such as businesses, are at greater risk of default than those that can use force or the threat of force, such as governments, to obtain the money to repay.

Therefore, in general, the lowest risk of money default (i.e. not being able to pay back the nominal money borrowed) is with sovereign borrowers borrowing in their own fiat currency (e.g. the US Treasury borrowing in dollars, the UK government borrowing in pounds). The next lowest risk category of borrowers is governments that have the power to tax, such as states and cities, provided that they don't borrow too much. The next lowest level of risk is so-called high-quality borrowers like well-established corporations, such as Disney. These corporations have lots of assets, generate lots of free cash flow (cash flow available to service debt), and have much more equity than debt.

The risk of default increases as borrowers have more debt relative to assets, less free cash flow relative to debt service, greater volatility of cash flow, and several other factors that influence the probability of them not being able to pay. These are generalizations. Over time, many governments, such as those of Greece and Puerto Rico, have proven to be very high risk (both have defaulted) despite their ability to tax. For you as an investor, this means that if you purchase government bonds, you will probably want to purchase bonds from governments that are unlikely to default in the future.

Many types of bonds are given a credit rating by a credit rating agency, such as Standard & Poor's (S&P), Moody, Fitch, A.M. Best, or Egan-Jones. There are many categories of rating, generally ranging from a top rating of AAA down to a low of C or so. These ratings usually provide a good general indication of the short-run risk of credit default, but there are many instances of the credit rating agencies completely missing the boat. Famously, prior to the mortgage-backed meltdown of 2008–2009, many securities received very high ratings and then defaulted within months of receiving those ratings. Table 3.1 lists the rating categories and their approximate meanings of the top three US rating agencies. The bonds at the top of the list receive a higher rating than the bonds at the bottom, meaning that these agencies consider them less risky. Table 3.1 shows this relationship.

Table 3.1 Categories for Top 3 US Rating Agencies

Bond Ratings	Moody's	Standard & Poor's	Fitch
Investment Grade	Aaa	AAA	AAA
	Aa1	AA+	AA+
	Aa2	AA	AA
	Aa3	AA–	AA–
	A1	A+	A+
	A2	A	A
	A3	A–	A–
	Baa1	BBB+	BBB+
	Baa2	BBB	BBB
	Baa3	BBB-	BBB-
Non-investment Grade	Ba1	BB+	BB+
	Ba2	BB	BB
	Ba3	BB–	BB–
	B1	B+	B+
	B2	B	B
	B3	B–	B–
	Caa1	CCC+	CCC+
	Caa2	CCC	CCC
	Caa3	CCC–	CCC–
	Ca	CC	CC
Highly Speculative	C	C	C
		D	D

Historical Experience of Defaults

The rate of default by investment-grade borrowers varies a great deal from time to time. However, unless you are a highly skilled analyst and trader (and maybe not even then), you are unlikely to be able to move into and out of bonds in advance of good or bad credit news.

Therefore, you should be more interested in the overall, cumulative experience of defaults of different ratings grades. We can see cumulative historic default rates in the table below.

Table 3.2   Cumulative Historic Default Rates, 1970–2006[14] (in percent)

Cumulative Historic Default Rates (in percent)

Rating categories	Moody's		S&P	
	Municipal	Corporate	Municipal	Corporate
Aaa/AAA	—	0.52	—	0.60
Aa/AA	0.06	0.52	—	1.50
A/A	0.03	1.29	0.23	2.91
Baa/BBB	0.13	4.64	0.32	10.29
Ba/BB	2.65	19.12	1.74	29.93
B/B	1.86	43.34	8.48	53.72
Caa-C/CCC-C	16.58	69.18	44.81	69.19
Investment Grade	0.07	2.09	0.20	4.14
Non-investment Grade	4.29	31.37	7.37	42.35
All	0.10	9.70	0.29	12.98

Source: US Congress, House Report 110-835, Section 205. Sept. 9, 2008, https://www.congress.gov/congressional-report/110th-congress/house-report/835/1

Notice that in the reporting period of 36 years, there were no AAA municipal (or muni) bonds that defaulted. However, this does not mean that if you had bought only AAA bonds you would have never experienced a default. Why? Because bonds can be, and often are, downgraded. Even so, however, since the end of the Great Depression, municipal bond defaults in the United States have been fairly rare. As this is written in early 2023, Puerto Rico is still trying to recover from a 2016 default on approximately $72 billion in debt. To date, this is the largest muni-bond default in US history. It has also been the case that large municipal bankruptcies are often politicized, and the outcome to bondholders may not follow the priorities they thought they were promised. This has been the case in Puerto Rico, with both general obligation bondholders and certain collateralized bondholders fighting over who has priority.

---

[14] These data apparently cover the years 1970–2006. Note therefore that these tables do not reflect the historically very high default rates that occurred in 2008 and 2009.

The best way to minimize your exposure to credit risk when investing in bonds other than home-currency bonds issued by a sovereign entity that prints its own currency (e.g. US government bonds denominated in US dollars; Japanese government bonds denominated in yen) is to buy a very diversified basket of bonds, and to stick with investment-grade bonds, preferably nothing below A rated. For the majority of individual investors who invest in bonds, it makes more sense to use one or more bond mutual funds than to purchase individual bonds.

Interest Rate Risk

All fixed-coupon bonds (most bonds except for adjustable or floating-rate bonds) are exposed to the risk of rising interest rates. Everything else equal, the longer the maturity of a bond, the greater the exposure to interest rate risk. The exposure of a bond to a change in interest rates is measured by a number called the bond's *duration,* which we discussed briefly in chapter 2. Duration has several definitions, but in this context we use it to mean sensitivity to interest rates. For example, as of this writing, the duration of the US government 10-year note (which is another name for "bond") is about 9.1. This means that for every 1% that interest rates rise, the value of the note will fall by about 9.1%. The current duration of the US government 30-year bond is 21.0. That is, if long-term interest rates were to rise 1%, the value of a 30-year bond would fall about 21%.

Duration is somewhat complex mathematically. One standard text on bond math (there's a lot of detail) is *Fixed Income Mathematics* by Frank Fabozzi, published by McGraw Hill. Unless you are a professional, you won't need 99.9% of it. In the next section, we'll try to give the minimum you should know.

Bond Math – The Absolute Minimum

If you invest in bonds, even if you do so through mutual funds, you need to know a few basic aspects of bond math. We just mentioned duration. Confusingly, a bond usually has more than one yield at any given moment. The three yields you need to know about are the *coupon yield*, the *current yield*, and the *yield-to-maturity*. Only when the bond is trading exactly at par (i.e. $100 market price for $100 principal value) do the three yields equal each other.[15]

The *coupon yield* is simply the stated yield on the bond. For example, suppose a bond is issued at par to yield 6%. For every $1,000 of principal value, it will pay $30 every six months, for a total of $60 a year. (Unlike our example of *bond 1* in chapter 2, in the United States, bonds usually pay interest semiannually.) The interest, $60, divided by the par value of $1,000, is 6%.[16]

---

[15] And even then, not exactly, because most bonds sold in the United States pay interest semiannually, so you need to consider compounding to get annual yields.

[16] The coupon is called the coupon because in the old days bonds were printed as physical pieces of paper with all the coupons attached. Each coupon had a date. When the date arrived, you had to physically clip the coupon (using scissors) and present the coupon at a bank for payment. They are no longer physical. Note that the coupons are semiannual (twice a year), and that the sum of coupons 3 and 4 equals 4.25% of the face value of the bond. Coupon 1 is for less because it was for a short period (i.e. not a full six months). There was probably another page of coupons that accompanied this bond when it was issued, as it appears to have a maturity in 1928.

The *current yield* is the dollar amount of the annual coupon divided by the current dollar market price. For example, suppose a $1,000 bond with $60 annual coupons was trading at a market price of 95, (bond prices are almost always quoted with 100 as par), meaning the bond has a current market value of $950. The current yield would be 60/950 = 6.316%.

The *yield-to-maturity* is the most complicated of the three yields, but the best way to compare one bond to another. Coupon yield overstates the true yield when a bond is trading above par, and understates it when the bond is trading below par. This is because if you buy a bond above par, the coupon yield ignores the premium that you will lose if you hold the bond to maturity. If you buy a bond at a price of $107.50, when it matures the principal payoff is $100, you lose the $7.50. This capital loss does not show up in the coupon yield. The same phenomenon is true with the current yield.

Yield-to-maturity solves the problem of considering both the coupons and the capital gain or loss on the difference between the price of a bond and its payoff value (which payoff value is usually 100.) Yield-to-maturity is the *internal rate of return* that equates all the bond's cash flows to its current market price. In other words, the yield-to-maturity is the rate of return (which we called r in chapter 2) such that the present value of all the bond's cash flows equals the bond's current price. Calculating a yield-to-maturity by hand is tedious. Almost everyone does it (if they must do it) using a computer or a calculator. If you choose to do the calculations yourself, you must learn the various conventions used by the software, and the conventions used in the market you are considering investing in.

Inflation Risk

Inflation is a risk for bondholders because most bonds have a fixed coupon. (Floating-rate bonds are an exception, which we do not deal with here.) If inflation turns out to be higher than the yield-to-maturity of the bond, the bondholder will have lost purchasing power, even if the bond pays in full and on time. Over the last approximately 100 years in the United States, as measured by an index of returns on US government 10-year bonds,[17] on average bondholders have earned a bit more than inflation, pre-tax, with long periods of both outperformance and underperformance. Since 1933, for example, the annual compounded total return on bonds (to 2012) was about 5.2%, compared to inflation over that period of about 3.6%.

Over the 84 years in NYU Professor Aswath Damodaran's data (see footnote 17), the total return on bonds has averaged 5.17%, while the coupon has averaged 5.05%. It is not a coincidence that the long-run return approximately equals the coupon. Over the long run, the only source of return is the coupon. This obvious truth must be given particular weight in environments of historically low interest rates, such as during mid-2021. If you buy a US Treasury 10-year bond (as bond buyers in mid-2021 may have done) at a yield of 0.9%, that's about what you should expect to get.

At such low rates, and in a world of fiat money where price inflation is the stated goal of the dollar's custodian,[18] owning 10-year government bonds can hardly be considered an investment (given our chapter 2 definition of an investment as "the exchange of cash for some other asset with the expectation of receiving in the future a greater value of cash in return"), because the interest on the bonds will probably not even keep up with inflation. During the "crisis" period of 2008 to 2015, when the Fed held interest rates at near zero and said it was worried about deflation, inflation as reported by the CPI averaged 1.7% per year, compounded. In 2021, the Fed publicly announced it would tolerate inflation higher than 2% a year. Sure enough, inflation skyrocketed during the latter half of 2021 and 2022. The Bureau of Labor Statistics reported official annual Consumer Price Index inflation rates of 8.5% for the year ending in March 2022.[19]

---

[17] There are many sources of data. We used data compiled by NYU professor Aswath Damodaran, who used numbers from the St. Louis fed. See www.damodaran.com.

[18] FRED Economic Data, St. Louis Fed, Graph of M2 Money Supply from 1960 to 2023, https://fred.stlouisfed.org/series/M2NS, accessed July 12 2023.

[19] Bureau of Labor Statistics, U.S. Department of Labor, The Economics Daily, Consumer prices up 8.5 percent for year ended March 2022, https://www.bls.gov/opub/ted/2022/consumer-prices-up-8-5-percent-for-year-ended-march-2022.htm.

Low Interest Rates as Financial Repression

For roughly eight years following the 2008 financial crisis, the Federal Reserve kept short-term interest rates at close to zero. This meant that savers holding cash and equivalents were losing value at the rate of inflation, because they earned no interest on their savings, but the value of their money decreased due to inflation (CPI a bit less than 2%). For the entire period from 2008 to 2020, savers in US dollars lost roughly 19% in real terms based on reported CPI.

An extremely rough measure of the amount of cash savings that might have been affected is the M2 money stock[20] which has averaged about $11 trillion over the 10 years (rising fairly steadily from about $8 trillion to $14 trillion) up to 2019. Because much of that money would have been earning interest, we can estimate that roughly 19% of $11 trillion, or about $2 trillion was transferred from savers to the borrowers who were able to borrow at or close to zero interest rates. The largest of these borrowers was the federal government, followed by banks.

In addition, for most of this time, the interest rate the government was paying on debt with maturity of less than five years was also below the CPI inflation rate. A rough estimate would be that the government borrowed an average of $5 trillion (in addition to the short-term borrowings already represented in M2) for eight years at a rate 1% below inflation. That would represent another $400 billion (because 1% of $5 trillion = $50 billion; that multiplied by 8 years = $400 billion) transferred from savers to the government, for a total of about $2.4 trillion, most of which went to the government with most of the rest going to banks.

(Note that the estimated transfer of $2.4 trillion would be about double if inflation really averaged close to 4%, as some people believe, rather than the officially reported 2% for the period.)

At near-zero interest rates, bonds are not an investment; they are a hedge against the possibility of collapsing equity prices, or, theoretically, against actual deflation.

[20] Bureau of Labor Statistics, U.S. Department of Labor, The Economics Daily, Consumer prices up 8.5 percent for year ended March 2022, https://www.bls.gov/opub/ted/2022/consumer-prices-up-8-5-percent-for-year-ended-march-2022.htm.

Chapter 4
Equities

What Are Equities?

Almost everything that is not a loan is an equity investment of some kind, or a combination of a loan and equity.[1]

Equity means ownership. When you own the common stock of a company, you own a small piece of the company. Legally, you have certain rights, and you participate in the profits and losses of the company. Virtually every publicly traded company has some form of limited liability, meaning that you cannot lose more than the amount you invest.

In practice, most of the time all you get is the up and down of the stock price on the stock market, and the dividends the company chooses to pay, if any.

The most obvious type of equity investment is ownership of stock in a company. But you also own equity if you own real estate, or if you invest in a partnership that engages in a business such as oil drilling or commodities trading. We will not discuss it further in this book, but you should be aware that certain types of partnerships (for example some oil drilling partnerships) can generate unlimited liability for the partners.

---

[1] Even complex contracts like options and futures can be modeled as packages of equity and debt.

Equity

As of 2014, the World Bank reported that there were 42,615 companies in 63 countries whose stock is listed on an exchange somewhere in the world. This almost certainly understates the true number, because the World Bank data is missing for some countries, such as Sweden and Finland, whose combined exchange lists over 300 companies. Following (Figure 4.1) is a graph showing the number of listed companies by country.

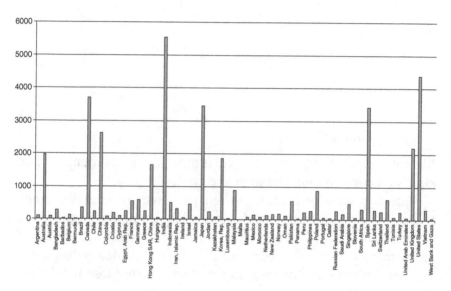

Figure 4.1   Number of Listed Companies by Country in 2014
Source: World Bank

In some sense, each of these 63 countries could represent a unique equity asset class, because returns may be more correlated within a country than between countries. However, most analysts don't consider each country, particularly small ones, as representing a meaningful asset class.

The number and identity of distinct equity asset classes will vary from analyst to analyst. However, for an American investor, most will suggest that the equity category contains the asset classes shown in Table 4.1:

Table 4.1 Equity Asset Classes

Asset Class	Brief Description
US large-cap companies	Companies with market capitalizations over $10 billion.
US mid-cap companies	Companies with market capitalizations between $2 and $10 billion.
US small-cap companies	Companies with market capitalizations less than $2 billion.
US REITs	Real Estate Investment Trusts.
International stocks	Stocks of companies based outside the United States, usually large-cap companies in the developed world.
Emerging markets	Stocks of large companies based in the developing world.
Gold-mining stocks	Gold-mining stocks have historically performed quite poorly since 1964, but have very low correlation with the S&P 500, and may be a hedge against inflation.

Additional Equity or Equity-Like Asset Classes That Might Be of Interest

In addition to the stock asset classes in Table 4.1, there are several other types of equity exposure that can be quite different. In the next section, we take a brief look at some of them.

What Generates Stock Returns

Benjamin Graham, the intellectual father of stock analysis, is often quoted as saying, "In the short run the stock market is a voting machine; in the long run it is a weighing machine."[2]

---

[2] The source for this saying of Graham's is his student, Warren Buffett. Buffett, in his 1993 letter to shareholders of Berkshire Hathaway, says, "As Ben Graham said: 'In the short-run, the market is a voting machine – reflecting a voter-registration test that requires only money, not intelligence or emotional stability – but in the long run, the market is a weighing machine.'" http://www.berkshirehathaway.com/letters/1993.html

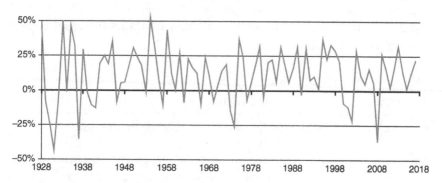

Figure 4.2   S&P 500 Total Returns 1928 to 2017
Source: http://www.stern.nyu.edu/~adamodar/pc/datasets/histretSP.xls

His comment contains two crucial insights. First, in the short run, stock returns are driven mainly by price changes. Over the short to medium term, stock prices can go almost anywhere. However, over the long term, the returns to stocks are driven mostly by earnings.

Let's digress on this subject for a while, because it all too often gets lost in the noise and hype surrounding stocks, investing, and the stock market.

Recall that returns are calculated by taking the difference between the ending price of a stock and its starting price, plus any dividends that you were paid on the stock.

Pretend for a moment that the stock market as we know it didn't exist; however, you could invest by buying small pieces of companies, which you would then hold for, say, 30 years. Your ownership would give you the right to receive your proportionate share of the earnings (if any) of the company. Together with your fellow owners, you would decide how much of the earnings to distribute to the owners each year (i.e. dividends), and the remainder would be reinvested by the business, ideally to earn good returns.

The primary way a business grows is by saving part of its earnings and reinvesting those earnings (called "retained earnings" by accountants) into the business. The amounts reinvested by the business increase the *book value* of the business. (Book value refers to what accountants call *stockholder's equity*, of which retained earnings is a part.)

You can see that over a long period of time, your return would consist of the dividends you receive (i.e. earnings that are paid out) plus the growth in the value of the business. That growth results primarily from reinvesting earnings. Therefore, the main source of your return over the long run is the earnings of the company.

That should be obvious, but it is sometimes obscured when media figures, talking heads, and various pundits discuss the stock market.

This insight is valuable enough that I will repeat it: Over the long run, the primary source of returns to owners of companies (i.e. stockholders) is the earnings such companies earn. If you remember this and always keep it in mind when investing, you will, we hope, avoid some of the greater follies that stock investors sometimes fall into.

Medium- and Short-Run Returns

Stock investing is made much more difficult by the large swings that can affect stock prices in the short to medium run. Often these swings have little to do with earnings or earnings power, but often it is unclear what is causing them.[3]

Over the short to medium term, most of the return (gains or losses) from owning stocks is generated by changes in prices (so-called capital gains or capital losses). These shorter-term swings are what Graham is referring to when he says in the short run the stock market is a voting machine. In the short run, the price of a stock can go almost literally anywhere.

---

[3] Many economists have tried to explain these short-run changes, but other than an essentially untestable hypothesis of changes in expectations, they haven't had much luck. See, for example, Stefan Avdjiev and Nathan Balke, "Stochastic Volatility, Long Run Risks, and Aggregate Stock Market Fluctuations," Bank for International Settlements Working Paper (October 2010).

For example, in 2018, the Canadian cannabis company Tilray, which had never earned a dollar and had barely any sales, saw its stock start trading in the public markets in the summer at $17 a share, which valued the company at $1.3 billion. That valuation was 8.5 times the book value, and the company had negative earnings (i.e. was losing money), negative cash flow (i.e. was using up cash, rather than generating cash), and small revenues. Nevertheless, within three months, the stock had (albeit briefly) shot up to $300 a share, theoretically valuing the company at over $22 billion, and 150 times book value! By the next day, the stock had dropped to $150 a share, cutting the market value of the company by $11 billion in mere hours.

Individual Stocks Versus "The Market"

The stock market is, by definition, the sum of the stocks that trade. One might expect that because every company is different, what happens to the price of one company over a day, a month, or a year would be completely independent of what happens to the price of another, unrelated company. But that is not the case. For whatever reasons, the short- and medium-term price movements of stocks tend to be correlated with each other.

Thus, it makes sense to speak of "the market" going up or down.

For the remainder of the book, we will focus not on individual stocks, but on stock markets (usually of different countries) and on stock market "segments" such as gold-mining stocks or real estate investment trusts.

Markets and Indices

While people often talk about "the stock market," we can be slightly more specific. For example, when we talk about the US stock market, we might be talking about the Dow Jones Industrial Average (DJIA), or the S&P 500 index. Each is an index designed to represent "the market" in the United States. Both do a pretty decent job, because both contain a significant fraction of the total value of the companies traded on the US exchanges, and because, as previously mentioned, stock price changes tend to be highly correlated.[4]

The valuation concepts that apply to individual companies apply to stock markets as well. Over the long run, the return that a stock market generates is mostly determined by the earnings of the companies that compose the market.

Over the short to medium term, the returns to a stock market are determined largely by price movements in the market.

Valuation Measures for Individual Companies

In theory, any investment asset is worth the present value of its expected future cash flows. In the case of equities, it is difficult to know what those future cash flows will be, and therefore difficult to calculate an appropriate present value of cash flows.

You could spend all your time trying to understand the expected cash flows of a company, let alone a large group or an entire market of companies. Fortunately, there are a few key summary valuation measures[5] that can be applied to companies and markets. We discuss two of them.

One key valuation measure for a company is its price-to-earnings (P/E) ratio. The price-to-earnings ratio is the company's price-per-share divided by its earnings-per-share. Equivalently, it is the company's market capitalization (which is the price-per-share times the number of shares, or the "price" of the entire company), divided by the company's total earnings.

A company's P/E ratio represents the price you are paying today for a dollar of annual earnings. For example, if a company has a P/E

---

[4] Although the DJIA has only 30 stocks, and is a price-weighted average, and the S&P 500 has 500 stocks and is market-cap weighted, for the 48 years from 1970 to 2018, the average annual return of the two indices differed by only a few hundredths of 1%. Over shorter periods, the performance can and has diverged significantly more.

[5] There is a common misuse of the term *metric* when what is meant is *measure*. According to the US National Institute of Standards and Technology, "The terms *metric* and *measure* have some overlap. We use *measure* for more concrete or objective attributes and *metric* for more abstract, higher-level, or somewhat subjective attributes. For instance, lines of code (LOC) is a measure: it is objective and concrete."

ratio of 10, this means that you're paying $10 for each $1 of earnings. While there is no certainty that the company will continue to earn the same amount per share, we have lots of historical data that enables us to identify "high" and "low" valuations.

There is no theoretically "correct" P/E ratio. We have historical data for thousands of companies, in some cases back to the nineteenth century, and this provides a background for considering whether a given P/E ratio is "high," "low," or neither. In general, taking the market as a whole, single-digit P/E ratios would be considered low, and ratios over about 30 would be considered high.

Another important valuation measure is the price-to-book (P/B) value. A company's *book value* is what accountants call *shareholder's equity*. On a company's balance sheet, shareholder equity is what remains after liabilities are subtracted from assets.[6] In financial accounting terms, *assets* include items that the company owns. Assets appear on the left-hand side of a balance sheet. Common categories include cash, property, plant and equipment, goodwill, intellectual property, and inventory.

Liabilities represent claims against the company. Liabilities appear on the right side of a corporate balance sheet. Common categories of liabilities include amounts that the company owes currently, such as accounts payable, and amounts that the company will have to pay later in the future, such as long-term debt.

The greater the excess of the company's assets over its liabilities, the higher the company's equity. Assuming the book values represent market value,[7] if the company sold all its assets and paid its liabilities, it would have the equity left over. Everything else equal, if a company has higher equity, it is worth more. The P/B value represents the price you are paying per dollar of book value. Like

---

[6] This is yet another example of a finance word having more than one meaning. We have been talking about equities as an asset class. Now we use the same word, asset, to describe a holding on the balance sheet of an individual company.

[7] In general, there is a difference between book value and market value of assets. This difference is explained in part by accounting rules, which require companies to carry assets on their books (i.e. on the balance sheet) at the lower of cost or market.

the P/E ratio, a low P/B ratio is "cheap," and a higher P/B ratio is "expensive."

It is important to note, however, that book value may not represent the full value of certain companies, including tech companies, which tend to have relatively low book values. Remember that book value represents assets minus liabilities. Tech companies, which tend to generate more value from their intellectual property than do other companies, may not be able to count this intellectual property as an asset. Alternatively, the intellectual property may be counted as an intangible asset, but such assets are difficult to value. So the intellectual property may be valued, on the balance sheet, at less than it is actually worth. Tech companies' book values may seem low compared to the company's true value.

Valuation Changes and Returns

Just as an individual company can have a price/earnings (P/E) ratio, so can an entire market. In essence, if you sum the earnings of all the companies in a market and divide by the total market value of the companies (the market value is the price per share times the number of shares), you will get an earnings-to-price ratio (also called an earnings yield) for the entire market. Take the reciprocal, and you have the P/E for the market.

P/E ratios for markets can be high or low, just as they can for individual companies.

Remember that over the long run the primary determinant of returns of a stock market is the aggregate earnings of the companies that compose the market.

However, over the short to medium term, changes in valuation levels, e.g. P/E ratios, dominate returns.

For example, daily changes of 1% in the value of the market are not uncommon. Because of the way companies actually earn money, and the way they report earnings, it is extremely unusual for the earnings of the market to change anywhere near 1% in a day. Many days the reported earnings of the market don't change at all. But days in which the market is open and prices don't change are exceedingly rare.[8] As previously mentioned, there may be no obvious, or even any discernible, reason for the price change. This observation of the apparently random movement of prices gave rise to the random walk hypothesis.

Noise – Information Versus Signal

In the pre-digital days of radio, it was common to fiddle with a radio dial trying to find a faint broadcast signal among the noise that fills the airwaves. Scientist Claude Shannon at ATT's Bell Labs developed a theory of information, and part of his theory involved this question of signal versus noise.

Shannon observed that the signal/noise problem exists in many situations outside of radio. In fact, the signal/noise problem exists anywhere that information coexists with a lot of random or seemingly random data.

Stock price information would seem to be an example of noisy data. If you watch the changes in the DJIA from minute to minute, most of it seems random. Randomness cannot be proved, only disproved. But we, and most observers, believe that most of the short-term movements in stock prices are random.

For most people, the fact that short-term stock price movements are mostly random means one thing: You can completely ignore the daily (or more frequent) reports of price movements and miss nothing that matters. The "tale of the tape" is mostly "sound and fury, signifying nothing."[9]

---

[8] You may object that the stock market is evaluating the present value of all expected future cash flows, and that therefore a small percentage change in, say, each of the expected future cash flows should produce a larger percentage change in the net present value, which is the sum of all those expected future cash flows. You would be right. Robert Shiller, author of *Irrational Exuberance*, looked at this question in a 1980 paper titled "Do Stock Prices Move Too Much to be Justified by Subsequent Changes in Dividends?" Robert J. Shiller, *The American Economic Review* Vol. 71, No. 3 (Jun., 1981), pp. 421–436. Shiller said the answer was yes. Economists continue to debate the question.

[9] Economist Paul Samuelson wrote one of the first papers suggesting that price movements are random in 1964. His memorable title, evoking MacBeth, was "Is Real World Price a Tale Told by the Idiot of Chance?" The phrase "tale of the tape" is an old Wall Street saying, and dates from the time before modern digital communications when stock prices were communicated by a specialized telegraph which printed them on long, thin strips of paper called ticker tape.

Valuation Changes

But you can't ignore valuation. If the market is trading at a P/E of 30, everything else equal, long-run returns are going to be lower than if the market is trading at a P/E of 10.

Two factors work against you when you invest in an "expensive" market. These factors are the low earnings yield, and the possibility that the market will "reprice" to a lower multiple.

Stocks, like other goods, come with prices, and those prices can be cheap or expensive. There are a number of different ways of determining whether a market is "cheap" or "expensive." CAPE, or cyclically adjusted price earnings ratio, is one of them. The CAPE uses the current value of the market as its numerator, and the inflation-adjusted 10-year average of earnings for its denominator. In a wide variety of markets around the world, the CAPE, along with similar valuation measures, has done a decent job of forecasting long-run returns from the stock markets.

Although there is quite a bit of noise, a high CAPE probably means a low return over the next decade or two. There are two factors associated with a high CAPE that tend to push future returns toward the lower side of the range. The first is the fact that a high CAPE means a low earnings yield. If there is no change in the valuation level, and no change in earnings, the return will approximate the earnings. The second factor is that a high CAPE has more room to revert to a lower CAPE than it does to move even higher.

Similarly, a very low CAPE means an increased probability of a high return over the coming decade or two. Again the two factors are at play. A low CAPE means a high current earnings yield. It's easier to earn high returns when you're getting 10% to start than when you're getting 3%. Second, if historical ranges provide a reasonable guide for the future, a low CAPE is more likely to rise as it reverts to the mean, than it is to fall or stay low.

Historic CAPE Versus Returns

The following chart shows the relationship between CAPE and subsequent 15-year returns for the US, Japan, Germany, and the world for the 34 years between 1979–2013. The relationship, while noisy, is clear. Higher CAPEs in the past 30 or so years are associated with lower returns, and lower CAPEs are associated with higher returns.

The fitted curve in Figure 4.3 showing CAPE versus subsequent 15-year annual real return is Expected Return $= -0.075\ln(x) + 0.2775$, where x is the current CAPE. For example, if the current CAPE is 20, the expected return is $-.075 \times 2.9957 + .2775 = .0528$, or 5.28%.

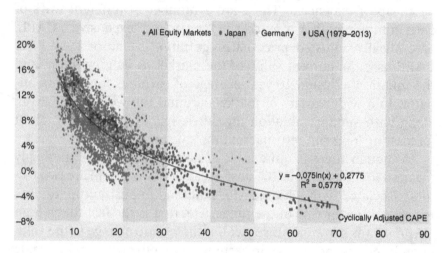

Figure 4.3 Connection CAPE vs. Real Returns of the 15 Following Years (p.a) in the period 1881–2013 (other markets). The US, Japan and Germany are higlighted as examples in a single perid 1979–2013. All returns-adjusted, in local currency, incl. dividend income and annualized.
Source: Star Capital

This graph may overstate the strength of the relationship because the points graphed are based on lots of overlapping data. That is, during the 132 years from 1881 to 2013, there are only 8 completely nonoverlapping periods. But these data would count, for example, the 15 years from 1985 to 2000 as one data point, and the 15 years from 1986 to 2001 as another.

What About Momentum?

Many people like to buy stocks that have been rising, because they expect that the stocks will continue to rise. The financial world term for this kind of strategy is *momentum*. Many academicians, and many professional investors, have studied markets around the world looking for evidence of *momentum*. Many have found that yes, indeed, there is, or has been, momentum in stock returns.

For example, in 2011, Jegadeesh and Titman[10] found:

"There is substantial evidence that indicates that stocks that perform the best (worst) over a three- to 12-month period tend to continue to perform well (poorly) over the subsequent three to 12 months. Until recently, trading strategies that exploit this phenomenon were consistently profitable in the United States and in most developed markets."

At around the same time, Cliff Asness, who earned his PhD at the University of Chicago under Eugene Fama, the father of the efficient-market hypothesis (EMH), argued that "momentum is a strong ex ante efficacious strategy around the world."[11]

Asness's company, AQR, runs a momentum fund that "employs a systematic approach to construct the portfolio that starts by identifying the investment universe, ranks the stocks in the universe by their total return over the prior 12 months excluding the last month, selects those that rank in the top third, weights them by market capitalization, and rebalances at least quarterly."[12]

There is quite a bit of evidence to suggest that momentum is "real," but the evidence that it is exploitable by individual investors is much less clear. Exploiting momentum is not easy.

We conclude that momentum is probably not an appropriate strategy for individual investors who don't want to devote a lot of their own time to study, and perhaps to trading.

[10] Narasimhan Jegadeesh and Sheridan Titman, "Momentum," *Annual Review of Financial Economics* 3 (December 2011): 453–509.
[11] Clifford Asness, "Momentum in Japan: The Exception That Proves the Rule," *Journal of Portfolio Management* 37 (Summer 2011): 67–75.
[12] "About the Fund," n.d., AQR Large Cap Momentum Style Fund, https://funds.aqr.com/funds/aqr-large-cap-momentum-style-fund#about

What Has Generated Historical
Returns in the US Market?

Changes in valuation matter, but as the time horizon gets longer, changes in valuation matter less, and earnings matter more. For example, suppose that earnings start at $1 and the market is priced at a P/E of 16.67 (i.e. an earnings yield of 6% which is 1/16.67). The "market" will be valued at $16.67 (because the "market" earns $1, and is valued at 16.67 times earnings). Let us suppose that the earnings are reinvested and the companies that compose the market earn the same return on the reinvested earnings as they had been earning on their original capital.

That is, if the market was priced at 16.67 times earnings, the earnings yield was (by definition) 6%. We will assume that the reinvested earnings also earn 6%. This is a complicated way of saying that we are assuming that the market will compound earnings at 6% per year. If earnings compound at 6% a year for 10 years, after 10 years, the market earnings will be $1 \times (1 + .06)^{10} = \$1.79$. If the multiple is still 16.67 times earnings in 10 years, the annual return for the 10 years will have been 6%, and the market which started at $16.67 will be worth $29.85. We calculate that future market by multiplying the earning in 10 years, 1.79, by the multiple, 16.67. (This is the market's earnings multiplied by the price/earnings, which gives us the market's "price," more commonly known as the market valuation.)

But the P/E multiple of the market tends to change over time. To simplify our model, let's assume that the P/E multiple stays constant at 16.67 (so we can reinvest and compound at 6% each year), but then right at the end the multiple jumps up to 28.

Now the value of the market at the end of year 10 will be its earnings, 1.79, multiplied by its P/E ratio, 28. The product of 1.79 and 28 is 50.12. The growth of 16.67 to 50.12 in 10 years is an annual compound rate of 11.7%.[13] The increase in the valuation multiple is

---

[13] $\left(\frac{50.12}{16.67}\right)^{\frac{1}{10}} - 1 = 11.7\%$

a very significant source of total return. Put differently, the market generated a compound annual return of 11.6%, of which 6% came from reinvesting earnings, and the other 5.6% came from an increase in how those earnings were valued, that is, an increase in the P/E ratio.

Now let's consider a period of 50 years, with the same 6% per year earnings being compounded. After 50 years the earnings will be $1 \times (1+.06)^{50} = 18.42$. If the multiple is still 16.67, the total annual return will be an average of 6%. But if the multiple jumps right at the end to 28, the market will have a value at the end of the 50 years of $18.42 \times 28 = 515.8$. The annual compound (or geometric) return is 7.1% per year. The valuation change still matters, but not nearly as much over a longer term.

Over the short to medium term, the return on the market is driven to a large extent by changes in how a dollar of earnings is valued. That, in turn, depends on investors' degree of optimism or pessimism. Hence, in the short to medium term, the stock market is a voting machine. But over the long term, mainly what matters is earnings; hence, says Graham, in the long run the stock market is a weighing machine.[14]

Long-Run Source of Returns to US Stocks

Most of our discussion of returns has ignored inflation. But a large part of earnings growth over the past century has been inflation.

Over the last century or so, depending on the exact period and the exact measurements used, US stocks have returned about 10.7% per year, compounded. These returns have been composed as shown in Table 4.2.

---

[14] Because we cannot observe directly why the market does what it does, this interpretation is only a theory, and is hard to falsify. There are other interpretations. One of the more interesting ones comes from economist/philosopher Erik Angner, who argues that the cheapness or expensiveness of stocks is driven mainly by the desire of institutions to hold equities, and this desire, it seems to him, is largely independent of their price or "value."

Table 4.2   Breakdown of Stock Return Data

Dividends	4.2%
Real earnings growth	2.5%
Inflation	3.5%
Valuation change	0.5%
Total	**10.7%**

But the 10.7% is somewhat misleading. To get an inflation-adjusted return, we must subtract out the inflation element. Subtracting 3.5% from 10.7% leaves a "real" or inflation-adjusted return of 7.2%. But if we want to use this historical number to project future returns, we should probably also take out the .5% which resulted from "valuation change."

The valuation change is the result of the expansion of the price/earnings ratio during the period studied. For example, in 1900, the P/E of the US stock market was about 13. Recently (2023) it was about 26. That increase in P/E over 123 years has added about 0.5% per year to the annual return. But there is no reason to expect that multiple to continue to expand.[15] It might expand, or it might contract; we just can't tell.

What Returns Can We Expect from US Stocks from Here?

As this is written in Q3 mid-2023, the CAPE of the US stock market is about 30, and the dividend yield is about 1.54%. By historical standards, the US market is in the expensive to very expensive range.

---

[15] Although there is no absolute theoretical maximum to the multiple at which equities can trade, the maximum for an entire developed market (excluding periods of severely depressed or negative earnings) that we are aware of was reached by the Japanese market in the late 1980s, when the P/E of the entire market was close to 100. I (Roger) was working in the Treasury group at the World Bank then, and I recall all of us marveling at the stratospheric heights the Nikkei was reaching. Disbelief set in when the Nikkei reached about 18,000, which would have been about 50 times earnings. It doubled from there, reaching an all-time high of 38,957 on December 29, 1989, before the bubble burst. Twenty years later, in 2009, the Nikkei finally bottomed, having fallen nearly 90%. Japanese stocks have still not recovered to their highs of 1989. In late 2023, it stands at around 31,200.

Over the long run, the nominal return should be the sum of earnings growth plus dividends and inflation. Ignoring inflation, if real earnings growth is 2.5% and the dividend is 1.9%, we can expect about 4.4% real return over the long run. (Note that 4.4% equates to a P/E ratio of 22.7, which is 1/(4.4).) If inflation averages 2% on top of this, maybe we can expect 6.4%. In the short to medium to even 30-year time frame, the result could be significantly lower if the market reprices to a lower P/E, as happened with Japan.

Another way of thinking about this gets us to a similar result. If we merely take the reciprocal of the CAPE (i.e. 1/30), we get 3.3% for a current earnings yield. This 3.3% becomes a reasonable estimate of long-run real return. If we add 2% inflation, we get an estimate of 5.3% long-run return.

Using data from Robert Shiller[16] we see the following relationship between CAPE and the real total return (i.e. price change plus dividends, adjusted for inflation) from the US stock market from the period 1881–2015. This graph is based on annual data. The graph maps the CAPE earnings yield (which is 1/CAPE) on the x-axis, versus the returns of US stocks for the next 10 years on the y-axis. The CAPE earnings yield is based on the average 10-year earnings of the past 10 years of the stock, whereas the 10-year returns were generated in the 10 years after the CAPE was measured. Thus, the graph establishes a relationship between the past CAPE earnings yield of the stock market and its future returns.

The slope of the fitted line is not statistically significantly different from one. That is, it is plausible to read this graph basically the same way we read the bond yield versus returns graph. That is, the earnings yield (based on 10-year average earnings) is a decent predictor of the total, real return over the next 10 years. (Note, however, the low R-squared which reflects that the line does not explain most of the observed variance. Nevertheless, the basic relationships seems consistent with the naïve view that future returns can be roughly estimated by the current CAPE earnings yield.)

---

[16] Based on data from Robert Shiller, available at http://www.econ.yale.edu/~shiller/data.htm

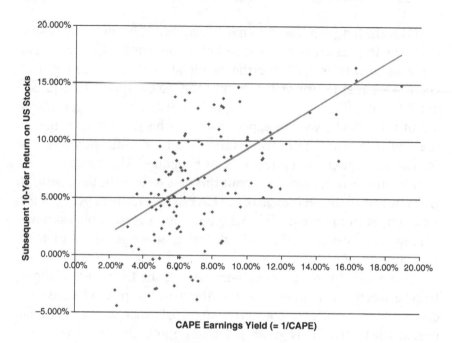

Figure 4.4 US Stock Market CAPE (P/E 10) vs. Subsequent 10 Year Real Return
Source: Robert Shiller

There are several differences between this chart and the bond chart. The most obvious is the amount of "noise" in the data. That is, for any given level of CAPE yield, the subsequent return might vary tremendously. For example, when the CAPE earnings yield was about 6%, (corresponding to a CAPE of 16.66), the subsequent 10-year real returns were as low as –3%, and as high as 13%.

The second is a statistical observation that wouldn't really affect our conclusions, but we note it because a careful reader might wonder about it. That statistical observation is that a line is unlikely to be the correct theoretical fit, because as the market gets more and more expensive, the CAPE yield gets smaller and smaller, and as the earnings yield approaches zero, the nonlinearity of the change increases.[17]

---

[17] There are actually a lot of standard statistical assumptions which this linear regression violates. The errors are heteroskedastic; the model seems fairly obviously misspecified; the data periods overlap which virtually guarantees that there is (impermissible) autocorrelation, and there are

The general trend of the graph indicates that if the CAPE earnings yield is low (in other words, that the P/E ratio, which is the reciprocal of the earnings yield, is high), then the subsequent 10-year returns will be low, and vice versa. However, as can be seen from the graph, this is not always the case.

But don't worry too much about the statistical methods. The fit of real-world data is so noisy that we can't do much more than observe that over the past 140 years, there has been a general tendency for high valuations (i.e. low earnings yields) to produce low returns, and low valuations to produce high returns.

Valuation Risk

The long run CAPE (for the past century or so) of the US market has averaged about 17. For the past couple of decades, the CAPE has averaged about 27. Some people argue that the market has permanently repriced to higher valuations.[18]

Other people believe that sooner or later the valuations will return to levels closer to their long run averages (i.e., they will *revert to the mean*).

There seem to be good arguments on both sides, but no one can guarantee that valuations will stay high. It is instructive to look at the potential effect on returns if valuations return to lower levels.

Medium-Term Expected Returns

Over the medium term, say 10–20 years, we should expect that the returns to the market may be influenced by the valuation reverting toward its mean.[19] The CAPE at 30 is much more expensive than its

---

probably others. In an ideal world, we'd use nonoverlapping periods, but we just don't have enough data to do so.

[18] See, for example, Rob Arnott, Vitali Kalesnik, and Jim Masturzo, CAPE Fear: Why CAPE Naysayers Are Wrong, ResearchAffiliates.com (January 2018).

[19] Whether or not the CAPE is mean-reverting is hotly debated. But the debate is really about the time frame. The CAPE cannot go anywhere. For a discussion, see Arnott et al., CAPE Fear: Why Cape Naysayers Are Wrong, ResearchAffiliates.com (January 2018).

long-run average of about 17. We can use the log-linear regression equation from earlier. This regression gives us an expected return of $-.075 \times \ln(30) + .2775$, which equals 2.2%. If instead we used the linear fit (the regression equation in the previous chart), we find $(.93) \times \left(\frac{1}{30}\right) = 3.1\%$.

We could also build a simple spreadsheet to model the growth of earnings, and the possible contraction of earnings multiples. For example, the following spreadsheet is based on actual S&P 500 numbers as of December 2020. We somewhat arbitrarily assumed that earnings would grow at an average of 5.5% per year (including inflation), and also arbitrarily that the P/E would contract by 1.2 per year, until it reached 26.2, still far above its long-term average, by the end of 10 years.

The spreadsheet in Table 4.3 shows the earnings of the S&P 500 growing while the P/E ratio is shrinking. Multiplying the S&P's earnings times its P/E ratio gives us its price. In our model, the level of the S&P growth varies from 3,700 to 4,242 over the scenario period. The return to owning the S&P 500, however, would exceed that growth because of dividends. Those calculations are shown on the right side of Table 4.3. Starting with 3,700, and reinvesting dividends, at the end of year 10 we have 4,900. The annual compound return comes out to 2.86%, which after adjusting for inflation might be small, zero, or negative. As this hypothetical example illustrates, even if earnings grow, investors can do poorly.

Variability

History tells us that there is a lot of variability and unpredictability about returns. The actual return over the next 10 years from the US stock market could be significantly better, or significantly worse, than any of our estimates. But the point of our estimates is that it seems extremely optimistic to expect real returns over the next decade anywhere close to double digits, and even 6% would seem quite unlikely.

Table 4.3 S&P 500 Earnings Change Due to P/E Ratio

Year	Earnings	P/E ratio	Level of S&P 500	Percent Price Change (%)	Payout Ratio	Beg Bal	Div	End Bal	Div Yield
1	100.00	37.0	3,700		0.49	3,700	48.93	3,749	1.32%
2	105.50	35.8	3,777	2.08%	0.49	3,827	51.62	3,878	1.37%
3	111.30	34.6	3,851	1.96%	0.49	3,955	54.46	4,009	1.41%
4	117.42	33.4	3,922	1.84%	0.49	4,083	57.46	4,140	1.46%
5	123.88	32.2	3,989	1.71%	0.49	4,211	60.62	4,272	1.52%
6	130.70	31.0	4,052	1.57%	0.49	4,339	63.95	4,403	1.58%
7	137.88	29.8	4,109	1.42%	0.49	4,465	67.47	4,533	1.64%
8	145.47	28.6	4,160	1.25%	0.49	4,589	71.18	4,660	1.71%
9	153.47	27.4	4,205	1.07%	0.49	4,710	75.09	4,786	1.79%
10	161.91	26.2	4,242	0.88%	0.49	4,828	79.22	4,907	1.87%
						Compound Annual Return:		2.86%	
11	161.91	25.7	4,161	−1.91%	0.49	4813.212	79.22	4,892	1.90%
12	161.91	25.2	4,080	−1.95%	0.49	4797.25	79.22	4,876	1.94%
13	161.91	24.7	3,999	−1.98%	0.49	4779.717	79.22	4,859	1.98%
14	161.91	24.2	3,918	−2.02%	0.49	4760.58	79.22	4,840	2.02%
15	161.91	23.7	3,837	−2.07%	0.49	4739.807	79.22	4,819	2.06%
16	161.91	23.2	3,756	−2.11%	0.49	4717.362	79.22	4,797	2.11%
17	161.91	22.7	3,675	−2.16%	0.49	4693.209	79.22	4,772	2.16%
18	161.91	22.2	3,594	−2.20%	0.49	4667.312	79.22	4,747	2.20%
19	161.91	21.7	3,513	−2.25%	0.49	4639.63	79.22	4,719	2.25%
20	161.91	21.2	3,432	−2.30%	0.49	4610.123	79.22	4,689	2.31%

Source: http://www.multpl.com/s-p-500-earnings/

71

Takeaways Regarding Returns

The key takeaways are as follows: Returns come both from changes in price and changes in earnings. When forecasting future returns, you should be aware of the market's current valuation, and realize that the market's valuation may revert to the mean. That is, expensive markets are likely to reprice downwards, and cheap markets are likely to reprice up. If the P/E ratio increases, everything else equal, your returns will increase. If the P/E ratio decreases, everything else equal, your returns will decrease.

Chapter 5

Real Estate

Measured by market value, real estate is the biggest asset class in the world.[1] A 2018 report[2] estimated that the value of the world's real estate at year end 2017 was $280.6 trillion. That was broken down as follows:

Category	$Trillions
Residential	220.2
Commercial	33.3
Agricultural and Forestry	27.1
Total	280.6

A huge fraction of this real estate serves as collateral for mortgage loans. Confusingly, those loans are also sometimes considered

---

[1] Almost certainly the most valuable identifiable class of capital is human capital, but it is not readily investable and is not an asset class. In 2020, the UN ILO reported average wages in the G20 countries of about US$45,000 equivalent in the "advanced" countries and $22,000 in the "emerging" countries. More than half of the subject population is in "emerging" countries, so we guess at a global average of $30,000 equivalent. If there are 1.5 billion workers, then total global wages would be $45 trillion. It doesn't take a very high multiple to see that human capital is the most valuable class of capital in the world.

[2] Paul Tostevin, "8 Things to Know About Global Real Estate Value," Savills.com (July 2018), https://www.savills.com/impacts/market-trends/8-things-you-need-to-know-about-the-value-of-global-real-estate.html

"real estate." In the United States, most residential mortgage loans are actually complex financial instruments composed of characteristics of both bonds and options.[3] We believe that their complexity makes them poor candidates for inclusion in most individual investors' portfolios.

Kinds of Real Estate

Broadly speaking, most investment real estate fits into one of the following categories: farmland; timberland; residential (houses and apartments); office buildings; commercial/industrial/retail; and special purpose (stadiums, concert halls, port facilities). For some of these categories, we have enough historical data to make some observations.

We will take a somewhat in-depth look at farmland, residential, and office buildings, and skim or skip others.

Farmland

The value of farmland is mostly driven by the value of the crops that can be produced on that land. When the farmland is in the path of growth, as happened around many US cities in the nineteenth and twentieth centuries, owners can make a fortune by selling the land at a high price to developers who value the land, not as farmland, but as land to build on. It is hard to predict, however, whether a specific section of land will be in the path of growth. There is a strong theoretical argument that the long-run returns to farmland are primarily from the cash flow that the farmland produces.

---

[3] Because most residential mortgages are long term, and can be prepaid, the lender is usually short a package of options. The investor in mortgages, such as the retail investor in a mortgage mutual fund, becomes the lender. The built-in options mean that the mortgage portfolio has a property called "negative convexity." Negative convexity means, approximately, that when interest rates are rising, the portfolio will act like a longer-term bond, and the value will fall a lot, and when rates are falling, the portfolio will act like a shorter-term bond, and not rise much.

As with stocks, over short to medium terms, the returns will also be influenced by changes in the valuation of those cash flows.

Over the past 30 years or so, US farmland as a whole has been an excellent investment. On the other hand, so have long-term bonds, and the longer the better. This is probably not a coincidence. Recall that theoretically, the value of an asset is the present value of its expected future cash flows. In the case of land, these cash flows can plausibly be considered to extend into the indefinite future. If the cash flows were fixed, that would mean that land could be valued as a perpetual bond. As such, we would expect the value of land to be sensitive to interest rates, for, as we discussed in chapter 2, the value of bonds is sensitive to interest rates.

Figure 5.1 shows a graph of the nominal and real price of the average US farm over the past half century.

In 1967, the yield on long-term treasury bonds was about 5.5%. In 2017 it was about 2.7%. From Figure 5.1, we see that the average acre of farmland in 1967 had an inflation-adjusted value of around $900, and by 2017 that inflation-adjusted value was about $2,700, which represents a tripling of real value.

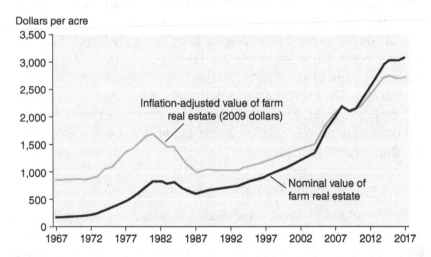

Figure 5.1 Average U.S. farm real estate valu, nominal and real (inflation adjusted), 1967–2017

Source: https://www.agrimarketing.com/s/112328

Falling Interest Rates Explain Half the Real Increase Since 1967 . . .

Recall that if we have an asset producing a perpetual cash flow, and an interest rate, the value of the asset is theoretically equal to the cash flow divided by the interest rate. Let us suppose that in 1967, the average acre of farmland produced $49.50 of cash flow. Using the 5.5% US Treasury long-term bond rate as the discount rate, we calculate $49.5/.055 = $900.[4] If that $49.50 remained unchanged, and we valued the asset again in 2017 using the 2.7% discount rate, the asset would be worth $49.5/.027=$1,833.

. . . But Falling Interest Rates Explain All the Real Increase Since 1987

Now let's do same analysis, but we'll choose 1987 as our starting year. In that year, the yield on the US long bond was about 8.8%. At 8.8%, every dollar of perpetual cash flow would be worth $1/.088 = $11.36, and at 2.7%, every dollar of perpetual cash flow would be worth $37.04. Note that 37.04 is 3.26 times 11.36. Thus, we can "explain" the entire increase in real (inflation-adjusted) farmland value between 1987 and 2017 by the change in interest rates.

Of course interest rates are far from the only factor. Farmland is not a bond. Changes in the availability and terms of loans, and changes in the price of farm products and inputs are also important factors. These other factors definitely play a role in the changes of farmland values. Even so, however, interest rates seem to be the dominant factor over the last 30 years, which is when most of the exciting returns took place.

Price/Earnings Ratio for Farmland

Much farmland in the United States is leased out for cash. These net cash rents (net of whatever costs are incurred; *net* refers to what is left over for the landowner, before interest and taxes) are

---

[4] We used $49.50 to keep this illustration simple. In the real world, farm returns are riskier than Treasuries, so everything else equal, they would require a higher discount rate.

economically very similar to earnings in a corporate setting. That means it is reasonable to look at a "price to rent" multiple for farmland, and this multiple is roughly analogous to a P/E multiple for stocks. Figure 5.2 shows a graph of that multiple for West Central Indiana farmland from 1960 to 2015.

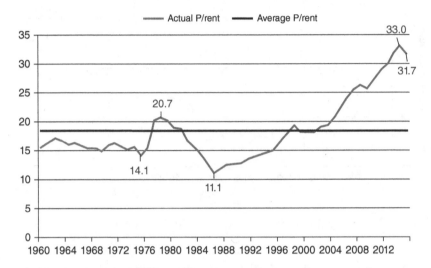

Figure 5.2 Farmland Price to Cash Rent Multiple for West Central Indiana. 1960–2015

Source: Purdue Agricultural Economics Report, August 2015, bdfcnmeidppjeaggnmidamkidd-ifkdib/viewer.html?file=https://ag.purdue.edu/commercialag/home/wp-content/uploads/2015/08/PAER-AUGUST-2015-Revised-.pdf

Note that the multiple ranges from a low of 11.1 (in the mid-1980s) to a recent high of 33. That increase is very close to the theoretical increase we calculated earlier due to changes in interest rates. Does the price/rent ratio of farmland predict future returns? Theory, and evidence from the past 60 years, suggest that the answer is yes.

If land is purchased at 31.7 times the cash rent, and that rent can be thought of like earnings, then it follows that the yield on the purchase price is 1/31.7 or 3.15%. (This is analogous to the earnings yield being the reciprocal of the P/E ratio.) In order for the return to increase, either rents have to rise or interest rates have to fall or both. Either is possible, but by historical standards rents are high and interest rates are low.

All Farmland

Figure 5.3 shows a chart of average US farmland rental rates (net of expenses) from USDA data. We were not able to find data from earlier than 1999.

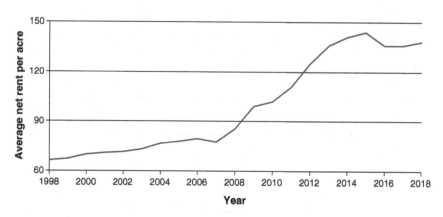

Figure 5.3   Average Net Cash Rental Per Acre for US Farmland
Source: USDA 60

We might wonder whether we can develop insight into what drove the large increase in rents beginning in the middle of the 2000s. Following are two graphs we put together using data from the USDA. We find them suggestive.

The graph in Figure 5.4 shows the average net farm rent per year and the price of corn.[5] Note that the price of corn began a steep and prolonged rise about 2006, and that rents began their steep rise with a lag. Can we understand anything about what caused the price of corn to jump? There is a strong circumstantial case that ethanol-burning is a prime suspect.

---

[5] The rent figure is a gross aggregate, and includes a very wide range of types of farmland, from low-rent, dry-land Montana to the high-rent coastal California and everything in between. The corn price is similarly an aggregate and average of many different prices averaged to a single number per year. I (Roger) should note that as I write this, the words "Crudest form of casual empiricism" are ringing in my ears. This was an admonition I heard in graduate school from my principal dissertation advisor, Anne E. Peck. This analysis is crude. But I'm trying to learn something, not publish an academic paper. We could do a bunch of sophisticated econometrics, but at the end I doubt we'd learn much if anything important that we don't learn from these graphs, and a bit of economic thinking.

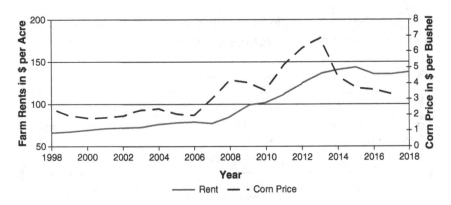

Figure 5.4   Farm Rents vs. Corn Price 50

We know that price is determined by the intersection of supply and demand. Everything else equal, a large increase in the demand for corn should cause the price of corn to rise. The graph in Figure 5.5 shows that beginning in 2005, the fraction of the corn crop used for ethanol[6] began a steep and prolonged rise.

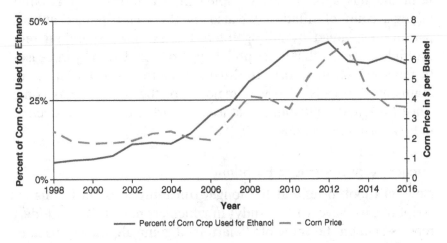

Figure 5.5   Corn Price vs. Percent of Corn Crop Used for Ethanol

---

[6] This increase is almost certainly due in large part to Congress's passing the Volumetric Ethanol Excise Tax Credit – a subsidy of 51 cents per gallon for ethanol – in late 2004. The total value of this subsidy has been in the neighborhood of $6 billion a year in recent years. That is a significant addition to the demand for corn, given that the total value of the US corn crop is in the neighborhood of $50 billion a year.

It is probably not coincidence that the corn price followed suit. Figure 5.6 shows all three factors on the same graph:

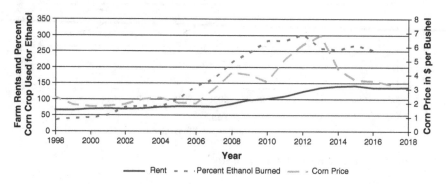

Figure 5.6   Farm Rents, Corn Price and Percentage of Corn Crop Used for Ethanol 0

Farmland – Summary

We saw that over the last 50 years, the value of prime Midwest farmland has approximately tripled in real terms, that is, after taking account of inflation. We also saw that that tripling is at least partially explained by falling interest rates, and expanding rent multiples. We saw that it has probably also been driven by increases in rents, which in turn were driven by increases in the prices of grains and oilseeds. The vast majority of the increase has come since 1987, and is attributable at least in part to the 30-year decline in long-term interest rates.

Longer-Term Returns to Farmland

Now let's look briefly at the longer-run returns to US farmland. Helpfully, we have a 1988 study[7] in which economist Peter Lindert reports data on the value of US farmland going all the way back to 1860.[8] Lindert's data enables us to look at the change in the real

---

[7] Peter Lindert, "Long-Run Trends in American Farmland Values," *Agricultural History* 62, no. 3 (1988): 45-85.

[8] Farmland prices in the South were cut in half during the Civil War decade, and remained depressed relative to the rest of the country until WWI.

(i.e. inflation-adjusted) price of farmland for the period from 1860 to 1986. During that long stretch, though there were long-term bull and bear markets, the overall average annual compounded growth rate was about 1% per year. For the shorter period between 1900 and 1986 (where the data are denser), the annual compound real return was also about 1%.

Lindert's data also include real rents. Between 1900 and 1986, the 10-year average of real rents also increased 1% per year.

So it seems plausible that farmland real values in the United States have increased at long-run trend of about 1% a year for the last century and a half. The great returns of the last 30 years can be entirely explained by increases in the cash rent multiple. And the increase in that multiple matches almost exactly the result we would expect if we viewed the stream of cash rents as a perpetual stream and discounted it at 30-year interest rates.

We saw that over the last 30 years, real farmland values have approximately tripled (due, we have argued, to the large drop in long-term interest rates). In addition, farmland owners have collected rents. The overall result has been very strong total returns. That has led some people to extrapolate those strong returns into the future. One of the arguments for continuing strong returns is based on the belief that per-acre grain yields will continue to rise. The essence of this argument is that if a given acreage produces more and more grain, then that acreage will become more and more valuable.

There is a certain plausibility to this increasing productivity argument, and it seems to be supported by the historical record of productivity growth. For example, Figure 5.7 shows a graph of US farmland corn yields.

Yields were essentially unchanged from the 1860s through the 1930s. Then, thanks to technology, primarily the application of fossil fuel powered machines to replace human and animal muscle power, they started increasing, and since the 1960s have been growing at an average of about 2 bushels per acre per year.

Looks great, right? Unfortunately for farmers, and therefore for landowners who rent to farmers, productivity growth does not

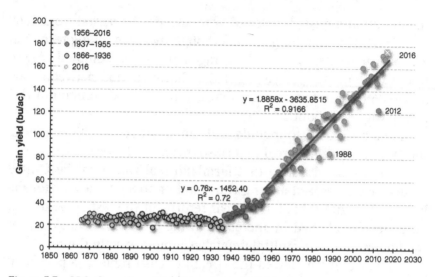

Figure 5.7   U.S. Corn Gran Yield Trends Since 1866
Source: Bob Nielsen, "Historical Corn Grain Yields in the US," *Corny News Network* (February 2023), https://www.agry.purdue.edu/ext/corn/news/timeless/yieldtrends.html

necessarily translate into profit growth. In practice, technological change has caused tremendous increases in productivity, but little increase in profits. This seeming paradox was dubbed the "technological treadmill" by economist Willard Cochrane way back in 1958.[9]

Cochrane noted that if you own the *only* farm that has increasing productivity, you can make out like a bandit, because you can produce and sell a lot more corn than your competitors, with little or no effect on the price. But if *everyone* is producing more corn, the supply of corn increases.

Everything else equal, when supply increases, market price must fall in order for the markets to clear. Over the past 80 years everything else hasn't been exactly equal, given that world population and demand for grains have grown. But on balance, the effects of increased supply and increased demand have mostly

---

[9] Willard Cochrane, *Farm Prices: Myth and Reality* (University of Minnesota Press, 1958).

canceled each other out, and the profits of farms have not increased nearly as much as productivity.[10] In other words, consumers of corn and grains benefit from lower prices, but producers don't. (More accurately, producers don't capture fully the benefits of increased efficiency. They do benefit, along with everyone else, from participating in an economy that is producing more wealth.)

Long-run evidence from the past 90 years suggests that overall increases in agricultural crop yield (as opposed to financial yield) will not translate into better returns to land. As seen in Figure 5.8, the costs of production have followed revenue fairly closely, leaving returns (i.e. profits) fairly stable over time.

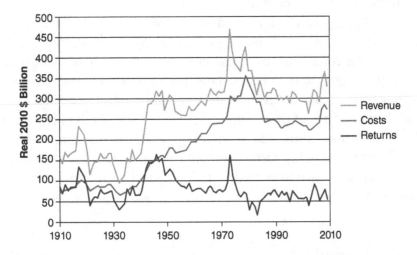

Figure 5.8 US Farm Revenue, Costs & Returns, Real Terms, 1910–2010
Source: Paul Mitchell, Presentation for course titled "Farming Systems Management," https://aae.wisc .edu/pdmitchell/

---

[10] The overall increase in farm productivity is termed the "green revolution" and Norman Borlaug is the person most associated with it. For billions of people in the world today, Borlaug is arguably the most important scientist ever, because without him there may have been no green revolution, and without the green revolution, billions of poor people could not be fed.

What Returns Should We Expect from Farmland?

The return to owning an asset is the capital gain or loss, plus the cash yield that the asset generates. In other words, it's the starting price minus the ending price, plus any yields such as dividends that you receive from the investment. There is evidence that the long-run price trend for US farmland is an increase in the real (inflation-adjusted) price, supported by increase in real rents, of about 1% per year.[11] So we might expect, over the long run, real capital gains of about 1% per year. In nominal terms, if we expect long-run inflation to average 3%, we might expect a long-run capital gain, or increase in the asset's price, of about 4% total.

To that capital gain, we would add the cash rent yield.[12] At today's valuations, farmland produces a cash rent yield in the neighborhood of 3%. So we might expect a total nominal return from farmland of 7% over the long run.

The history of US farmland since 1860 shows that farmland prices have experienced several generation-long swings in value. If that pattern continues, from the current high levels of valuation, there is a significant risk that land prices will fall in real terms, perhaps for decades. Given that land prices are at the very high end, in real terms, of their long-term trend, if prices fail to rise, or if they fall in the coming 15- to 30-year period, the real returns over that period to owning farmland could be quite low, given that all the return will have to come from already low yield in the form of cash rents.

---

[11] And maybe not even 1%. Simon Huston, et al., in their paper "Two Centuries of Farmland Prices in England," *Journal of Property Research* 35 (2018): 72–94, found that from 1801 to 2013, the average annual real (geometric mean) price return to farmland in England was about 0.7%. Christophe Spaenjers reports that US farmland produced a real (inflation adjusted) annual price return of 0.9% (geometric mean) during the period 1910–2014, in "The Long Term Returns to Durable Assets"; Chapter 5 in *Financial Market History*, David Chambers and Elroy Dimson (eds.) (University of Cambridge Press, 2016): 89.

[12] A cash rent yield would be the net cash rent divided by the market price of the land. For example, if the net cash rent were $30 per acre, and the market value of the acre were $1,000, the cash rent yield would be 3%.

Timber

In the US, there are over 500 million acres of timber. But there are only a few REITs that own timber. The historical performance of these REITs has suggested that timber REITs may provide some valuable diversification benefits, but probably do not provide long-run returns any greater than other REITs.[13] Timber REITs' returns are likely to come from sales of timber, organic growth of the trees, and changes in valuation. Timber is a long duration asset, and therefore from a theoretical viewpoint timber lands are likely to be very sensitive to interest rates.

Office Buildings

Retail investors can invest in office buildings through REITs. Over the long run, the value of an office building is primarily a function of the rental income it generates. You might think that office buildings are a great hedge against inflation, or a way to profit from owning property in a booming city.

For example, suppose you could have bought office buildings in New York City at the beginning of the twentieth century, and held them for the following century. Few cities in the world, if any, boomed more than New York during the twentieth century. How would you have fared financially?

Perhaps surprisingly, there's quite a bit of evidence to suggest that your returns would have been decent, but that you would not have earned extraordinary returns. For example, William Wheaton and colleagues studied 86 transactions in which the same office building in New York was sold more than once during the twentieth century. They found that, after adjusting for inflation, "commercial office properties were 30% lower in 1999 than they were in 1899."[14] There have been long periods when values rose sharply, and there have also been long periods when values fell

---

[13] Bin Mei and X. Piao, "Comparing the Financial Performance of Timber Reits and Other Reits," *Forest Policy and Economics* (June, 2016): 115–121.

[14] William Wheaton et al., "100 Years of Commercial Real Estate Prices in Manhattan," *Real Estate Economics* 37 (2009): 69–83.

sharply. They conclude, "long-term historic return to New York commercial property must mostly comprise yield with capital gains limited to general inflation."

If the pattern of the last century holds for the coming period, returns from New York office buildings (and probably the same pattern holds for other cities though we don't have the data) over the coming 15–30 years are likely to be low. Current cap rates in 2021 (which are roughly equivalent to the net rental yield, before considering financing and taxes, and are analogous to earnings yields for stocks), are somewhere around 3%.[15] If the real return from the changes in capital value are flat or negative, total returns will be quite low.

Returns to Land

The statement, "Buy land. They're not making any more of it"[16] seems intuitively true. And yet, that wisdom does not necessarily translate into investment returns. Since 1860, the population of the United States has grown at an average rate of somewhat over 1%, but the growth rate was higher in the nineteenth century, and the growth rate, while positive, has fallen since roughly the beginning of the twentieth century. During that same period, farmland values have averaged 1% real growth, with large swings uncorrelated with population growth.

The assumption implicit in the earlier Will Rogers quote is that "land" is a fixed resource. In a purely physical sense, of course, the amount of land on earth is fixed (subject to small natural fluctuations due to forces like erosion and volcanism). But as economist Julian Simon pointed out,[17] a "resource" is not a resource until

---

[15] Welcome to ReitNotes, https://www.reitnotes.com/cap-rate-by-real-estate-properties-in-US-cities/

[16] The actual Will Rogers quotation is "I had been putting what little money I had in Ocean Frontage, for the sole reason that there was only so much of it and no more, and that they wasent [sic] making any more . . ." according to the Will Rogers Today website, https://www.willrogerstoday.com/will_rogers_quotes/quotes.cfm?qID=7

[17] The Ultimate Resource (Princeton University Press, 1981).

people figure out how to use it. Petroleum, for example, has been known since antiquity, but its widespread use as a fuel wasn't innovated until the mid-nineteenth century.

So while land itself is "fixed," its use isn't. Builders in New York have figured out how to multiply a square foot of land by a factor of 10, 20, or 50 by building higher. Farmers (actually, an entire industry of innovators) have figured out how to multiply an acre of farmland by getting more and more yield from a given acre.

Of course, it must be the case that there is some limit. A building can go only so high, and only so much corn can be grown on an acre. But we are probably nowhere near those limits. For example, given existing technology, it is believed to be possible to build an office tower a mile high. And in 1985, Matthijs Tollenaar, a researcher at the University of Guelph in Ontario, Canada, calculated that the maximum theoretical potential corn from an acre was 502 bushels.[18] But in 2014, David Hula of Charles City, Virginia, actually grew 542 bushels of corn on an acre.[19] Also in 2014, Evan DeLucia and a team published a study in which they estimated that the theoretical limit of total potential plant productivity for human use (i.e. food, fuel, and fiber) is as much as 100 times current production levels.[20]

While no one can know for certain, the theoretical limit of land's productivity is not an issue to worry about for the foreseeable future. Both history and ongoing research strongly suggest productivity will continue to rise. For example, scientists are working on enhanced photosynthesis, and have already demonstrated in field tests that it can increase productivity by 40% in some plants.

---

[18] Matthijs Tollenaar, "Proceedings of the Conference on Physiology, Biochemistry and Chemistry Associated with Maximum Yield Corn," Foundation for Agronomic Research and Potash and Phosphate Institute, St. Louis, Missouri, November 1985.

[19] https://www.dtnpf.com/agriculture/web/ag/news/crops/article/2017/12/19/hula-sets-new-world-corn-yield-542

[20] E. DeLucia et al., "The Theoretical Limit to Plant Productivity," *Environmental Science & Technology* 2014: 48, https://pubs.acs.org/doi/abs/10.1021/es502348e

Homes

How much has the average American home appreciated, after adjusting for inflation, between 1890 and 2018? Even including the huge increase in prices since the end of the financial crisis, the compound annual growth of prices, after adjusting for inflation, has been less than 1/2% per year.[21]

International data also seems to support the idea of a low, but positive, real return to home prices over the past 150 years or so. A comprehensive study[22] of 14 advanced economies (all European except Canada, United States, and Japan) found that home prices increased on average about 1% a year in real terms, with the great majority of that rise coming since 1950. The data also show that the volatility of returns has increased since then.

In the United States (and perhaps many other countries), single-family homes, which constitute the vast bulk of owner-occupied homes (a small fraction are condos or townhomes) tend to be significantly more expensive to live in than rental apartments on a current cash flow basis. For example, in 2019, the median monthly rent in suburban Los Angeles was $3,950, while the median home price was $1,144,000[23].

A 30-year mortgage on that median-priced house will require a down payment of about $228,000 (20%), to qualify with good credit for a loan with an interest rate of about 4%. To that interest rate, we must add a number of annual expenses that will likely be absent for renters. The biggest of these is property taxes. In Los Angeles today the property tax rate is about 1.4% per year. In addition, most homeowners will carry insurance, which might add .25% per year. All homes have maintenance; the amount can vary all over the map. It could easily run a 1/2 percent to 1 percent or more of home value. We'll use 1/2% for this calculation. If we add up these extras, we get 2.15% of additional costs that a renter likely doesn't face. So

---

[21] Based on data from Robert Shiller, available at http://www.econ.yale.edu/~shiller/data.htm.
[22] Katharina Knoll et al., "No Price Like Home: Global House Prices, 1870-2012," Federal Reserve Bank of Dallas Working Paper #208, October, 2014.
[23] According to zillow.com as of February, 2019.

the total estimated annual cost of owning (to simplify we'll assume 4% interest cost on the down payment amount, although of course depending on where that down payment comes from, it may be a high or low assumption) is 6.15% of $1,144,000, which comes to $5,863 a month.

We have not counted the transaction cost of buying a home, which is likely to be in the neighborhood of 8% of the price of the home (consisting mostly of a real estate commission of 5–6%, loan fees of 1–2%, and other miscellaneous closing costs).

In this example, the up-front cost of owning is significantly higher than renting. This has usually been the pattern. However, if we assume that rents will continue to rise at the historical average rate (somewhat below the overall rate of inflation), over a 30-year time horizon it is likely that the overall cost of owning will be lower if – and this is a big if – home prices rise from here at the rate of inflation plus 1%.

The problem is that, as is the case with stocks, home prices seem to be quite volatile. And, if home prices have a tendency to revert to the long-run trend, it seems that reversion could put significant downward pressure on home prices over the period of a generation or so given that home prices have been historically high in the past few decades.

Our conclusion is that a home shouldn't really be thought of as primarily a financial investment because it is not likely to generate sufficient returns to be a good investment. It should be considered a consumption good, and possibly a hedge against high inflation. If you don't overpay, a house in a good location (based on historical patterns) will likely hold its value and appreciate slightly in real terms. If past patterns continue, the long-run cost of owning (after inflation) should be less than the cost of renting, though likely with the financial benefits of ownership being back-loaded (i.e. later in time; put differently, you'll pay more to own, possibly for many years, before the long-run increase in rents catches up and puts the value of ownership ahead of the value of renting). In the current home market of 2023, in many parts of the United States, it would be hard not to overpay, at least by historical standards.

Owning Apartments as Investments

We view residential real estate as generally the most attractive type of investment real estate for passive portfolios primarily because we believe that there is less long-term economic risk for apartments than for commercial, industrial, retail, or specialized property.

Although apartments can and do age, wear out, or become obsolete, they seem to do so at a slower rate than most other types of property. Many people have no problem living in a building that is quite old, even more than 100 years in many places. But there are few if any industrial facilities that old that have not been mostly or completely rebuilt. Similarly, the trends and fashions in retail – away from downtowns, then to malls, then to big-box stores and category killers, and now to internet and delivery-based retail – make it harder to predict the future value of retail real estate.

We believe apartments are generally better investments than houses because houses usually command a premium (that is, sell at lower cap rates) to apartments. Also, because apartments are easier to invest in (via REITs), we believe apartments are arguably the best candidate for including real estate in an investment portfolio.

Source of Return

Apartments are a business in which a large amount of fixed capital is invested to provide a largely fixed stream of services. That is, a building is built with a certain number of rental units. To a first approximation, that number of rental units is fixed. You can't move it. You can't unbuild it (in any economical manner). And you can't usually expand it.

To a first approximation, apartments are a commodity, and it is hard or impossible to earn profits above the market rate. Bad management can drive away customers, drive costs up, keep revenues down, or any combination. Good management, again to a first approximation, can earn the market rate of rent.

Apartments are, then, somewhat comparable to farmland as a generator of rental income. They are a long-duration asset that we expect would, as a result, be quite sensitive to interest rates.

Rents, when aggregated at the national level, have tended to rise at almost the rate of inflation over the long term. That is, since 1933 (the last year of the gold standard), rents have risen at a compound annual growth rate of about 3.2%[24] versus the CPI of all items increase of 3.5% over the same period.

If we assume that rents will continue to keep up with inflation, then, everything else equal, it is reasonable to assume that the real cash flows from apartments will keep up with inflation. While individual properties and markets will almost certainly do better and worse, there is no obvious reason to think that the overall future of rents will diverge significantly from inflation.

Economic Theory

Economic theory provides a convenient, simple (and probably correct) argument for why rents should roughly follow inflation. The argument is that housing is basically a commodity, and it is a commodity that has a fairly elastic supply[25] in the long run, and fairly inelastic demand[26] in the long run.

On the supply side, houses (and apartments) are basically just a bit of land, some wood, some concrete, some metal, some

---

[24] Federal Reserve Bank of St. Louis FRED, "Consumer Price Index All Urban Consumers – Rent," https://fred.stlouisfed.org/series/CUUR0000SEHA

[25] *Price elasticity of supply* is a measure of how much supply of a good will increase for a 1% change in price. In the case of housing, increases in price will tend to bring new supply to the market, but it requires fairly deep and sustained price decreases to cause supply to be withdrawn. (Instead, when rents fall and stay down, the quality of housing is likely to deteriorate, even as the buildings themselves remain for years or decades.) Dixie Blackley estimated long-run supply elasticity for new housing in the United States at between 1.6 and 3.7, which is pretty elastic. Dixie Blackley, "The Long-Run Elasticity of New Housing Supply in the United States: Empirical Evidence for 1950 to 1994," *Journal of Real Estate Finance and Economics* 1999: 25–42.

[26] *Price elasticity of demand* is a measure of how much demand changes for a 1% change in price. Many studies have found that demand for housing, even in the long run, is inelastic. See, e.g., David Albouy, et al., "Housing Demand, Cost-of-Living Inequality, and The Affordability Crisis," NBER Working Paper 22816 (2016).

plastic, some labor, building materials, and other expenses. In the United States, in many areas, there is plenty of additional land, and where land is not available (e.g. Manhattan Island), it is usually possible to build vertically. So broadly speaking, in most places there are no physical constraints to building more housing units.

In most places where there are tightly binding constraints, (e.g. Silicon Valley in California) the most binding constraints are political. Other than local political limits, which restrict building in some places, there is no practical limit to the number of apartment units that can be built over time. So supply, unless restricted by politics, grows as demand grows, keeping prices (rents) from increasing much beyond the cost of new construction.

On the demand side, long-run demand for housing is mostly a function of population. Barring some kind of demographic disaster (e.g. a plague, or giant natural disaster such as eruption of the Yellowstone volcano or large meteor strike, or war or civil insurrection), the US population is likely to keep growing. The US Census Bureau predicts[27] that over the next roughly half century, the US population will grow at about 0.6% per year. But, you should take that projection with a large dose of salt. Demography is not an exact science. During the twentieth century, the World Bank and the United Nations made a series of predictions about country populations for the year 2000. Not surprisingly, the earlier the predictions were, the greater their ultimate error proved to be. From 1972 to 1994, both organizations consistently reduced their estimates, but they all turned out to be high. Figure 5.9 offers a chart. Don't worry if you don't understand it.

Logic and historical studies suggest that population must, over the long run, drive demand for housing. Droes and van de Minne[28] looked at about 200 years of data for housing in Amsterdam and found, not surprisingly, that population was the major demand variable over the period. Over shorter periods, income and interest rates are also important factors driving demand for housing.

---

[27] Sandra Colby and Jennifer Ortman, "Projections of the Size and Composition of the US Population: 2014 to 2060," US Census Bureau (March 2015).

[28] Martijn I. Droes and Alex van de Minne, "Do the Determinants of House Prices Change over Time? Evidence from 200 Years of Transactions Data," ERES 2016_227, European Real Estate Society (ERES).

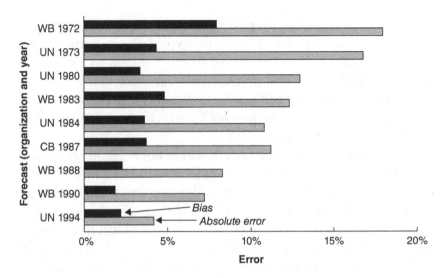

Figure 5.9   Mean bias and mean absolute error in country population projections for the year 2000, by source and date of forecast
Source: John Bongaarts and Rodolfo Bulatao (eds.), *Beyond Six Billion: Forecasting the World's Population* (National Academies Press, 2000).

It seems likely that the US population will continue to grow, possibly at a declining rate of increase, resulting in a slow but positive long-run increase in demand for housing. And it seems likely, based on theory and experience, that the supply for housing will be very elastic over the long run. That is to say, it seems likely that the increasing demand for housing as a result of population growth over the long run is not likely to drive up prices very much. Over shorter periods, which might still be a generation or so, other factors including income and interest rates may well have large influence on demand and therefore on prices.

This analysis of long-run supply and demand is consistent with there being relatively little real (i.e. after inflation) capital gain return to housing, including apartments, over the long run. If so, then the long-run returns to apartments must be mostly from current cash flows, with price rises reflecting mainly inflation.

And if we are right that the returns from apartments must, over the long run, come from the rental cash flows, the long-run return from apartments, as is also the case from businesses, must be mainly a function of the rate of such cash flows.

Good data regarding long-run (i.e. a century or so) returns on apartments and rental housing is hard to find. For a shorter period, however, almost half a century, we have good data in the form of equity REIT dividend yields. These data suggest that equity real estate behaves roughly like a long-duration asset. But as the data also suggest, there may be periods in which the behavior differs sharply from that of bonds.

Unlike bonds, real estate cash flows are not fixed. Rents can and do fluctuate, and over long periods of time rents can adjust for inflation. Furthermore, real estate companies, including REITs, can and do access the capital markets for debt, and their effectiveness or lack thereof can affect returns. But by and large, the return from owning real estate is the current cash flows, and the growth in those cash flows. Figure 5.10 below shows the Equity REIT dividend yield versus the US Treasury 10-year yield.

It is also the case that REITs, particularly in times of stress, such as the financial crisis of 2008–2009, may lose significant market value apparently unjustified by their long-term prospects. Even so, looking at monthly data from 1994 to 2019 for apartment REITs, we see that the dividend yield at the beginning of the period was a pretty good predictor of the total return over the next 10 years. Please see the graph in Figure 5.11.

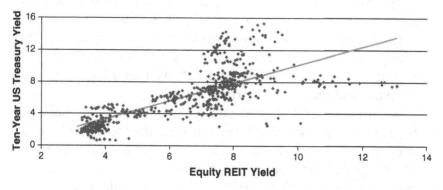

Figure 5.10   Equity REIT Dividend Yields vs US Ten Year Yields Monthly Data Jan. 1972-Feb. 2021
Sources: FTSE NAREIT and St. Louis Fed FRED

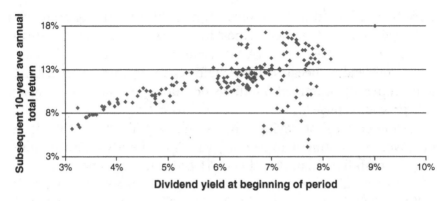

Figure 5.11 Apartment REIT Yields vs. Subsequent 10 Year Total Return 1994–2009

Many of the points in the lower-right-hand side of the graph correspond to 10-year periods that ended in months in 2008–2009 when the entire market, including REITs, had fallen by roughly half.

Over long periods of time, rents have tended to rise at about the rate of inflation. Perhaps, if we are optimistic, we believe that good management can contribute to real growth in cash flows, but it is hard to see how this could be more than perhaps 1% per year.

If current cash flow yield on US equity REITs is 3.9%, and inflation is 1.9%, it seems logical that the long-run real return we can look for is in the 2% (the cash flow yield minus inflation) range. Perhaps it will be as high as 3%.

However, we note that real estate is a long-duration asset. That is, real estate values are sensitive to interest rates. See in Figure 5.11 the close connection between REIT yields and 10-year US Treasury yields. If (when?) yields on 10-year treasury bonds rise significantly, it seems to us almost a matter of certainty that the yields investors demand on real estate will also rise. Recall that with equities, the reciprocal of yield is the P/E ratio. As yields rise, P/E ratios fall.

In real estate, it is more common to hear the term "FFO" multiple instead of P/E ratio. "FFO" stands for "funds from operations" and is a non-GAAP measure intended to capture the ability of a REIT to generate operating cash flow. (GAAP stands for "Generally

Accepted Accounting Principles" and is the accounting standard followed by the SEC as well as most businesses in the United States.) Many people believe that GAAP accounting for equity real estate can be misleading because depreciation is an expense under GAAP, and properly maintained buildings do not depreciate as rapidly as GAAP would suggest.

Another way of saying this is that equity real estate is a tax-favored investment, and equity REITs frequently produce more net free cash flow than they do GAAP or taxable income.

From a valuation standpoint, it doesn't matter whether you call the cash flow "earnings," "FFO," or "Florence." Investors will value cash flows at lower multiples when interest rates are high than when interest rates are low. Thus, when interest rates are low by historical standards, it seems likely that there is significantly more opportunity for real estate valuation multiples to come down in the medium-term future than for them to increase. Contractions in multiples can mean decreasing prices, even if rents and free cash flow are rising.

Summary

We have seen that returns to farmland, apartment REITs, and office buildings, all of which are assets that have cash flows that can be expected to continue into the indefinite future, come from two factors: rents and changes in the multiple that investors are willing to pay for those rents. This is analogous to stocks, which produce earnings, and are valued at varying P/E ratios.

Over long periods of time, nominal rents have historically tended to rise at about the rate of inflation, meaning that real rents do not increase, or if they do, they do so at a very low rate.

Real estate is a long-duration asset. As such, real estate market values are likely to be exposed to the risk of interest rate increases.

The best estimate for the long-run return from investment real estate is probably the current yield on the real estate, perhaps plus a small growth factor, and perhaps plus an adjustment for inflation.

Single family homes have historically appreciated at only half a percent per year in real terms. Given that homes are expensive to live in (e.g. property taxes, maintenance), the historical data show that as pure investments (ignoring the fact that you have to live somewhere and the associated consumption benefits of owning a home) homes have not been great. Homes should be viewed as a consumption item, not an investment.

Chapter 6
Gold and Gold Stocks

Is Gold in a Class by Itself?

Because of gold's long history as money, there is a good argument that gold is in an asset class of its own. Most of the world's central banks, and many people, as a practical matter consider gold to be a close substitute for money, although it is not de facto or de jure money anywhere at this time.[1] The US Federal Reserve does include its gold holdings in its calculations of the *monetary base*. In addition, despite the fact that for almost half a century gold has not officially backed any country's currency, most of the world's central banks have either held onto their gold, or acquired more.

From an accounting perspective gold is not money, because accounting rules define a *base* or *functional* currency, such as the US dollar for Americans, and measure everything in terms of that functional currency.

---

[1] Money is the commodity (or abstraction) that is most widely accepted in the market. Instead of saying that gold is *money*, it might be more accurate to think of gold as possessing some of the characteristics, especially the store of value characteristic, that are desirable in money. It would be relatively easy for gold to become money again in the sense of being the most widely used medium of exchange.

However, gold is unique both in its physical properties, and in its place in the history of civilization. Gold has been prized since at least 5000 BCE, and the naturally occurring alloy of gold and silver called electrum formed the first known coins in the Kingdom of Lydia in Asia Minor about 2,600 years ago. Ever since, gold has usually been used as money.

Unlike all forms of paper money, gold cannot be conjured out of thin air by governments that refuse to live within their means. Perhaps this is why governments, via their central banks, are by far the largest holders of gold in the world.

A Brief History of Gold

Gold is not an investment because you cannot expect it to grow in real terms over time, and because it does not generate a dividend or similar cash flow.[2] If history is a guide, gold is money. From the first known coins, minted by King Croesus of Lydia about 2,600 years ago, until 1971, there was never an extended period of time in which it was not the dominant practice of market economies to use gold and/or silver as the basic monetary medium.

In 1933 Franklin Roosevelt devalued the dollar by about 75% by redefining the dollar as 1/35th of an ounce of gold, instead of the former approximately 1/20th of an ounce. Americans were not permitted to own gold, but the dollar was still exchangable into gold in international trade.

Under the terms of the 1944 Bretton Woods agreement, the currencies of most non-Communist developed countries were tied to the US dollar, and the dollar in turn was fixed at $35 per ounce of gold. Foreign governments were supposed to be able to get gold at the fixed exchange rates established under the Bretton Woods agreement.

---

[2] For large institutional holders, such as central banks, there is a market for lending gold, and earning interest.

In 1971, President Nixon, for personal domestic political purposes,[3] defaulted on the United States' Bretton Woods obligations. He "closed the gold window," that is, he refused to honor the US commitment to accept dollars from foreign central banks at the promised rate of $35 per ounce. This reckless and unilateral act severed the last remaining official link between gold and money, and led directly to the undeclared worldwide depression of the 1970s.[4]

As a consequence of abandoning the gold standard, the 80 years following 1930 have seen more inflation (defined as a general increase in price or fall in the purchasing power of money), in absolute and percentage terms, than occurred in the prior seven centuries combined. In the seven centuries between 1200 and 1930,

---

[3] Recent scholarship, based on analysis of the Nixon tapes, finds compelling evidence that Nixon willfully and knowingly abused the power of the presidency to bully Fed Chairman Arthur Burns into expansionary monetary policy (printing money). As Milton Friedman had personally warned Nixon, this policy led to price inflation and a weakening of the dollar's value against other currencies. Predictably, foreign governments then sought to exchange dollars for gold at the official rate of $35. Nixon, rather than permit Burns to take steps to reduce inflation (as Carter and Reagan permitted Paul Volcker), chose to sever the link to gold. Nixon committed many crimes as president (probably among the least of these was his involvement in Watergate), but it seems possible that this single act – severing the link to gold – has caused more domestic and international havoc than any act of any other president going back to Woodrow Wilson. See Burton Adams and James Butkiewicz, "The Political Business Cycle: New Evidence From the Nixon Tapes," *Journal of Money, Credit and Banking* 44, no. 2–3 (March/April 2012). Books could (and should) be written on other presidential acts that have caused untold havoc. Among these presidential acts was Franklin Roosevelt's mandate that the federal government purchase silver at a price 50% above market price, thereby subsidizing silver producers in the seven Western "silver bloc" states. Roosevelt needed their votes for his unprecedented interference in the markets by causing the US government to purchase silver (which the United States had demonetized in 1873) at more than double the then-prevailing world price. Roosevelt had been warned that this policy would be disastrous for China, which was then on the silver standard. The policy caused silver to drain out of China, with significant negative effects on the Chinese economy. The Japanese benefited (to the great detriment of the Chinese) as later did the Chinese Communists (to the even greater detriment of ordinary Chinese). See, e.g. Milton Friedman, "Franklin D. Roosevelt, Silver, and China," *Journal of Political Economy* (1992). And while we're reviewing Roosevelt's record, we must hold him partially accountable for the fiat money mess in which the world finds itself today.

[4] As economist Michael Bordo writes, Nixon abrogated the promise to redeem dollars for gold, "for political and doctrinal reasons . . . [and] blamed the rest of the world rather than correcting mistaken U.S. policies. In addition . . . Nixon adopted wage and price controls to mask the inflation, hence punting the problem into the future." Michael Bordo, "The Imbalances of the Bretton Woods System 1965 to 1973: U.S. Inflation, The Elephant in the Room," Economics Working Paper 18115, Hoover Institution, Stanford University (August 2, 2018).

prices increased 21 times, for an annual rate of approximately 4/10ths of 1% per year. From 1930 to 2010, prices increased by 52 times, an annual rate of 5%. Thus, during the period of fiat money following 1930, prices increased 12 times faster than during the previous 720 years.

You can see this clearly on the graph in Figure 6.1 showing UK inflation from 1209 to 2010, based on data from economist Greg Clark.[5]

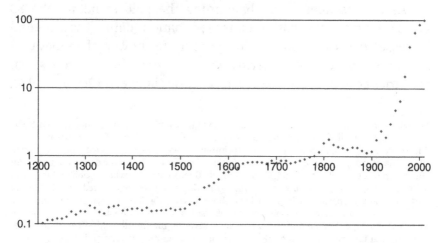

Figure 6.1   Cost of Living, UK

The vertical axis on this chart is logarithmic. The increase from .1 to 1 represents a tenfold increase in prices, as does the increase from 1 to 10, and 10 to 100. Notice that for most of the period on this chart, the price level is relatively constant, showing no trend. Of the eight centuries here, virtually all of the sustained price increase occurs in just two: the sixteenth century, and the last 100 years.

The sixteenth century inflation is known to economic historians as the "Price Revolution" and was caused by the influx of silver from the Old World, which increased the money supply without

---

[5] *Average Earnings and Retail Prices, UK, 1209–2010*, Gregory Clark, UC Davis (October 30, 2011).

a corresponding increase in real goods and services. During the 70 years from approximately 1530 to 1600, prices rose by about 5 times, which works out to an annual compounded rate of 2.3%. (The "low" inflation of 2% that the Fed targets will reduce the value of the currency by 80–90% during the life expectancy of people in developed countries today.[6]) The Price Revolution was caused by the tremendous flow of silver from the New World to Spain and Europe.[7]

But even the Price Revolution is dwarfed by the inflation that has occurred since 1930, about the time that most developed countries abandoned the gold standard. According to Clark's data, during the eight decades since 1930, prices have risen not 5 times as during the Price Revolution, but over 50 times! The annual compound rate of inflation, in Clark's data from 1930 to 2010, is 5%.

In 1930, an ounce of gold in the United States was $20.67. That is, the dollar was defined so that an ounce of gold was equal to $20.67. Some actual prices from 1930, and from 2015, suggest that gold is not an investment in the sense that we should not expect it to return a greater purchasing power in the future, but that it does maintain its purchasing power. Here are some examples that do not prove that gold maintains its purchasing power, but do suggest that in many cases it has held its purchasing power, even as the value of the dollar has declined by 98%.

In 1932, the *New York Times* carried an advertisement for an experienced public accountant. The job paid $45 a week,[8] or 2.18 ounces of gold. Today that 2.18 ounces, at $1,250 per ounce, would be worth $2,721. That translates into a yearly salary of $141,000. Indeed.com states that the average salary in 2016 for a CPA in New York City is $112,000.

---

[6] Assume an 80-year life expectancy. A price index starting at 100 in year 1 that grows at 2% per year will grow to 487.5 in year 80. That represents a loss of about 80% of the starting purchasing power.

[7] See Douglas Fisher, "The Price Revolution: A Monetary Interpretation," *Journal of Economic History* 49, no. 4 (December 1989).

[8] All 1930s prices in this section are sourced from Scott Derks, *The Value of a Dollar, 1860–2004*, 3rd ed., Grey House Publishing (2004).

Also in New York, an office assistant job was offered at $15 per week, or $780 per year, in 1932. At 1932's $20.67 per ounce of gold, that $780 represented 37.73 ounces of gold. Fast-forward to today's (August 2023) dollar price of gold of about $1,895, we find that the 37.73 ounces would be worth about $71,500. Although there is quite a bit of variation in people and in jobs, today indeed.com lists several office assistant jobs that pay in the low $60,000s to low $70,000s in New York City.

A pair of "plain-toe Oxford tie shoe; black calf-grain leather" men's shoes was offered for $2.48 in the Montgomery Ward catalog in 1932. That price equates to .12 ounces of gold, which at $1,750 per ounce would be $210. Today, Allen Edmonds offers a "Park Avenue Cap-toe Oxford" men's shoe for $199.97.

Gold's Place in a Portfolio

Over long periods of time, gold tends to hold its value. Gold does best when paper currencies are at their worst. But there are long periods during which the price of gold can decrease in terms of paper currency, even in the presence of inflation. The most recent major example occurred during the two decades from 1980 to 2000, during which time gold declined from a daily high of over $800 per ounce to a low in 1999 and 2000 of about $250 per ounce. During those two decades, according to the US government's CPI, the dollar lost over half its value, as inflation averaged 3.75%.

However, that average inflation was less than half of the inflation rate during the 1970s, and the annual rate tended to drop during the period.

Interestingly, the gold price soared during the next decade, from 2000 until 2011, increasing from the low of $250 to a daily high of over $1,800, an increase of 7.2 times, or an annual compounded rate of over 19%. During that same 11-year period, inflation continued, but at a relatively low rate (by fiat money era standards) of 2.5% per year. See Figure 6.2.

Over long periods, gold tends to hold its value. Gold is the only money in the world today that cannot be printed, and that

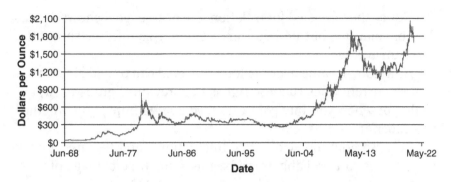

Figure 6.2 Gold Price in US$ per Ounce (London AM Fixing)
Source: FRB St. Louis FRED

does not represent someone else's liability. Unless you believe that modern technology,[9] or something else, will repeal the empirical regularity of 2,500 years, you should be comfortable that over the long run, which could easily be a quarter century or more, gold will tend to hold its value against a wide variety of goods.

But there is no tendency over the long run for gold to gain purchasing power. Figure 6.3 shows a graph of the price of gold in US dollars divided by the US CPI; in other words, it is the price of gold adjusted for inflation as measured by the CPI.

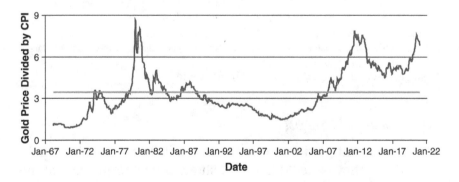

Figure 6.3 Gold Price per Ounce Divided by CPI (April 1968 to February 2021)

---

[9] E.g. bitcoin or something similar.

Notice that adjusted for inflation, the price of gold shows a great deal of volatility, but no real trend. The horizontal line shows the long-run average.

As a store of value over the long run, gold can provide insurance against currency destruction. But as the previous figures show, the timing of when you buy gold can have a large impact on whether you experience large losses.

Because gold has wide price fluctuations, and because it does not grow, it can probably serve best as a small percentage of your portfolio as a hedge against high and unexpected inflation.

In terms of where gold is valued relative to its history, Figure 6.3 suggests that at current levels ($2,000 per ounce and the CPI at about 302, for a ratio of 6.6) the gold price, adjusted for inflation, is relatively high. However, an almost opposite conclusion can be drawn from the following chart in Figure 6.4, which shows the gold price in terms of M2 money supply.

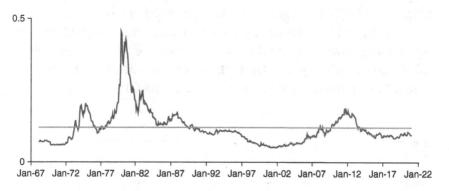

Figure 6.4   Gold Price ($/oz.) Divided by M2 (in Billions)

What About Gold Stocks?

We've seen that gold is not an investment. But what about gold stocks? Are they better? Figure 6.5 shows a long-term chart of the Barron's Gold Mining Index of gold mining stocks. Notice that in

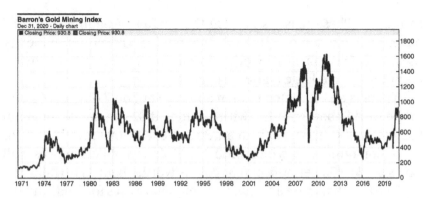

Figure 6.5 GBMI – Barron's Gold Mining Index
Source: http://www.goldchartsrus.com

2016, the index was at about 400, and in 1971 was about 150. This is a compounded return of about 2.2%. But look at that wild ride! Since 1971, the index has had bear markets in which it has declined over 50% seven times. Seven bear markets in 46 years is an average of one every 6.5 years.

Gold stocks are much more volatile than gold, and indeed they are much more volatile than stocks in general. Perhaps surprisingly, the greater volatility as compared to gold may mean that gold stocks can play a valuable role in a portfolio. However, given the volatility, it may mean that if you decide to include gold stocks, you should consider a systematic rebalancing program so that when they have done very well, you sell some, and when they have done poorly you add to them.

Silver

Silver, like gold, has a long history of serving as money. However, there are three major reasons that we believe that in the modern world, gold is the more suitable of the two metals to serve as a store of value, and perhaps at some future time again be widely accepted as money. These reasons are: (1) the greater per-ounce and total market value of gold; (2) the fact that gold has fewer nonmonetary uses; and (3) the fact that world central banks and sovereign investment funds hold large amounts of gold.

There is an estimated total of about 30 billion[10] ounces of silver in the world above ground, with a value (at $25 an ounce) of about $750 billion. Compare this to an estimated 187,000 metric tons, or 6.6 billion ounces, of which probably 90%, or 6 billion ounces, still exists. At $1,850 per ounce, that gold is worth about $11 trillion.

The fact that there are fewer nonmonetary uses for gold, and the biggest of those is jewelry, means that it would be less disruptive to industrial markets if gold were remonetized, as compared to silver.

The third reason probably reflects the first two, and as all money is money only because other people want it as money, the fact that central banks already hold a lot of gold makes it more likely that they would agree in the future to remonetize gold.

If gold is money that also has commodity-like properties, silver is more like a commodity that has some monetary properties. Silver has a long and successful history as a monetary metal. For centuries, both gold and silver circulated as money, and sometimes they did so in a formal, fixed ratio. A fixed-ratio regime is called a bimetallic regime.

Formal bimetallism only works when the relative demand for and supply of gold and silver remain in a narrowly balanced. For various technical economic reasons we believe that bimetallism is not efficient,[11] and seems inferior in practice to a gold standard.

Summary

Gold is not an investment in the sense that it can't be expected to produce a stream of earnings or to grow in real terms. It can be expected,

---

[10] The US Geological Survey estimates that 1.74 million metric tons of silver have been mined. This equates to about 60 billion ounces. No one knows how much of this silver is still available, but 1/2 is a common guess.

[11] See, e.g., François Velde and Warren Weber, "A Model of Bimetallism," *Journal of Political Economy*, 108, no. 6 (December, 2008).

however, to hold its value in real terms. Gold is the only commodity with a proven track record of serving as money in both the ancient world and the modern, global economy.

Gold stocks are volatile and fluctuate widely. But because gold stocks have historically had a low correlation with other asset classes, and they have high volatility, according to the concepts of modern portfolio theory, gold stocks can have a place in "efficient" portfolios.

Chapter 7
Futures and Commodities

This chapter will explain what futures contracts are and, in order to do so, we will first explain the concept of arbitrage. We will also clarify how futures contracts relate to commodities, define commodities, and discuss whether there are yields on commodities.

Arbitrage

Arbitrage refers to the opportunity to buy a security (or other fungible[1] asset) at one price and simultaneously sell it at a higher price. In theory, an arbitrage transaction involves no risk. The *arbitrageur* (the person performing the arbitrage) makes a profit on the difference in prices. For example, if an investor sees that the price of IBM stock is $125 per share on the New York Stock Exchange, but the same stock sells for (the equivalent of) $127 on the London Stock Exchange, the investor has the opportunity to buy stock on the NYSE and sell it in London, earning a profit of $127 minus $125 minus any transactions costs. This is an example of arbitrage.

---

[1] The word *fungible* refers to the interchangeability of items that are all "alike." For example, dollar bills are fungible, because each one is as good as any other one. We offer an additional explanation later in this chapter.

When trying to determine whether or not there are arbitrage opportunities in a given market, it may be useful to ask, "What must be true in order for there to be no arbitrage opportunities?"

In the previous example of the investor who notices arbitrage opportunities between the United States and England, it is evident that once a single investor notices the opportunity, other investors are likely to see it as well. When British investors begin to buy the IBM stock from the United States, the increase in demand will push up the price of IBM stock in the United States. Similarly, the increase of supply to the UK will push down the price. Eventually, as more investors take advantage of the arbitrage opportunity, the UK price will converge to the US price, and the opportunity will disappear.

In other words, if there's a profitable arbitrage opportunity, arbitrageurs will notice it and seize it, causing it to disappear.

The fact that arbitrage opportunities tend to disappear will help us understand the pricing of futures contracts.

Futures Contracts

Futures contracts are highly standardized contracts that allow investors to enter into a contract today, at today's specified price, which commits them to buy or sell the good in question at a specified future date. For example, a buyer of gold futures may buy a contract today which gives the buyer the right and obligation to buy an ounce of gold in one year at the price of $2,100 per ounce. The exchange of cash will not take place for a year. The price of gold today is called the *spot price*. The price associated with the right and obligation to buy gold in one year at the price of $2,100 is called the *futures price*.

Futures contracts are useful for producers of commodities who need to be sure that they can sell their products at a specified future price. For example, grain farmers may find it beneficial to sell futures contracts, guaranteeing they will sell a specified amount of grain at a specified price one year in the future. The futures contract protects farmers (technically this protection is called a *hedge*) from the possibility that grain prices may decrease, which would mean that farmers' profits would decrease as well. Grain prices could decrease due to factors completely outside the farmers' control, such as an increase in grain supply because of an especially abundant year of crops.

Similarly, buyers of futures contracts may wish to assure themselves of a certain price for commodities they will not actually need until some future date. Petroleum users, such as airlines, for example, may wish to buy futures contracts for oil to protect against the possibility that the price of oil could increase. Futures contracts help producers and users be more certain about the price of goods that are essential to their businesses.

Pricing of Futures Contracts

There is a great deal of misunderstanding about the way that futures prices are determined. In this section we will explain the correct way to understand what futures prices mean, and do not mean.

The key fact to remember is that for storable commodities, it is possible to convert a commodity today into a commodity tomorrow by storing the commodity, but it is not possible to convert a commodity tomorrow into a commodity today.

Let us illustrate with an example from the gold market.

For the sake of this example, let us assume that there is a single, riskless interest rate of 10%, and that arbitrageurs can borrow or lend any amount at that interest rate. Let us further assume that the price of gold today (the *spot price*) is $2,000 per ounce. Let us assume that the futures price for gold to be delivered in one year is $2,300. Further assume for simplicity that storage of gold is riskless and costless.

A potential arbitrageur will look at the spot price of gold, the futures price, and the interest rate to see if there is an arbitrage opportunity. If an arbitrageur lends $2,000 at 10%, he will earn $200 in interest by the end of the year, meaning that he will have $2,200 total after one year. If he borrows $2,000, he will owe $2,200 at the end of the year.

Arbitrage involves the simultaneous purchase and sale of *the same item* on two different markets. To be valid arbitrage, the arbitrageur must make sure that no matter what happens, he will not have a net position. In the case of arbitrage between spot and futures prices, the arbitrageur will make or lose money in accordance with the difference between the futures price and the spot price, *not* because the price of the commodity goes up or down.[2]

Let us consider an example from the gold market. Suppose the futures price is $2,300, the spot price is $2,000, and the interest rate is 10%. Arbitrageurs could profit by simultaneously selling futures contracts and purchasing spot (actual, physical) gold today. In this example, we will assume that the arbitrageur borrows the $2,000 to purchase the gold. Note that the arbitrageur is long spot gold, meaning that he owns spot gold, and short gold futures, meaning that he is obligated to deliver the gold in the future. Being long and short equal amounts of gold, the arbitrageur has a zero net position.

When the arbitrageur sells a futures contract, he will receive $2,300 in one year, at which time he will be obligated to deliver the gold. To implement this arbitrage trade, the arbitrageur borrows $2,000 today and buys gold, holding it for one year. At the end of the year, he delivers the gold and receives $2,300 as per the futures contract. The arbitrageur then uses the $2,300 proceeds to pay back the $2,000 loan plus the $200 of interest that accrued on the loan, for a total of $2,200. The arbitrageur has earned $100 profit and was not exposed to changes in the price of gold during the year.[3]

Now let's assume the futures price is only $2,100, but the spot price remains at $2,000 and the interest rate is 10%. The arbitrageur would need to choose another method to make a profit. He could short the spot, or, in other words, borrow gold and sell it at the spot price. (This highly simplified example assumes that the arbitrageur does not incur costs to borrow the gold. In the real world, arbitrageurs of gold would likely have commercial

---

[2] 87% of commodity traders are men. https://www.zippia.com/commodity-trader-jobs/demographics/

[3] This is a simplified model. In the real world, he may have margin calls (i.e. be required to put up additional cash or other collateral) on his futures position, his loan, or both.

interests and would hold gold in the normal course of business, so they may not need to borrow gold. While there is a market for the lending of gold, most physical commodities cannot be literally borrowed. In fact, one of the important economic functions of futures markets is to make the "lending" of physical commodities more feasible.[4])

The arbitrageur sells the borrowed gold at the spot price of $2,000, and thus receives $2,000 today. In order to make sure he receives his ounce of gold, the arbitrageur simultaneously buys a futures contract, but will not have to make any payments until he takes delivery of the gold in a year. In the meantime, he takes the $2,000 received today and lends it out at interest. In one year, he will have earned $200 (10% on the original $2,000), meaning that he has a total of $2,200. As per the futures contract, he will owe $2,100 for the ounce of gold on the futures contract. Thus, one year from now, the arbitrageur will receive one ounce of gold, and will pay it back to the gold lender. The arbitrageur has now earned a profit of $2,200 – $2,100 = $100. Assuming that the arbitrageur has not paid to borrow gold, he will earn a profit of $100.

If, however, the futures price of gold were $2,200, the arbitrageur could not profit by selling futures contracts, borrowing money, and investing that money in the meantime, as he did in the first part of this example. For example, assume the arbitrageur sold a futures contract and borrowed $2,000 to buy gold at the spot price. In one year, the arbitrageur would owe $2,200, but would also receive $2,200 from the buyer of the futures contract. The arbitrageur would neither make nor lose money.

Neither could the arbitrageur profit by borrowing gold, selling it at the spot price, and buying a futures contract. He would receive $2,000 today for the gold, which he could invest or lend out at the rate of 10% per year. In one year, he would have $2,200. However, the arbitrageur had also bought a futures contract to ensure

---

[4] See *The Economic Function of Futures Markets*, Jeffrey Williams, Cambridge University Press, 1989.

that he would receive his ounce of gold back, so he would owe $2,200 to the seller of the futures contract.

In order for futures contracts to be priced such that arbitrage will not occur, the price of the futures contracts needs to track closely with the cost of holding and storing the cash commodity. In this example, the only cost we considered was the prevailing interest rate. In the previous example, in order for no arbitrage to occur, the futures price would need to be $2,200, so that an arbitrageur could not make money by lending in the present and buying a futures contract.

If you want to understand how futures contracts are priced, you must understand how arbitrage can be used to keep prices "in line," that is, such that there are no opportunities to earn big profits through arbitrage.

Commodities

Some people consider commodities to be an investment asset class. We don't think they are, because, for reasons we'll explain, we don't think they pass the "reasonable expectation of getting back more than you put in" test. We will ask for your indulgence as we review a bit of theory and history to explain why.

By *commodities*, people generally mean a weighted index of certain commodities, such as the *Dow Jones – UBS Commodity Index. Commodities* are goods which are *fungible*. A good is fungible if any unit of the good is interchangeable with any other unit of the good, and if no user or seller will make any distinction between units. For example, corn, soybeans, and coffee, properly defined, are commodities. Many of the terms of a futures contract describe the commodity in detail. For example, the Chicago Mercantile Exchange's corn contract calls for par delivery of #2 Yellow corn; the USDA in turn has an extensive definition of #2 Yellow corn. All the commodities traded on organized exchanges are carefully and extensively defined.

As of this writing, the DJ-UBS index is composed as follows:

Commodity	Weight %
Gold	10.92
Natural Gas	9.39
WTI Crude	8.68
Corn	7.35
Copper	6.52
Soybeans	6.21
Brent Crude	6.14
Aluminum	4.54
Sugar	4
Unleaded Gasoline	3.74
Silver	3.65
Heating Oil	3.41
Coffee	3.28
Wheat	3.25
Live Cattle	3.1
Soybean Meal	3.01
Nickel	2.73
Soybean Oil	2.68
Lean Hogs	2.46
Zinc	2.17
Cotton	1.5
Kansas Wheat	1.27

Another index, upon which the largest commodity EFT (exchange-traded fund) is based, goes by the mouth-filling name of *DBIQ Optimum Yield Diversified Commodity Index.*

Commodity	Base Weight
Aluminum	4.17%
Brent Crude	12.38%
Copper – Grade A	4.17%
Corn	5.63%

(continued)

Commodity	Base Weight
Gold	8.00%
Heating Oil	12.38%
Light Crude	12.38%
Natural Gas	5.50%
RBOB Gasoline	12.38%
Silver	2.00%
Soybeans	5.63%
Sugar #11	5.63%
Wheat	5.63%
Zinc	4.17%

You can invest in the DBIQ index via the exchange-traded fund called *Powershares DB Commodity Tracking ETF*, whose ticker symbol is DBC. This ETF had net assets of about $1.8 billion as of March 2019, and traded an average of about 2,100,000 shares per day over the preceding three months. The fund charges a management fee of .85% per year. It rebalances the portfolio to the base weights once a year.

The rationale for including commodities in a portfolio is that over long periods of time, commodities should provide an inflation hedge, and even over shorter periods of time, the returns from commodity indexes have low correlations with the returns of the stock market.

Holding different asset classes that have low correlations with one another means that when one drops, the others will likely hold their value. This type of diversification works even better when assets have negative correlations. Negative correlation means that, on average, when the returns from one asset class are negative, returns from the other will be positive. The long-run correlation between commodity returns and stock returns seems to be close to zero. But what about the returns to owning commodities?

Commodity returns can be tricky to calculate, and depend on the monetary regime in place during the period under consideration. During the first 150 years of US independence, when the dollar was backed by gold, or returned to gold after a temporary, unbacked period, commodity prices fluctuated a great deal, but showed no long-term trend up or down. Over very long periods of time, commodity prices can do surprising things. Figure 7.1 shows seven and a half centuries of wheat prices in England.[5]

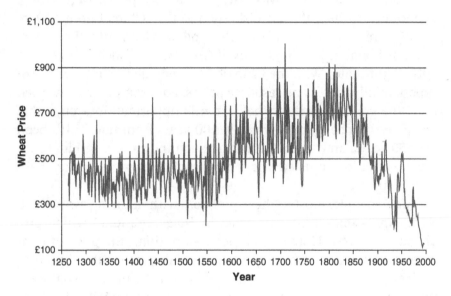

Figure 7.1 Wheat Prices in England, 1274–1996 Price per 1996 UK Pounds per Tonne (1 Tonne = 1,000 kg)

Though volatility is huge, the wheat price shows no trend, up or down, for the 300 years from about 1250 to 1550. The price then rises rapidly, with high volatility, for about 100 years. These are the years of the Price Revolution, caused by the huge influx of silver from

[5] Makridakis, Wheelwright, and Hyndman, *Forecasting: Methods and Applications*, Wiley (1997). Also available at https://ourworldindata.org/food-prices#data-sources

the New World. The rapidly falling prices of the final 150 years are probably a reflection of the repeal of Britain's Corn Laws[6] in 1846, the opening of the American great plains to grain production, the sharp drop in transportation costs made possible by railroads, and the huge increase in farm productivity made possible by the Industrial and Green revolutions.

During the 1970s, when inflation was rampant throughout the world, there was widespread belief that we were "running out of resources," and that was why commodity prices were rising. Economically illiterate alarmists such as the "Club of Rome" were vocally predicting, essentially, the end of the world. In a now infamous book titled *The Limits of Growth*, published in 1972, the authors (affiliated with the Club of Rome) made dire predictions of exponentially increasing resource prices. For example, they warned that "the great majority of the currently important non-renewable resources will be extremely costly 100 years from now."[7] It's been over 50 years, and so far there is no such indication. In Figure 7.2 are the inflation adjusted prices of nine of the most important base metals since 1972.

Many people, most of them probably without being aware of it, were expressing an implicit belief in *Hotelling's Rule*[8] which predicted that, given Hotelling's strict assumptions, the price of non-renewable resources would rise exponentially, at the rate of interest.

The theory predicts, for example, that if the price of coal were $100 per ton on January 1, and the interest rate were 5%, a year later the price of coal should be $105 per ton. The graph in Figure 7.3

---

[6] The Corn Laws were a set of import tariffs and other restrictions on import intended to keep the price of grain high in Britain. *Corn* in nineteenth-century British English was more or less synonymous with twenty-first-century American usage of the term *grain*. What Americans call *corn*, much of the rest of the world calls *maize*.

[7] D. H. Meadows, D. L. Meadows, J. Randers, and W. W. Behrens III, *The Limits to Growth* (Universe Books, 1972): 66.

[8] Economist Harold Hotelling published a paper in 1931 describing a theory that the price of "non-renewable" resources should rise. Hotelling and other economists who adhere to this theory fail to understand that the "resource" is not just the stuff in the ground and "other things" are never equal. The very fact of rising prices will cause more human ingenuity to be deployed to find better ways, alternative ways, and other approaches, so that Hotelling's predicted exponential rise never lasts, if it happens at all.

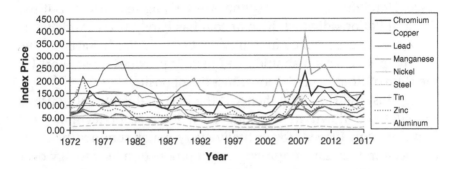

Figure 7.2 Inflation-Adjusted Metal Prices, 1972–2017
Source: NBER Working Paper 18874

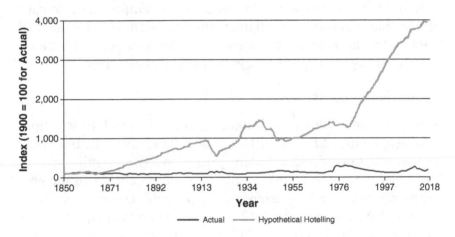

Figure 7.3 Inflation-Adjusted Coal Price – Hotelling Prediction Versus Actual

shows what has actually happened with coal prices since 1850, and compares it to the Hotelling prediction.[9] Both the actual price and the Hotelling predicted price are after adjusting for inflation.

As Figure 7.3 shows, the actual price of coal over this 168-year period behaved not even remotely like the Hotelling predicted

---

[9] The Hotelling prediction was calculated by taking the starting value and compounding it forward at the real rate of interest derived from the constant maturity US Treasury 10-year yield and the CPI or similar inflation index.

price. Hotelling predicted exponentially rising real prices. But the actual inflation-adjusted price of coal has barely risen. And coal is not a special case. No commodity, not even oil, has behaved as the Hotelling Rule says it should. And history provides no support for the Club of Rome's predictions. Just the opposite.[10]

Against the Hotelling theory is the idea that commodity prices should trend down in the long term because of technological improvement. Indeed, for virtually every major commodity, there has been tremendous improvement in production technology over the past century.

So, which view is right? Economic theory does not tell us; however, history does. Over the past century and half, according to Paul Cashin of the International Monetary Fund, empirical evidence[11] shows that, adjusted for inflation, the long-term trend is for real commodity prices to decline, on average, about 1% per year. At least over his study period, technology was ahead of difficulty.

Monetary Regime Matters

Note, however, that Cashin's findings applied to real, or inflation-adjusted, commodity prices. In actual dollars, also called *nominal* or non-inflation-adjusted dollars, prices have risen significantly in the paper-money era. Since Franklin Roosevelt abrogated the government's promise to redeem dollars for gold, commodities have increased at approximately 3.4% per year,[12] compounded. There has also been a great deal of volatility of commodity prices, with repeating cycles of boom and bust. We can see a graph of nominal and real price indices for industrial commodities, as follows in Figure 7.4.

So, in a period of paper money, if the long-term trend of commodity prices is up because of inflation, it would seem that there is a strong case to own an index of commodities as an inflation hedge. But, a closer look casts doubt on that seemingly logical conclusion.

---

[10] Charles Maurice and Charles Smithson, *The Doomsday Myth*, Hoover Institution Press (1984) offers a long-term historical look at resource "crises" that were feared but never really materialized.

[11] Paul Cashin and John C. McDermott, "The Long Run Behavior of Commodity Prices," *IMF Staff Papers* 49, no. 2 (2002).

[12] Commodity prices are a component of inflation calculations, but the relationship between inflation and commodity prices is not stable, and complex. See Fred Furlong and Robert Ingenito, *Commodity Prices and Inflation*, FRB St. Louis, No. 2 (1996).

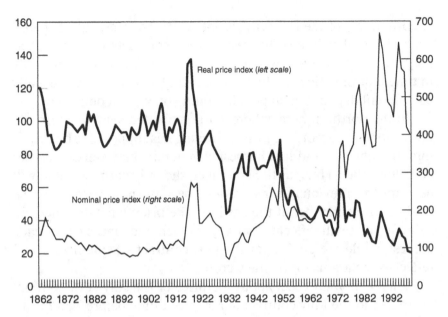

Figure 7.4 Nominal and Real Price Indexes for Industrial Commodities, 1862–1999

Source: Cashin, "Long Run Behavior of Commodity Prices": 185.

Are There Commodity "Yields"?

I (Roger) studied the commodity futures markets in great detail when I earned my PhD in the 1980s. My doctoral dissertation was an empirical study of the pricing of several agricultural commodities and their futures contracts. And my master's thesis focused on the pricing of the Treasury Bond contract. The specifics of some of the markets have changed, but the underlying principles and economic mechanisms have not changed at all.

So I was very surprised when, as I read in preparation for writing this section, that the people who award the CFA[13] are teaching that commodity futures offer three supposed "yields."

Before we can explain these "yields," we need to explain a little about futures markets. Consider the corn futures market. At any given time, you can buy or sell a contract that will call for delivery

---

[13] Chartered Financial Analyst, the most respected "investment-related" credential on Wall Street. I obtained my CFA in 1990.

of corn in any of the following months: March, May, July, September, or December. In all other respects, the contracts are identical, as they promise to deliver the exact same physical goods, differing only in time. But the price at which you can buy or sell corn will usually be different depending on which month you want it delivered.

In the northern hemisphere, corn is planted sometime around March to May – according to an old saying it is supposed to be "knee-high by July"[14] – and it is harvested generally between September and November. Thus, until September, the only corn available will be from the previous year's harvest, because new corn won't be ready until September at the earliest. The pricing for the May and July contracts will reflect the supply and demand for the prior year's harvest, while the pricing for the next contract – September – will reflect expectations for the new crop.

What can you expect about the price of the July corn contract compared to the May contract at any given time before May? Consider that no new corn will be harvested. So the supply in July will have to be no greater than the supply in May, and probably it will be less because some corn will be consumed but none produced in those two months. Also, it is possible to convert corn in May to corn in July by storing corn from May until July, but it is impossible to do the reverse. Therefore, we would expect the price of corn usually to be higher in July than in May, because the supply of corn in July (preharvest) will not be higher than in May, and will probably be lower.

But, that does not mean you can profit by buying corn for delivery in May and holding it until July. Why not? Because it costs money to store the corn. In fact, the best predictor of the difference between the price of May corn and July corn is precisely the cost to "carry" it from May to July. As a result, the usual arrangement of futures prices, other things equal, is to differ by carrying costs,

---

[14] According to an article in the July 4, 2013, issue of *Bon Appetit* online, Keith Alverson of K2 Farms in Chester, SD, said, "It always used to be knee-high by the Fourth of July, but in the last 15, 20 years or so ... it's gotten bigger. We've pushed to earlier planting dates now, mostly because we can control weeds with new technology." So here is an example, in the last couple of decades, of a significant improvement in the production technology for a major commodity.

with the later months being higher than the earlier months by their carrying costs. This condition is known as "positive carry" or "contango."[15]

We can now return to the three supposed yields of *spot price* yield, *roll* yield, and *collateral* yield. The spot price yield is merely the gain or loss from change in the spot price. It is misleading at best to call it a yield. It is not a yield. Furthermore, it is so unpredictable that short-run price movements are hard to distinguish from random walks.

I was surprised that I had never heard of a roll yield, because I had spent years studying this subject quite closely. The reason I had never heard of roll yield is that it too is not really a yield. The roll yield is supposed to be the "yield" that the investor earns by selling the nearby month and buying a more distant month. As we have seen, this procedure will usually cost the investor money, not earn him a yield.

It turns out that roll yield is a modern version of an idea that goes way back to John Maynard Keynes's and John Hicks's theory of "normal backwardation." This armchair hypothesis assumed that futures markets were dominated by producers on the sell side, and speculators on the buy side. Supposedly, producers transferred risk to speculators, and the speculators could expect to earn a "risk premium" or compensation for taking extra risk, because the futures price was below the expected future spot price. Speculators would profit because they could receive the goods in the future at a price lower than the expected future spot price. In other words,

---

[15] The term *contango* appears to originate in the mid-nineteenth century among traders on the London Stock Exchange. It has no obvious meaning, but I think many people use it today because they think it makes them sound smart. I prefer the term *positive carry* because it is more informative and more intuitive. *Full carry* is the maximum amount by which the later contract can exceed the earlier contract. A carry amount in excess of the full cost of carry would create an arbitrage opportunity, and arbitrageurs would buy the nearby contract, bidding up its price, and sell the distant contract, pushing down its price, until there were no further arbitrage profits to be earned. Indeed, in the mid-1980s I was an intern for GT Capital Management in Hong Kong. The Hang Seng Stock Futures contract was brand new, and traders were overpricing it. I laid out an arbitrage strategy, which basically consisted of buying the spot and selling the futures, and earning the excess returns. GT implemented the strategy, and earned consistent returns for about a year until others caught on and the opportunity was arbitraged away.

Keynes/Hicks said that buyers could expect to make money because they were getting paid to take the risk of holding the commodity.[16]

Ultimately this is an empirical question. My reading of the evidence suggests that even if there is a "risk premium" built into futures prices, it is small and unreliable, and likely to be overwhelmed by other factors.

The fact is that most physical commodities not only offer no yield, they cost money to store. The only exception I can think of is that on occasion gold could be lent out to generate a yield. But most commodities, as varied as oil, live cattle, orange juice, and lumber, are expensive to store. Financial commodities, for different reasons, will rarely if ever offer systematic opportunities to profit merely by "rolling" from one contract to another.[17]

Collateral Yield

The final type of yield promised on commodity index funds is *collateral yield*. This amounts to interest on money that the index funds hold. It is easy to understand once you understand how a commodity index fund works.

A fund does not actually buy and hold commodities. Instead, it buys futures contracts on those commodities. The index is supposed to be unlevered. That is, if you invest $100,000 into the fund, you are supposed to get the price change on $100,000 of the index. However, to achieve this amount of exposure, the fund may need to post only, say, $20,000 of so-called *margin*[18] money with the futures exchange. The remainder of your $100,000 (in this case, $80,000)

---

[16] Though you would not likely learn it from modern discussions of commodity futures pricing, which if they look at the issue at all tend to regurgitate some version of the erroneous "normal backwardation" hypothesis, the issue was addressed in the academic literature at least as long ago as 1961. See Roger W. Gray, "The Search for a Risk Premium," *Journal of Political Economy*, Wol 69, No. 3, June, 1961.

[17] The reason is that these markets are subject to arbitrage. Well-positioned and sophisticated arbitrageurs (if you're one you know you are) may earn such profits, and in doing so make the markets sufficiently efficient that retail investors cannot earn such returns.

[18] This margin money is a good-faith deposit. It is not borrowed money in the sense that stock market retail investors borrow money on margin. Futures margins are required by the exchange clearinghouses to protect themselves from losses if one of their clients experiences a loss on a trade. The use of the term *margin* to mean different things in seemingly similar financial contexts is one of the annoying facts that students just have to put up with.

will be invested in money market instruments. The yield on these money market instruments is what the promoters mean by *collateral yield*. This is not properly a return to commodities, because you could earn it even if you didn't invest in commodities. You'd earn a similar return if you invested only in money market instruments.

Commodity Index Funds Have Negative Expected Real Returns

The only return you can expect on a commodity index fund is the long-run return due to inflation. However, when you use no leverage, as commodity index funds tend to do, your long-run return before costs would only be, based on the historical average, 3.4% a year or so. From that, you would have to subtract the fees charged by the fund, the commission costs of trading the futures, and the carrying costs of the commodities because you are, in effect, on average paying the carrying costs.

For these reasons, although there may be periods of significant positive performance for a commodity index ETF, there are probably better ways to incorporate futures into a portfolio.

Managed Futures Funds

We have just seen that commodities as an asset class might enhance a portfolio if you considered only the change in spot price, but that the costs of storage, financing, and insurance (the carrying costs) and the cost of index management probably offset the inflation hedge benefits of owning a commodity index as a permanent portfolio allocation.

Before we decide not to invest in commodities, however, it makes sense to look at a different approach to commodities, called *managed futures*.

We saw in the previous chapter that a futures contract is a highly leveraged contract on the future price of a commodity. There are also futures contracts on stock indices, a wide variety of government bonds, and foreign exchange rates, in addition to the more familiar physical commodities.

Most financial economists believe in the *Efficient Market Hypothesis*, or EMH. The Efficient Market Hypothesis states that financial markets, including the stock, bond, and futures markets, are efficient in a technical sense. The essence of that technical efficiency is the proposition that a trader cannot earn excess returns using only publicly available information. There are hundreds, perhaps thousands of academic papers reporting evidence of one or more instances of the Efficient Market Hypothesis.[19]

If the Efficient Market Hypothesis were true, it would not be possible for investment managers to consistently beat the markets.

And, in fact, in the stock and bond markets, very few investment managers do consistently beat the market. That is why, as we will discuss later, index investing in stocks and bonds, as opposed to selecting individual stocks that you think will outperform the market (called "stock picking"), has a lot to recommend it.

But, for some reason that we do not understand, a small corner of the financial world, known as the managed futures industry, does succeed in consistently beating the market using only publicly available information. (Brian Hurst, a principal at hedge fund management firm AQR Capital, suggests that managed futures returns are explained in a statistical sense by serial correlation in futures price changes,[20] a finding with which most futures managers would readily agree. It is widely known that most successful managed futures programs are based on trend following,[21] but to an economist, this doesn't explain anything, because we still have no idea why price changes would exhibit such serial correlation.)

---

[19] For a review of the literature on the EMH by one of its proponents, see Burton Malkiel, "The Efficient Market Hypothesis and Its Critics," *Journal of Economic Perspectives* 17, no. 1 (2003).
[20] Brian Hurst et al., "Demystifying Managed Futures," *Journal of Investment Management* 11, no. 3 (2013).
[21] See, for example, Andreas Clenow, *Following the Trend*, Wiley (2013).

Barclays CTA Index

In the United States, managed futures are regulated by the *Commodity Futures Trading Commission* (CFTC). The CFTC refers to the investment managers in the managed futures business as *Commodity Trading Advisors* (CTAs).

As the name implies, managed futures are actively managed accounts. Therefore, it is a bit misleading to speak of an index. However, the hedge-fund reporting firm Barclays has for almost three decades compiled the results of most of the leading managed-futures advisors into an index of sorts.

The BarclayHedge CTA index is an index of the returns of selected managed futures programs since 1980. The index began in 1980 with only 15 programs and has grown since then as the market has grown. In 2015 the index included 535 programs.

The performance of the index, according to the Efficient Market Hypothesis,[22] is impossible, because the index has had a compounded return over 35 years of almost 10% per year. Over that same period, it has had a low annual standard deviation of 11.7%. The returns are also essentially uncorrelated with the returns from stocks and bonds. As we will see, correlations are important in constructing portfolios with as little risk as possible for a given level of return.

However, the Barclay CTA index probably doesn't have a future expected return of 10%. For the first five years of the CTA index, there were 31 or fewer programs in the fund. There is an old rule of thumb in statistics[23] that says you need about 30 observations under certain assumptions to make reliable inferences.

---

[22] There are many forms of the Efficient Market Hypothesis (EMH), but the core idea is that all publicly available information is already reflected in the market prices quoted on the exchanges. In this case, the relevant version of the Hypothesis is the so-called *weak form*. Therefore, the theory says, no strategy that relies only on publicly available information can be consistently profitable. Most CTAs use only past prices to predict future prices. The consistent long-run profitability of these systems would seem to disprove the EMH, at least with respect to the futures markets.

[23] For explanation of this rule of thumb, see Gerald van Belle and Steven Millard, *STRUTS: Statistical Rules of Thumb*, Chapter 2, Wiley-Interscience (2008), available at http://www.nrcse.washington.edu/research/struts/chapter2.pdf.

If we exclude the first 5 years of the index under the reasoning that there were too few data points (i.e. managers), the compound return for the remaining 30 years is about 7.3% per year compounded. Still impressive, especially for a market that most financial economists would say should be efficient,[24] but significantly lower than the 10% of the full data. (Note that the first 5 years cover the first 5 years of the 1980s, which were a period of record-high interest rates. It is likely that those high interest rates contributed to the returns of the CTA index in those years.)

Over the 10 years 2006 to 2015, inclusive, the index return has been just 3% per year compounded, compared to the S&P 500 compounded return over the same period of 6.5%. However, the S&P 500 provided a wild ride over those 10 years, with a standard deviation of return in excess of 17%, against the uncorrelated CTA index's annual standard deviation over the period of under 6%. And, significantly to most investors, the CTA index's best year during those 10 years was 2008, exactly the year that the stock market had its worst year in decades.

There is some evidence to suggest that in periods of great financial market stress, CTA returns will tend to be positive. One possible explanation for this periodic inverse correlation is that managed futures returns are positively correlated with market volatility, and that market volatility tends to spike when financial crises and stock and bond market crises occur. In other words, because most CTAs are trend followers, CTAs don't care whether markets are going up or going down, because they can make money being long or being short (buying futures or selling futures) with equal ease. When markets "crash," as in times of financial stress, the very process of crashing creates a strong trend, typically generating strong positive returns for trend-following CTAs.[25]

---

[24] And therefore the trend following should produce, on average and before costs, a return of zero.

[25] Though it is of course possible that a CRT could be caught "long" in a number of markets as they crash, and if the crash is fast enough, as for example the day in October 1987 when the US stock market lost 20%, the long CTA could suffer terrible losses.

The main argument for including managed futures in a portfolio is that a managed futures fund can have reasonable expected returns, and very low, even zero, expected correlation with the other asset classes in the portfolio. This means that adding managed futures to a portfolio, despite the fact that the managed futures component is quite volatile, can actually reduce the expected volatility of the overall portfolio.

We cannot offer specific investment advice in this book. However, we have long standing relationships with several CTAs who have been very successful for decades. Please feel free to contact us if you'd like an introduction. Email CTA-Intro@SterlingFoundations.com, and reference this book and this offer.

Chapter 8
Mutual Funds

Mutual funds are not an asset class, but are rather a vehicle to invest in one or more asset classes.

A mutual fund is an investment fund designed to allow many small investors to pool their money so they can take advantage of the benefits of diversification, access to markets, and professional management that they probably could not get on their own. Individual investors pay a generally small annual management fee for the convenience and the opportunity to achieve diversification.

Open-Ended Funds Versus Exchange Traded-Funds (ETFs)

As of Sept 2023, the largest fund is Vanguard Total Stock Market Index, with assets of approximately $1.4 trillion. This fund is available as an open-ended fund, and as an Exchange-Traded Fund (ETF).

Open-ended funds differ from ETFs in three main ways: the frequency with which investors can buy or sell, the pricing of the funds, and the fees associated with owning the funds. Open-ended funds trade once per day, at the end of the day, while

ETFs – like stocks – trade continuously through the day while the market is open. The frequency of ETFs' trades means that the price is always fluctuating, analogous to the fluctuation of stock prices. The price of open-ended funds, however, is calculated at the end of the day, after all the trades have occurred. This price per share is called the Net Asset Value (NAV), and investors can purchase shares of an open-ended fund at the NAV when the market reopens. ETFs tend to charge lower management fees than open-ended funds. But overall, both kinds of funds will have essentially the same returns.

Open-ended funds tend to have slightly higher minimum initial investment amounts than the equivalent ETF. A typical open-ended fund might require a minimum initial investment of $2,500 or more, while in theory (it might not make sense in terms of transactions cost) you could buy a single share of an EFT, which might cost as little as $15 or so.

Advantages of Fund Investing

To buy the stocks in the S&P 500 in the same proportions as they are in the index would require the investment of hundreds of thousands, or perhaps millions, of dollars. The commission costs, if you paid the common minimum of around $10 per company, would be $5,000. In contrast, if you invest in an S&P 500 index fund you don't even have to know what companies are in the S&P 500, or what weights they have, or when they change. You don't have to reinvest dividends. The fund management, for which you pay perhaps 5 to 15 basis points per year ($5 to $15 per $10,000 of investment), takes care of all these things for you.

Index Funds

Index funds are a type of mutual fund that attempts to track a specific index. For example, an index fund may try to mimic the S&P 500, or a similar index. Index funds aim to achieve the same returns as the index they are tracking, rather than outperform the index, whereas other types of mutual funds may attempt to "beat" an index. Funds that follow an index are called *passively managed* funds, whereas *actively managed* funds usually attempt to outperform an index. Actively managed funds may charge higher management fees than passively managed funds.

Major categories of index funds include US-focused index funds and internationally focused index funds, as well as sector funds. US-focused funds invest within the United States. For example, Vanguard offers a variety of US bond funds as well as US stock funds. While these funds can help investors diversify their holdings within the US, they do not provide the opportunity to diversify outside the US.

International funds offer US-based investors the opportunity to diversify their portfolio holdings outside of the US. The wide variety of funds allows investors to choose whether to invest in a specific international geographic region, such as Europe or Asia, as well as whether to invest in a specific type of market, such as emerging markets. (Emerging markets refers to the markets of developing countries, which may not adhere to accounting standards and regulatory structures accepted by established markets such as the United States and Japan. The International Monetary Fund classifies Argentina, Brazil, and Russia as emerging markets, for example.[1])

Alternatively, an international fund may have a very broad focus, such as Vanguard's World Ex-US Fund, which invests in Europe, Asia, the Middle East, and emerging markets. The fund's largest holdings include Chinese tech company Alibaba, Japanese auto company Toyota, and Swiss pharmaceutical company Novartis. International funds provide investors with the opportunity to achieve a high degree of sector and geographic diversification at relatively low cost.

Sector Funds

Sector funds offer investors an opportunity to invest in a specific market sector or industry, such as the energy sector, the financial

---

[1] International Monetary Fund, https://www.imf.org/en/Publications/WEO/Issues/2020/09/30/world-economic-outlook-october-2020

sector, or the technology sector. Vanguard, for example, offers a Vanguard Energy ETF which invests in companies that are involved in oil and gas drilling, exploration, and refining services. As of October, 2023 its top two holdings are Chevron and Exxon Mobil.

Sector funds allow investors to remain concentrated in a single sector while simultaneously achieving some diversification through investing in multiple companies of one sector. Investing primarily in one specific sector, however, can increase the potential for downside in your portfolio if something should happen to devalue an entire sector.

Hedge Funds

Hedge funds are usually structured as limited partnerships, and typically use riskier investment strategies than mutual funds. Because of SEC regulations, hedge funds are usually open only to accredited investors. In August 2020, the definition of "accredited investor" was amended. Previously, the definition had required individuals to meet a minimum net worth criteria, but was amended to allow investors to be considered "accredited" based on a "clear measure of financial sophistication."[2] The definition is somewhat complicated, but includes banks, 501(c)(3) charities whose assets exceed $5 million, and individuals or couples filing jointly whose net worth exceeds $1 million.[3] Young or beginning individual investors probably don't need to concern themselves with hedge funds.

Individual Bonds Versus Bond Mutual Funds

For individual investors, mutual funds (open-ended or exchange-traded) usually provide more value than individual bonds because, as compared with individual bonds, funds offer more diversification, more liquidity, and probably lower total costs. A typical

---

[2] "SEC Modernizes the Accredited Investor Definition." SEC.gov. https://www.sec.gov/news/press-release/2020-191
[3] Cornell Law School, https://www.law.cornell.edu/cfr/text/17/230.501

bond mutual fund will own hundreds, or even a thousand or more, different issues. Only the wealthiest investors could achieve that level of diversification directly.

Your holdings in an open-ended mutual fund are usually completely liquid, meaning you can sell all or part of your holdings easily, and without suffering any price penalty, any day the markets are open.

Noted financial author William Bernstein has argued that open-ended funds may be superior to ETFs for bonds because, in the event that the bond market seizes up like it did for a while during the 2008 financial crisis, the investor is less likely to be hurt by lack of bond market liquidity.[4] His reasoning is not free from doubt (little is in investing), but we think he's probably right. However, for most people it probably doesn't matter.

A low-cost mutual fund or ETF probably offers the lowest total costs unless you plan to invest in government bonds, in which case direct purchase may save you some money.[5] With a low-cost mutual fund, such as the Vanguard Total Bond Market Fund ETF (symbol BND), you will probably incur management costs of about 1/20 of 1%, also called *5 basis-points*, per year. The same fund is available as an open-ended fund at the same management fee. In practice it would not be feasible for most people to do as well on their own either in terms of diversification or costs.

Are Mutual Fund Expenses a Good Value?

When you hold a mutual fund, the fund company charges you a fee, and the other expenses of the fund come out of your money. Annual fees and expenses in municipal bond funds might be about 20 basis points, if you use a low-cost fund. In corporate bond funds, you may be able to find lower annual costs, perhaps about 10 basis points.

---

[4] William J. Bernstein, *Rational Expectations* (Efficient Frontier, 2014): 169.
[5] For example, Vanguard's Intermediate Treasury Fund has a policy of holding Treasuries with an average maturity of 5 to 10 years. For investors with less than $50,000, the expenses are .2% a year, and over that .1% a year. An investor with $50,000 in the fund would pay about $100 of fees. An investor with $1 million in the fund would pay $1,000.

At these cost levels, for every $100,000 you have invested, you are paying $200 a year for municipal bond fund management, and $100 a year for corporate bond fund management. Given the time it would take, the reduction in diversification, and the higher bid-offer spreads you would incur doing it yourself, it seems unlikely that most people would be better off buying individual bonds themselves, even through a discount broker.

Therefore, for the majority of investors, bond funds are preferable to owning individual bonds, except possibly US Treasuries, because you can buy them at issue without a fee. Similarly, most individual investors probably are better off owning diversified stock funds, because it would require more money and time to assemble a properly diversified stock portfolio than most beginning investors probably have.

Chapter 9
Basic Portfolio Theory

In most business schools and university economics departments today, there are several related prevailing ideas about financial markets. Here is a short discussion of the four big ideas of modern finance theory. These ideas are the *Markowitz Model* (also known as the *Modern Portfolio Theory* model); the *Capital Asset Pricing Model*; the *Random Walk* model; and the *Efficient Market Hypothesis*. Together, these ideas are often grouped under the name *Modern Portfolio Theory*.[1]

Markowitz Model

Every investor wants to get the highest possible returns while taking the least possible risk. In the 1950s, economist Harry Markowitz described a formal, mathematical method for selecting a portfolio of assets that would have the maximum possible return for each level of risk.

To do this, Markowitz defined the risk of a security, or a portfolio of securities, as the variance[2] of returns. Markowitz defined

---

[1] For a relatively nontechnical and brief history of portfolio theory before "modern" portfolio theory, see Harry Markowitz's article "The Early History of Modern Portfolio Theory: 1600–1900," *Financial Analysts Journal*, July/August (1999).

[2] Variance is a statistic defined as the average of the squares of the difference from the mean. It roughly corresponds to what most people think of when they think of the volatility of a security price.

the return as the expected return from the security. He then considered how correlated the return of each security was with every other security.[3] For example, the returns from the 30-year US Treasury bonds are highly correlated with the returns from the 10-year US Treasury.

Markowitz then made some further assumptions, and described a method for calculating the optimal portfolio; that is, the portfolio that has the maximum expected return for a given level of risk.

Markowitz won the Nobel Prize for this work. In practice, however, for most people it has little value. The problem is not with Markowitz's math,[4] nor is the problem with computing power. The problem is that there is no known way of accurately predicting the inputs to the model, and the model tends to be very sensitive to small changes in the inputs when there are more than two assets or asset classes.[5]

In our experience, the model will tend to "load up" the recommended portfolio with one risky asset or asset class. For example, suppose you are trying to find the optimal portfolio and are selecting from cash, short-term bonds, long-term bonds, REITS, US stocks, and developed country foreign stocks. Of these asset classes, REITS and the stocks are probably going to have the highest expected returns. But instead of weighting each of them, the model is likely to choose the one it calculates is best. So the model will choose a portfolio that has a lot of the "best" asset, but very little of the others.

---

[3] The set of all these pair-wise correlations is called the covariance matrix.

[4] If you want to learn about mean-variance optimization, you can find an extensive treatment in a finance text such as Edwin Elton and Martin Gruber's *Modern Portfolio Theory and Investment Analysis*, now in its 9th edition (Wiley, 2013). Any reasonably recent edition should be fine. Older editions can be found used for just a dollar or two.

[5] The statistical logic and machinery behind the MPT and mean-variance optimization is intellectually attractive. If you delve into and find it so, please also read Scott Summer, Mark Riepe and Laurence Seigel's article "Taming Your Optimizer: A Guide Through the Pitfalls of Mean-Variance Optimization" in *Global Asset Allocation: Techniques for Optimizing Portfolio Management*, Jess Lederman and Robert Klein (eds.), (Wiley, 1994). At a minimum, make sure you understand the section titled "The Beguiling Effects of Estimation Error," the main point of which is that small amounts of uncertainty in the data (e.g. the standard error of the mean, discussed in the appendix to this chapter), can vitiate the results of mean-variance analysis.

That would be okay, except that when you make small changes to the expected returns, the expected variances, or the expected covariances, then the model might make big changes to the optimal portfolio. Worse, because of the way the math works, the model is quite likely to choose the asset in which you made the biggest overestimate of return or the biggest underestimate of risk.[6] In the real world, this is problematic because it is very likely that the expected variances will change. This means that your optimal Markowitz portfolio could look completely different depending on small changes you make to the assumptions.

Perhaps for this reason, when people have tested the model against simpler methods of selecting a portfolio, the simpler methods have consistently outperformed the Markowitz method.[7]

The Markowitz Model yields portfolios that are said to lie on the *efficient frontier*. The efficient frontier (see Figure 9.1) is graphed as the curve of points having the maximum return for a given level of risk (where risk is defined as the variance of returns or, as it is more usually reported, the standard deviation of returns, which is the square root of variance).

Although the concept of the efficient frontier is useful for thinking about portfolios, when there are more than two assets (as in the real world), most people probably will not want to use the mathematical machinery of the Markowitz Model for personal financial planning or investment allocation due to its propensity to overweight the assets with the greatest estimation error.

But even though you probably won't find use for the Markowitz Model itself, the concept of the efficient frontier is important to the next model we will discuss, the Capital Asset Pricing Model.

---

[6] This effect is analogous to the Winner's Curse first described by Capen, Clapp, and Campbell in "Competitive Bidding in High Risk Situations," *Journal of Petroleum Technology* 23 (1971). They observed that in bidding for oil leases, "a lease winner tends to be the bidder who most overestimates reserves potential." In much the same way that an auction will award the lease to the bidder who has most overestimated the value, the Markowitz Model will allocate assets to the asset whose value (i.e. contribution to the model's objective function subject to the cost it contributes against the constraint) has been most overestimated.

[7] Victor DeMiguel et al., "Optimal Versus Naive Diversification: How Inefficient Is the 1/N Portfolio Strategy?" *Review of Financial Studies* 22, May (2009).

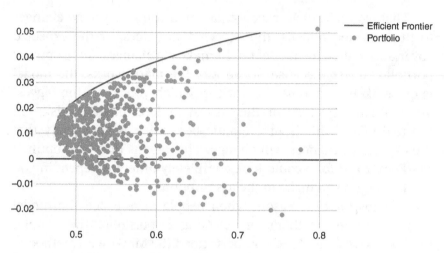

Figure 9.1 Markowitz's Efficient Frontier and Portfolios
Source: https://plot.ly/~chtan/98.embed

Capital Asset Pricing Model

The Capital Asset Pricing Model builds on the Markowitz Model, and expands the idea that return is a function of risk. The model assumes that investors can borrow or lend (generally at the so-called risk-free rate, which is the best rate available in the market), and thereby use a combination of risk-free assets and the optimal risky asset to construct a portfolio of any return. These possible portfolios are said to be on the *Capital Market Line.*

One of the most usable conclusions to come out of the Capital Asset Pricing Model's way of thinking is that there is some risk that an investor can reasonably expect to get paid for, and there is risk that a reasonable investor cannot expect to get paid for.

The risk an investor can expect to get paid for is *market* risk or *systematic* risk. Systematic risk is inherent to the entire market rather than to one specific company. Systematic risks include such risks as increases in interest rates, market crashes, economic recessions and depressions, war, and (as we saw in 2020) epidemics.

An investor cannot expect to get paid for *unsystematic risk*, because such risks can be avoided through diversification. Therefore, unsystematic risk is also known as *diversifiable* risk. Unsystematic risks are inherent to one specific company or segment of companies. For example, the risk to Tesla that Toyota will capture its sales of electric vehicles is an unsystematic risk, as it affects only specific companies. The concept of diversifiable risk can be illustrated by considering betting $1,000 on the outcome of a coin flip.

How and Why Diversification Can Reduce Risk

Suppose that you were offered a bet in which you bet $1,000 on a coin flip. If the coin comes up heads, you get $2,100, and nothing if it comes up tails. The expected value of this bet is $50. (Calculated as follows: $0.5 \times 2100 + .05 \times 0 - 1000 = 50$). Your range of possible outcomes is wide: you will end up either with a loss of $1,000 or a gain of $1,100.

Compare that to making 1,000 smaller bets on separate flips of the coin. Each bet is $1, and will pay off $2.10 if the coin comes up heads, and zero if it comes up tails. The expected value of each little bet is $.05 (calculated as follows: $0.5 \times 2.1 + .05 \times 0 - 1 = .05$), and the expected value of 1,000 bets is just 1,000 times $.05, or $50. So the expected value of the 1,000 smaller bets is the same as with the single big bet. But the range of likely outcomes is much narrower. We'll skip the math here, but now the chance of actually losing money is less than 7%, instead of the 50% chance with just one bet.

Diversifying among several stocks offers a similar way to reduce the risk of stock investing. For example, when an investor buys the Dow Jones Industrial Average (DJIA), he can expect to earn the return for taking the market risk. If that same investor were to buy, say, three randomly selected stocks from the DJIA, his expected return would be the same as if he had invested in the entire DJIA, but his risk (measured as variance of returns) would be higher. Just as in the coin flipping example, the risk of the first bet was greater than the risk of the second bet, but the expected value of the bets was equal. Similarly, the risk of investing in just a few companies is greater than the risk of investing in a broad swath of the market, but the expected returns are the same. The investor cannot reasonably expect to earn a return for *unsystematic* or *diversifiable* risk – which he could, if he chose, diversify away by buying a broader basket of stocks.

One implication of the Capital Asset Pricing Model is that if a class of stocks has persistently higher returns (say, small stocks versus large stocks), the class with the higher returns will also have higher systematic (non-diversifiable) risk. In other words, higher returns come at the expense of incurring higher risk. (This observation should not be misunderstood as claiming that all risks come with higher expected returns. It is only carefully managed risk that may be expected to bring higher returns.)

Let's look at how the Capital Asset Pricing Model might be useful in thinking about the returns to a specific company (we'll use Apple), and then an index (we'll use the Invesco QQQ ETF, which is heavily weighted toward tech stocks).

Mathematical Underpinnings of the Capital Asset Pricing Model

The Capital Asset Pricing Model assumes that, the return on a security can be modeled by a simple linear equation,

$$r = \alpha + \beta M \tag{1}$$

The left side, r, is the expected return. This return is assumed to be a function of some "risk-free" rate, called α (alpha), and some coefficient called β (beta) times the so-called *market* return. In the model, β is a measure of the volatility of the stock compared to the volatility of the market. The more volatile a stock, the higher its β.[8]

For example, if the market is defined as the S&P 500, and the asset whose return we are seeking to explain is Apple, over the

---

[8] The β is the ratio of the covariance of the return on a stock vis-à-vis the market to the variance of the market returns themselves. The academically inclined reader may note that we have slightly simplified the model from the full academic version in which the left-side return, r, is defined as the expected *excess* return.

period July 2014, to July 2019, the relationship of daily returns turns out to be:[9]

$$r_A = 0 + 1.2M. \tag{2}$$

That is, we find that Apple's *alpha* over the period was zero, and Apple was (roughly) 1.2 times as volatile as the market. The daily returns of Apple and the market are shown in the graph in Figure 9.2:

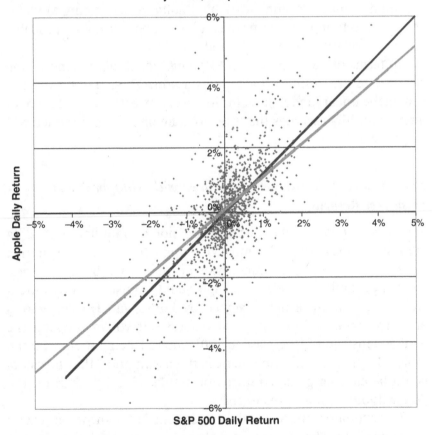

Figure 9.2 Capital Asset Pricing Model for Apple, July 2015 to July 2019 (y = 1.2x; R-squared = .43)

---

[9] We found this relationship by least-squares regression.

The lighter, dotted line in the figure is a slope of 1, while the heavier, solid line has a slope of 1.2. That is the fitted line for Apple according to the model. (If Apple had the exact same returns as the S&P 500, the fitted line for Apple would map exactly to the lighter, dotted line, the slope of which is 1.)

In academic finance, which has made its way to Wall Street and beyond, it is common to talk about a stock's *beta* as a measure of its riskiness. In the model, by definition, the market has a beta of 1. In this case, Apple has a beta of 1.2. Implicit in such talk is the assumption that this single-variable Capital Asset Pricing Model is correct, and that everything we can know about a stock's probable return is explained by its *alpha* and *beta*.

In terms of the Capital Asset Pricing Model, *alpha* amounts to risk-free return. Alpha shows up as a nonzero value of the intercept in the linear model. It seems like every investor who talks about alpha naturally assumes that the alpha he or she will produce will be positive.

Don't Mistake Beta (Returns Correlated with Risk) for Alpha (Risk-Free Returns)

Sometimes, people who perhaps are not as familiar with data analysis as they might be mistake a high beta in an up market for alpha. For example, marketwatch.com (owned by Dow Jones, Inc.) is generally considered a high-quality consumer investment website. A feature article[10] signed by Philip Van Doorn, who is an "investment columnist," told readers, "If you're tracking the S&P 500 instead of [the Nasdaq 100], you're leaving money on the table." Implicit in this statement is the assumption that investors could be earning greater returns on the Nasdaq 100 than on the S&P without taking a greater risk.

Unfortunately, the text of the article added little substance to this headline claim. The article talked about Invesco's Exchange-Traded

[10] Peter Van Doorn, "If You're Tracking the S&P 500 Instead of This Fund, You're Leaving Money on the Table" MarketWatch.com, March 15, 2019, https://www.marketwatch.com/story/if-youre-tracking-the-sp-500-instead-of-this-fund-youre-leaving-money-on-the-table-2019-03-13

Fund (or "ETF") called "QQQ," which tracks the Nasdaq 100 index, and claimed that the QQQ outperformed the S&P 500 over the last 20 years. It did. But Modern Portfolio Theory asks us to examine whether the extra return came from *alpha*, from *beta*, or perhaps from something else.

Alpha, as we said, is excess return that is earned without taking extra risk. In Figure 9.2, it would show up as the fitted line crossing the y-axis above zero.[11] Beta is the slope of the line. Higher returns for the asset on the y-axis would be reflected in a slope greater than 1, as in the figure. It is also the case when comparing the QQQ with the S&P 500.

Modern Portfolio Theory, particularly the Capital Asset Pricing Model, asserts that over the long run, return is a function of risk. As noted elsewhere, risk in the Modern Portfolio Theory world is usually defined in terms of the variance or standard deviation of returns.

Assessing the Risks and Returns of the QQQ Versus the SPY

Over the 20 years from 1999 to 2019, the QQQ returned an average of about 7.16% per year (CAGR of price change), while the S&P 500 (represented by *the SPY*) returned about 5.96%. Over the same period, the annualized standard deviation of the QQQ was about 27.7%, and of the SPY (an ETF that tracks the S&P 500) was about 19.0%.

In terms of return per unit of risk, (measured by annual return divided by annualized standard deviation), the QQQ ratio is .258, and the SPY ratio is .313. So on this basis it is the case that the SPY generated more return per unit of risk than did the QQQ.

Another way to look at that data is to ask the hypothetical question: What would our returns and risk have looked like if we leveraged the SPY by buying 120% (e.g. by borrowing 20%, assuming

---

[11] In the period considered, Apple produced a higher return than the market, but in Capital Asset Pricing Model terms, the higher return was attributed to the higher risk (measured as volatility). That is, the alpha was zero, and the beta was 1.2.

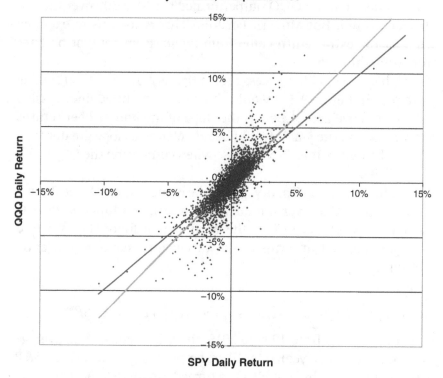

Figure 9.3 Daily Returns 1999 to 2019; QQQ vs SPY (y = 1.207x; R-Squared = .69)

we can borrow for free, just to keep the analysis simpler.)[12] (See Figure 9.3.)

If we did that, the compound annual return over the period from the 120% investment in the SPY would be the same as with the QQQ, but with somewhat lower volatility. In the parlance of Modern Portfolio Theory, the QQQ is not on the *efficient frontier*. That is, compared to the leveraged SPY, the QQQ has additional risk (in the form

---

[12] The "real" Capital Asset Pricing Model does not make this simplifying assumption directly. Instead, it looks at rates of return in excess of the risk-free rate, and then asks what would happen if we were able to borrow at the risk-free rate.

of volatility) that the investor was not paid for. The greater risk of the QQQ is clearly visible in the following graph, which shows the value of a dollar invested in the QQQ and in the SPY over the 20-year period 1999 to 2019. Note that from 2001 to 2008, the returns to the QQQ were lower than to the SPY (see Figure 9.4).

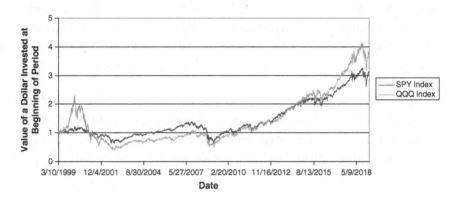

Figure 9.4   QQQ Is More Volatile Than SPY

Drawdowns

Although not much discussed (if at all) in the Modern Portfolio Theory literature, the concept of drawdown is important to most investors. The concept is simple: How much has my portfolio dropped from its maximum? For example, if you invest $1,000, it increases to $2,000, then drops to $1,750, you experience a drawdown of $250. Even though you are up from your starting point, you have a loss from your maximum. This loss from maximum is the *drawdown*.

In the period 1999 to 2019, the QQQ experienced a maximum drawdown of 82%. That is approximately the drawdown experienced by the Dow Jones Industrial Average from the 1929 high to the 1932 bottom. Over the same 1999 to 2019 period, the maximum drawdown of the SPY was 55%. That's still big, but not quite as devastating as 82%. Even leveraged to 120%, the maximum drawdown of the SPY would have been 66%—huge, but still less than the QQQ's 82%.

It may be the fact of drawdowns, more than any other factor, is what makes investing difficult. All rational investors dislike drawdowns. But drawdowns are unavoidable, even in the most successful investments. For example, suppose you had invested $290 in a share of Warren Buffett's Berkshire Hathaway in early 1980.

By May 2021, your $290 would have grown to $435,000. We've yet to find someone who would say that was not a good investment.

Yet, despite that world-beating performance, you would have been in a drawdown over 91% of the time! And at one time you would have seen the value of your investment decline by more than half.

Drawdowns are a fact of life in investing. And although we don't know in a deep philosophical sense why they occur, the persistence and pervasiveness of drawdowns is entirely consistent with the statistical model of investment returns known as *random walk*.

Random Walk

A random walk is a sequence of random outcomes. For example, suppose you were flipping a coin over and over, and counting the number of heads minus the number of tails. This number of heads minus tails is said to follow a random walk.

In 1965, Eugene Fama published a paper[13] suggesting that stock prices follow a random walk with drift.

If you flip a fair coin, the expected number of heads equals the expected number of tails. But suppose the coin were weighted to come up heads 60% of the time. Then you'd expect that over time the number of heads minus the number of tails would keep growing, but in a random sequence. That would be an example of a *random walk with drift*.

Fama suggested that daily, weekly, monthly, or yearly returns from stocks caused stocks to follow a pattern like a random walk with drift. That is, he suggested, stock prices move in a manner

[13] Eugene F. Fama, "Random Walks in Stock Market Prices," *Financial Analysts' Journal* (1965).

similar to how they would move if they were in fact a random walk with a slightly higher probability of going up than of going down.

Princeton's Burton Malkiel seized on this idea, and used it for the title of his bestseller *A Random Walk Down Wall Street* in 1973. Reasonable minds might differ, but my reading of the evidence is that while stocks do not, in general, follow a strict random walk, the price movements are random enough that most investors should treat them as though they were random.

If stock markets indeed follow a random walk,[14] then the strategies of so-called "chartists" and "technical analysts" who attempt to time the markets by predicting whether stock prices will go up or down should not provide superior returns compared to the returns on the index. Technical analysts examine the charts of past stocks, and base their investment decisions on patterns they observe on the charts. If the random walk theory holds true, such decisions are no better than the random flipping of a coin.[15]

Efficient Market Hypothesis

Fama and several other researchers built on the idea of randomness to propose the *Efficient Market Hypothesis*. If price changes are random, it follows definitionally that they are not predictable. If stock price changes (technically, returns to stocks) are not predictable, then no available information could be used to earn superior returns. The claim that no information available or even theoretically available can be used to beat the market is the basis of the Efficient Market Hypothesis.

---

[14] Financial academics distinguish between the path followed by prices and the path followed by returns. But we can, and do, ignore the difference in this discussion.

[15] Indeed, Malkiel, a professor of finance, tells a story in his book about his students producing a stock chart simulation by flipping a coin. When the coin turned up heads, the students recorded that the stock's price went up, and when the coin turned up tails, the simulated stock price went down. One coin flip simulation showed "a very bullish formation," which Malkiel showed to a technical analyst friend. The friend, greatly excited, advised investing in the stock right away, as it would continue to go up. (He was displeased when told that the chart was merely a simulation derived by coin flips.)

There are three forms of the Efficient Market Hypothesis (EMH). Fama outlined the three versions of the hypothesis, calling them the *weak* form, the *semi-strong* form, and the *strong* form. The unifying idea behind these three forms is that competition between markets will cause persistent profit opportunities to attract capital, and therefore will be bid away.

The weak form states that there is no useful information in the history of prices. If the weak form of the hypothesis holds, so-called *technical analysis*, also called *chart reading*, will not enable a trader or investor to earn above market returns.

The semi-strong form states that in addition to past prices, all other publicly known information, such as earnings, stock splits, and product announcements, is also already incorporated into the market price. Thus, for example, a trader or investor could not earn above-market returns by studying, say, the history of earnings, the ratio of market price to earnings, or the history of price book value.

The strong form states that even nonpublic information (e.g. "inside information") cannot be used to beat the market.

Fama, and those who follow him, believe that, for the most part, the stock markets (most of the studies have focused on US stock markets) are pretty efficient. Fama says, "With but a few exceptions, the efficient markets model stands up pretty well."[16]

For an example of how competition opportunities may originally arise but be bid away by multiple investors, suppose that one day of rising prices was followed 60% of the time by a second day of rising prices. In this example, we will call the fact that the market is up on a given day the *signal*, because the market being up signals that there's a 60% probability that it will be up again the next day. Some investors would recognize the signal. Some would then reason, and act, as follows. If the price is up today, I know there's a 60% chance it will be up again tomorrow. But because I know it will probably be up tomorrow, I should buy it today before the close.

---

[16] Eugene Fama, "Efficient Capital Markets, a Review of Empirical Theory and Work," *Journal of Finance* 25, no. 2: 383–417, Papers and Proceedings of the Twenty-Eighth Annual Meeting of the American Finance Association New York, N.Y. December 28–30, 1969 (May, 1970), https://www.jstor.org/stable/2325486

The Efficient Market Hypothesis says, in effect, that such extra buying will cause the price on day 1 to rise by more than it otherwise would have, because the extra demand for the stock will drive up the price. Eventually, it will rise enough so that the entire gain that would have happened on day 2 instead happens on day 1. Now the signal no longer works.

The Efficient Market Hypothesis, on a day-to-day basis, does a pretty good job of describing most markets most of the time. It is very difficult to earn excess returns, precisely because so many investors are competing to earn those returns.

There are hundreds of academic studies looking at one or another suspected exception to the Efficient Market Hypothesis. Many of these papers have reported exceptions, or as they are known in the finance lingo, *anomalies*. Many of these anomalies are small, abstruse, and/or evanescent. Probably many of these reported anomalies are the result of statistical chance, or of "p-hacking" on the part of financial researchers.[17] In nontechnical terms, p-hacking amounts to looking at your data six ways to Sunday until you find a "statistically significant" result. Or, as Nobel Prize–winning economist Ronald Coase put it, "If you torture the data long enough, it will confess."[18]

But markets are not automatically efficient. One of the big weaknesses of modern mainstream economics is a frequent failure to appreciate the crucial role that investors (often pejoratively termed *speculators*) play in risking their own capital and in the process constantly moving markets toward "correct" prices.[19] We believe it is likely that many real anomalies are discovered, exploited, and ultimately eliminated by hedge funds or similar investors. It is possible that some of the observed anomalies which Hou says were the

---

[17] Kewei Hou and his colleagues say, "The anomalies literature is infested with p-hacking." Kewei Hou, Chen Xue, Lu Zhang, Replicating Anomalies, Fisher College of Business Working Paper 2017-03-010, June 2017.

[18] Daniel B. Klein (ed.), "A Plea to Economists Who Favor Liberty: Assist the Everyman," *Institute of Economic Affairs* (2001): 84. This citation is to Gordon Tullock, who states "I have heard him [Coase] say this several times."

[19] Fama's colleague Sherwin Rosen has written about the issue. See, for example, Sherwin Rosen, "Austrian and Neoclassical Economics: Any Gains from Trade?" *Journal of Economic Perspectives* 11, no. 4 (Autumn 1997).

result of p-hacking were real, but were arbitraged away by firms like Renaissance Technologies. Renaissance, started by mathematician James Simons in 1982, is a quantitative hedge fund that manages about $60 billion. Simons himself has made about $20 billion.[20]

But over longer periods of time, there appear to have been several anomalies, or measurable tendencies for the market to diverge from strict efficiency. Probably the most significant of these is the *value anomaly*.

In the following section, we'll examine several perceived anomalies, including the *value anomaly*, the *size effect*, and the existence of momentum in managed futures.

Significant Exception to the Efficient Market Hypothesis: The "Value Anomaly"

Perhaps the most robust and well-demonstrated anomaly is the *value anomaly*. The value anomaly is the name given to the historical observation that on average, over time, stocks that trade at lower valuations (usually measured as low price/book, low price/earnings or similar measure comparing financial statement numbers to market price) have higher total returns than stocks that trade at higher valuations.

Value Versus Growth Stocks

People who study stock investing frequently speak of "value" stocks and "growth" stocks. Generally, stocks are categorized according to one of several quantitative measures. One common such measure is the ratio of a stock's price per share to its book value per share. The book value of a stock can be read from the company's balance sheet. In brief, the book value of a company is the accounting net worth

---

[20] In the process, Simons has helped make the markets more efficient. From a social point of view, efficient markets are a good thing, because to the extent that markets are efficient, they convey correct information about the relative values of different resources, and thereby help assure that the resources that are available will be used by those who value them most highly.

of the company. For example, if a company holds assets on its balance sheet at a value of $1 billion, and has balance sheet liabilities of $300 million, it has a book value of $700 million. If that same company has 7 million shares outstanding, it has a per-share book value of $100. If the stock is trading at $130 per share, the company is said to have a price/book ratio of 1.3.

Every publicly traded company must publish financial statements, and so it is possible to calculate a price/book ratio for every public company. Many people have done so, and gone back many years. Over very long periods, it seems to be the case that the one-third of stocks with the lowest price/book ratios have performed better than the rest of the stocks with higher price/book ratios.[21] There is also evidence to suggest that the very bottom decile of stocks by price/book ratio performs worst of all the deciles.

While the outperformance of low price/book stocks seems real and significant (perhaps 1 to 2% per year on average), there are long periods when they have underperformed. And of course there is no guarantee that low price/book will outperform in the future.

International Evidence

Fama and French published a paper in 1998[22] in which they found that value, as measured by price/book ratio, outperformed growth in 12 of 13 national stock markets during the period 1975 to 1995. The year 1975 marked a major long-term bottom in many world stock markets, and 20 years is too short a period from which to draw conclusions, but the evidence suggests that value outperforms internationally as well as in the United States. Value-oriented investment management firm Brandes Investment Partners published a study of international value covering the period 1980 to 2012, and found a persistent outperformance of value over growth. Figure 9.5 shows a graph from the publication illustrating the performance

---

[21] One often-cited paper by Eugene Fama (who received the 2013 Nobel Prize in economics) and Kenneth French is "The Cross Section of Expected Stock Returns," *Journal of Finance* 47, no. 2 (June 1992).

[22] Eugene Fama and Kenneth French, "Value vs. Growth: The International Evidence," *Journal of Finance*, 53, no. 6, (December 1998).

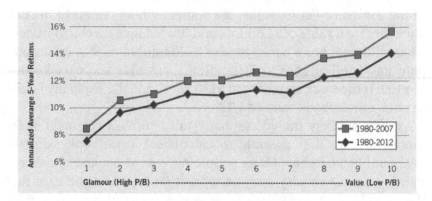

Figure 9.5 Global All Cap Value Premium (P/B Deciles, June 30, 1980 – June 30, 2012

Source: Worldscope via FactSet, The Brandes Institute; as of 6/30/2012. Past performance is not a guarantee of future results.

of stocks by price/book decile. The most expensive stocks, in the first decile, returned the least, and the "cheapest" stocks, in the 10th decile, returned the most.

This anomaly has been observed across many decades, and across many international markets, and seems to be real. If it is real, one possible reason it persists and is not "arbitraged" away is that it can take years for a "value" portfolio to outperform the market, and a value portfolio will underperform in many years. Portfolio managers are often judged on a shorter time frame, such as quarterly or yearly. If a manager is judged on the time frame of a year, and a value strategy can be expected to pay off only over a significantly longer time frame, the manager who adopts a value strategy incurs a significant career risk.

It has also been argued[23] that value stocks' higher returns are explained by value stocks' higher risks. And just to keep things interesting, it has been argued that in fact value stocks are not riskier.[24]

---

[23] E.g. by Nai-fu Chen and Feng Zhang, "Risk and Return of Value Stocks," *Journal of Business*, 71, no. 4 (October 1998).

[24] E.g. by William Bernstein – http://www.efficientfrontier.com/ef/902/vgr.htm – who bases his opinion on historical returns and standard deviations of Fama/French value and growth indexes for the period 1963–2002.

What About the "Size" Effect?

For decades in the United States, it has been widely believed that small company stocks have historically delivered higher returns than large company stocks. For example, the famous Ibbotson data[25] reported for decades that small stocks had yielded higher returns than large stocks. The impression was so strong that it led to the widespread belief that there is a continuum of expected return which is inversely related to company size. In other words, it is widely believed that small stocks have the highest potential returns, midsize stocks have potential returns in the middle, and large stocks have the lowest potential returns.

But even such a seemingly simple effect is not free from doubt. When researchers have looked more closely at the size effect, they have found that, for some unknown reason, almost all the effect seems to occur in January![26] Furthermore, since its discovery in the early 1980s the effect seems to have greatly diminished in the United States, and seems to be hard to detect in non-US markets. This effect has also been known as the *January effect*, and as of 2016, financial researchers have reported that the January effect no longer exists.[27] It makes sense that this effect has been discovered by the public at large since the 1980s, and competed away.

There is also a question of whether an effect that shows up in historical data can be captured by real investors. For example, it seems that a large fraction of the historically observed small-cap outperformance has come from illiquid, microcap stocks. If a stock is illiquid, it can be difficult to buy and sell, and even if you can buy or sell it, you might incur a large transaction cost for the trade. These transaction costs might consume all or part of the apparently available outperformance.

---

[25] Total return series for a number of different asset classes, going back to 1926, and published annually in as the Ibbotson *Stocks, Bonds, Bills & Inflation* (SBBI) yearbooks.

[26] See, for example, Michael Crain, A Literature Review of the Size Effect, October 29, 2011, available at http://ssrn.com/abstract=1710076

[27] Jayen Patel, *Journal of Applied Business Research*, https://www.clutejournals.com/index.php/JABR/article/view/9540

Nevertheless, in the United States in the past, there has been long-run outperformance by small stocks, as compared to the large-cap S&P 500. There seem to be good reasons, however, to doubt whether small-cap stocks will deliver a premium in the real world to investors going forward.

"Cheap" or "Expensive"? Volatility of Stock Prices Versus Earnings or Dividends

Perhaps of even greater significance than the value anomaly is the variation of entire markets between "cheap" and "expensive." Robert Shiller of Yale, and many others since him, examined the historical volatility of both stock prices and dividends.

You will recall that over the long run, the real return to owning stocks is driven by stocks' earnings. Other than changes in valuation multiples, over the long run there isn't anything else that can drive returns.

Logically then, Shiller suggests, stock prices should be no more volatile than earnings. But stock prices, Shiller finds, move far, far more than turns out after the fact to have been warranted by changes in earnings, or dividends.

Shiller applied the term *irrational exuberance* to the phenomenon of stocks running up to levels that are not justified by earnings and are very unlikely to be justified by future earnings. He wrote a book with that title.

During stock market booms, sometimes investors get carried away and entire stock markets get valued at very high levels. And sometimes the pendulum swings the other way, and stock markets get very cheap.

An objective measure of "fair value" is the holy grail of investors. The approach Shiller came up with was to use a 10-year average of earnings to look at the long-run average multiple of those earnings. That is similar to the approach Benjamin Graham applied 70 years ago.

We can never know before the fact what will happen with a stock market. But history does teach us that usually when it feels safe to buy a market, that market is not cheap, and when a market is cheap, it usually doesn't feel safe to buy that market.

The relationship between how cheap or expensive a market is, (measured by CAPE, by price/book ratio, or some similar measure) and subsequent 10- to 15-year compound average return is noisy, but real. On average, cheap markets lead to higher returns and expensive markets lead to lower returns.

Can You "Beat the Market"?

Unless you are planning to be an investment professional, or a very serious and dedicated amateur, you will most likely be better off not trying to "beat the market."

By "beat the market," we mean earning returns that are significantly and consistently above the return that can be earned by owning an index fund in the market under consideration.

For example, suppose we consider the US stock market. Perhaps the most representative index of that market is the S&P 500. There is of course no way of knowing how many individual investors bought and sold stocks and earned a higher return over any given period.

However, there are good, publicly available data on how many mutual funds were competing with the S&P 500, and how they did in comparison with a fund that passively owned the S&P 500 stocks.

The large majority, perhaps 75–90% of funds, do worse over most longer time frames. Whether the funds that do better do so as a result of skill or luck is hard to determine. More importantly, it seems to be very difficult to select a fund in advance that will outperform the index.

In 2005, for example, you might have been very excited to invest in the Legg Mason Value Trust, which, under the direction of manager Bill Miller had beaten the S&P 500 every year since 1990. But you would probably have been disappointed, because during the next 10 years, the fund was trounced by the S&P 500, not quite managing to earn positive returns over the entire period.

Although it is not certain, we believe that for the typical investor looking for US stock market exposure in their portfolio, the best approach is to use diversified low-cost, low-turnover funds.

Why Don't Professionals Beat the Average?

How can it be that 90% of the funds are below the average, as measured by the index? Answers vary, but the two main reasons probably are fees, and the fact that actively managed funds usually hold a certain percentage of their assets in cash.

Effect of Fees

The effect of fees is simple. The S&P 500 index itself includes no fees at all. Any real fund incurs some costs, such as trading and administrative, and every real fund management company charges at least minimal fees. The average actively managed fund probably incurs expenses of about 1% per year. So, for example, if in a year the S&P 500 index generated an 8% return, and a fund exactly matched that return before fees and expenses, but incurred 1% in expenses, the fund would return to investors 7%. The average funds fees and expenses of about 1% thus represent quite a handicap to overcome, and most funds don't.

Effect of Cash Holdings

The second factor working against funds beating the S&P 500 is that actively managed funds usually keep a certain percentage of their assets in cash while they wait for opportunities to invest it, and because they need to keep a certain amount of cash to meet withdrawal requests. On average, cash yields significantly less than stocks. Historically, the long-run average return to stocks has exceeded the return to cash by about 6 to 7%. If there is an average 7% extra return to stocks over cash, and a fund holds 10% of its assets in cash, that cash will on average cause the fund to perform about 0.7% a year worse than the overall stock market.

In fact, that is just the empirical finding of a study published in 2000 in the *Journal of Finance*.[28] The study found that the professional stock pickers actually do beat the index before costs and before the drag of nonstock investments (e.g. cash). But from the point of view of the investor, all that matters is the net result, which is worse than the average about 90% of the time.

Enhanced Index Strategies

The S&P 500 index, like most major indices, is market-cap weighted. That is, bigger companies have more weight in the index than smaller ones. For example, as this was written, Apple was the company with the largest weight in the S&P 500 index, at 3.81%, while Chesapeake Energy had a weight of .0155%. Suppose for sake of discussion that Apple could return 100% (e.g. the stock doubled overnight) while the rest of the index remained unchanged. The return from Apple would mean that the index had a return of 3.81%. Now suppose that Apple and the rest of the index companies remained unchanged, but Chesapeake returned 100%. The move in Chesapeake would generate only a .0155% return for the overall index.[29]

That means that companies with large market values count more in the index than do smaller companies. The reason for market-cap weighting is that market-cap weighting makes it possible for large funds to actually buy the index. The total market capitalization of the S&P 500 varies every day as the stocks go up and down. At year-end 2017, it was about $23 trillion dollars. Against that, S&P says that about $9 trillion is invested in some kind of S&P 500 tracking fund.

---

[28] Russ Wermers, "Mutual Fund Performance: An Empirical Decomposition into Stock-Picking Talent, Style, Transaction Costs, and Expenses," *Journal of Finance* 55, no. 4 (August 2000).

[29] I do not mean to suggest this is the exact procedure by which index returns are calculated. It is not, and the actual procedure is more complicated. The point is to explain the key idea of how market-cap weighting works. Also, after this was written, Chesapeake was removed from the S&P 500, and Apple, though not overnight, did double (and then some).

Notice that there is nothing magic about the index. It is not special, and there is nothing about the way it is selected that causes it to outperform most stock pickers. It outperforms because it has lower costs, and stays 100% invested all the time. In theory, if a manager or a strategy could overcome both of these sources of drag, they could consistently beat the index.

One such strategy that attempts to beat the index is called "equal weighting." There are 500 stocks in the S&P 500. In the "equal weighted" S&P 500 index, each stock contributes 1/500th of the value of the index.

One downside of a market-cap weighted index is that it gives more weight to high fliers, and less weight to companies that are out of fashion. Equal weighting avoids this particular bias. Does it work?

Since 1990, the answer seems to be yes. According to S&P, the equal-weighted version of the index has outperformed the market-cap weighted version by about 1.5% a year, but not consistently, and the equal-weighted version has had higher volatility. Since 2004, it has been possible to invest in an exchange-traded fund that seeks to track the equal-weighted S&P. That fund, named Guggenheim S&P 500 Equal Weighted ETF, ticker RSP, has outperformed as shown in the chart of actual prices in Figure 9.6.

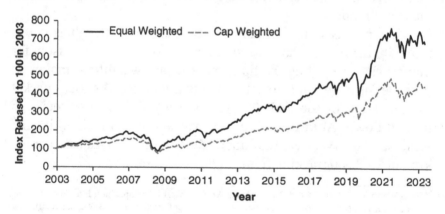

Figure 9.6   S&P 500: Equal Weighted Versus Cap Weighted

If you look closely at the chart, you will see that when the market goes down, as it did from late 2007 to 2009, and again in 2011, the equal-weighted index declined more than the market-cap weighted index. Is this because the equal-weighted index is higher risk, consists on average of smaller companies, or for some other reason? There is not enough data to answer the question.

However, over the quarter century following 1990, the equal-weighted index has outperformed the market-cap weighted index by an average of about 1.5%. That is a huge compounded effect, and could be because the capitalization-weighted index systematically overweights overvalued companies, or it could be a size effect, or it could be because the equal-weighted index takes more risk, or it could be something else.

In addition, if you were planning to own the investments in a taxable account, you would need to compare the after-tax returns of the equal-weighted index to the after-tax returns of the market-cap weighted index. It is possible that the equal-weighted index incurs more realized capital gains, and therefore generates more taxes, because it systematically sells "winners" to bring the weights back down to 1/500th. However, it may earn higher or lower dividends, which would also have an effect on the tax consequences.

Which Index?

As we saw previously, actively traded stock strategies have a steep hill which historically most have not overcome. But there is not simply one "correct" index. As we saw, is the "correct" index for the US market the S&P 500, the equal-weighted S&P 500, or something else? There is no correct answer.

The market-cap weighted indexes (e.g. S&P 500, Dow Jones Industrial Average), give most of their weight to the biggest handful of companies in the index. For example, in early 2016, the top 4% of companies in the S&P 500 accounted for about 25% of the index's value.

Alternatives are mid-cap indexes, such as the Vanguard Mid-Cap index, which is traded as the Vanguard EFT ticker VO.

The expense ratio on VO is currently .09% per year, versus the Guggenheim equal-weighted S&P 500 ETF's (ticker RSP) expense ratio of .40% per year.

The two funds have very highly correlated returns, with daily returns showing a correlation of .98 over the 13 years to January 2016. Over the 13 years that both funds have been in existence, VO has outperformed RSP by an average of .65% per year. VO has had slightly higher volatility during the period.

Does it matter? Does this performance have any meaning for the future?

Unfortunately, we cannot really say. There is a good theoretical and empirical argument that (ignoring taxes), the frequent rebalancing of an equal-weighted index adds value in the long run. There is also a good theoretical and empirical argument that lower fund fees, everything else equal, add value relative to higher fees in the long run.

Conclusion

The case for the Efficient Market Hypothesis is strong. However, markets and individual stocks are not always priced "correctly." It has historically been the case that only a small percentage of professionally managed mutual funds have outperformed the market after fees and expenses. It has also historically been the case that "value" stocks have tended to outperform the market, but there have also been long periods (10 years or more) during which they have underperformed.

Chapter 10
Financial Leverage

L everage refers to the practice of using borrowed money to invest. Most companies use some amount of borrowed money in their businesses. Some companies, such as high cash-generating tech firms (e.g. Apple, Microsoft) use relatively little borrowed money, while at the other end of the spectrum, banks (e.g. Bank of America, Citibank) use almost all borrowed money.

Everything else equal, the more financial leverage a company has, the riskier it is. That financial leverage risk is a big reason that tech stocks tend to trade at much higher valuation ratios than do banks.

Individual investors can also use borrowed money to invest. While for simplicity many academic models assume that investors can borrow at the "risk-free" rate, in the real world, few or no individual investors will be able to borrow at the "risk-free" rate. The usual way of borrowing to buy stocks, called *margin*, tends to be very expensive. Buying on margin refers to the practice of borrowing money to purchase stock. For individual investors borrowing on margin, interest rates tend to be much higher than the "risk-free" rate.

Smaller loan amounts face higher margin interest charges, while the largest accounts receive the lowest rates. For example, in October 2023, when the Fed Funds rate was about 5.25%, Fidelity offered margin loans at rates from 9.25% for loans over $1 million, to 13.575% for loans under $25,000. The lowest rate available was 5.83% for amounts over $200 million from Interactive Brokers, which positions itself as a low-cost shop. This 5.83% is determined by the Fed Funds rate. It was calculated by adding 50 basis points to the overnight Fed Funds rate.[1]

Reg. T.

In the United States, margin loans are regulated by the Federal Reserve, under its Regulation T, also known as "Reg. T." The regulation, which has the effect of law, limits retail investors to no more than 50% margin at purchase. For example, if you want to purchase $100 of stock, you must put up $50 and may (under Reg. T.) borrow $50. Once you own the stock, you must meet a "maintenance margin" requirement. Maintenance margin must be at least 25% under Reg. T., but many brokers require more than that. For example, Vanguard currently requires 35%, but reserves the right to increase that at any time without notice.

Effect of Leverage

Suppose you had the bad luck to buy $120 of SPY at its peak immediately before it declined by 55%, and that you had bought it using $100 of your own money, and $20 of borrowed money, so that your expected return would equal the return of the QQQ (assuming we could somehow know in advance that the 1.2 beta would apply).

When the SPY had dropped 55%, your stock would be worth $54, of which $20 would be the margin loan, leaving you with an equity

---

[1] The Fed Funds rate is the most important benchmark interest rate in the money markets. The Fed Funds rate is the rate at which US banks lend money to each other in the overnight market. The Fed Funds rate is manipulated by the Federal Reserve Bank.

of $34. You would still have plenty of margin, because $34 of the total of $54 is your equity, meaning that your margin loan is 37% (which is 20/54), still under the 50% initial limit. Your equity has declined from $100 to $34, a loss of $66 or 66%, as we calculated above.

In this historical example, you would not have been forced out by having your margin loan called. (When a lender *calls* a loan, he demands that it be repaid immediately.[2]) But, if the SPY had dropped more, you could have faced that situation. Whether or not such a margin loan would have actually been better than owning the QQQ depends to some extent on the interest rate. The extra 20% increased your return over the holding period from 5.96% to 7.16%, which is an increase of 1.2%.[3] But you would have gained less than 1.2%, because you had to pay margin interest on $20 of your initial cost.

Over time, as your investment gained in value, that $20 became a smaller fraction of the total. Let's make a wild guess and say that on average you paid margin interest on 10% of the value of your portfolio.[4] Let's make a further wild guess and say that the average interest rate was 5% per year. If so, margin interest would have reduced your total return by about .5% per year, to an annual average of 6.66% (i.e. 7.16% − .5% = 6.66%).

Let's round 6.66% to 6.7%, then recompute the return per unit of risk on your leveraged SPY position. The standard deviation was 22.8%. Return was 6.7%, so return per unit of risk is 6.7/22.8, or .292.

---

[2] Margin loans are callable at any time. Most mortgages and treasury bonds are not callable. Many, but not all, bank loans are callable. Call provisions are actually options, and have value. If you borrow money and the loan is callable, you are technically short the call option.

[3] I.e. 7.16 − 5.96 = 1.2. The fact that 1.2 resembles 120% is coincidence. Here's how we got the two return numbers. The actual return over the SPY was 5.96% per year. We'll show the analysis for a single year because it's simpler. If you invested in $100 of the SPY for a year, you'd gain $5.96. If you invested $120, you'd gain 5.96% of $120, which is $7.16. If you had been able to borrow the $20 extra that you invested, and pay zero interest on it, your return for the year would be $7.16. But your equity was only $100 (because you borrowed the $20), so your return on equity was 7.16%.

[4] You pay interest on the money you've borrowed, regardless of the value of your portfolio. We are showing the example here so that we can make a guess about the interest cost as a percent of the portfolio.

This is still higher than the QQQ's return per unit of risk of .258. Because of the cost of margin, however, we didn't match the QQQ's return.

To match the QQQ return after paying for interest on the borrowed margin money, we'll need about 30% margin. That would give a gross return, before margin interest, of 1.3 x 5.96%, or 7.75%. We estimate that the cost of the margin interest would cut about .7% from our return, for a net of about 7.15%, which is essentially the same as the realized compound return of the QQQ. This 1.3x leverage increases the volatility of the returns of the levered SPY to about .25, which is almost as high as the volatility of the QQQ.

It is important to note that once we start adding margin borrowing to our calculations, the results are very sensitive to the margin interest rate, the margin requirements, and to the path that the stock price takes. The stock price path means: Does the stock go up first, or down first? The path will affect the margin coverage. For example, if we borrowed 30%, say $30 on $100, then the market dropped by 55% (as the SPY did), our portfolio would drop in value by $71.50, because $71.5 is 55% of $130. That $71.50 is 71.5% of our initial $100 equity, and would trigger a margin call. Thus, even though borrowing 30% is "less risky" in terms of standard deviation of return, in the real world, such borrowing creates the risk of being forced out by the need to meet the margin call.

To a first approximation, then, if you have to borrow to leverage up the SPY, the cost of borrowing wipes out the benefit, and creates a different risk.

Borrowing on margin exposes you to a host of risks, some of which are hard to quantify. The biggest such risk, of course, is that an unexpectedly severe market downturn causes your equity to drop below the brokerage's (or the legal) requirements, and your position is sold out near the bottom, locking in your losses, and knocking you out of the game. But there are other, less subtle risks.

Some of these "hidden" risks are a consequence of the income tax laws, and others arise from the way that brokers are permitted to use your margin account holdings.

Securities Lending

Market professionals, such as hedge funds, often sell short individual stocks. When a short-seller makes a short sale, he is supposed to obtain the stock he has sold by borrowing it, and deliver that borrowed stock to a new owner.

He borrows the stock from a brokerage firm which has the stock, and is willing to lend it to him. The brokerage firm, in turn, is usually not long the stock for its own book, meaning that the brokerage firm does not own the stock itself. But one or more clients of the brokerage firm may own the stock. And because the brokerage firm has access to the stock, the firm may be able to borrow stock from clients, and then lend the stock.

If you hold your securities in a margin account, the brokerage firm has the right, under your account agreement with the firm, to lend out shares of stock that you own in your margin account. If the brokerage firm does lend out your shares, this creates at least two risks for you, and you get paid nothing for bearing these risks.

The main risks to you, the stock owner, from the brokerage firm lending out your stock are: (1) payments in lieu of dividends, and (2) hypothecation risk.

Payments in Lieu of Dividends

When the broker lends your stock, the borrower is required to pass along any dividends paid on the stock while the stock is lent out. However, the tax character of those payments may be different from the tax character of dividend payments. Some dividends are "qualified" to be taxed at the lower long-term capital gains rate. But payments in lieu of dividends are generally taxable as ordinary income, which is taxed at a higher rate than capital gains.

Most brokerage firms bury this information in the fine print of their margin account agreements. Fidelity actually has a program called "annual credit for substitute payments" specifically designed to "make whole" on an after-tax basis its clients who have received payments in lieu of dividends.

Fidelity doesn't necessarily do this out of the goodness of their hearts. Brokers who lend your securities receive collateral (generally cash) in an amount roughly equal to the value of the securities lent. (This is quite parallel to the way that repurchase agreements work in the bond market.) The broker then usually invests that cash collateral in interest-bearing securities (including possibly bond-backed repurchase agreements). The broker usually keeps the interest so generated.

That last point bears repeating. The brokerage firm lends out your securities. The brokerage firm receives cash collateral. The brokerage firm earns interest on that cash. The brokerage firm keeps the interest. (Some brokerage firms, such as Fidelity, allow the customer, under some circumstances, to receive part of this interest.)

Securities Lending Is a Complicated Tax Area

If your securities are lent out, it could create negative tax consequences for you. Securities lending transactions involve complicated tax law in the United States, and international lending may be even more complicated. In general, the US tax consequences are discussed in IRC Section 1058. "Under 1058, taxpayers do not have to recognize gain or loss from the transfer of securities if the exchange agreement requires the return of identical securities, if interest or similar payments accruing from holding the security are paid to the transferor during the covered lending period, and if there is no reduction in the transferor's risk of loss or its opportunity for gain. The statute also gives Treasury the authority to issue regulations adding other requirements."[5]

It seems possible, however, that if you lend out stock and the borrower sells or rehypothecates the shares, you could be deemed to have sold the stock, potentially triggering the recognition of income. We are not aware of cases where small shareholders

---

[5] Alston and Bird, News and Analysis, July 25, 2011.

(e.g. normal retail investors) have experienced this outcome. There are larger cases, involving millions of dollars, which were heavily lawyered and then challenged by the IRS, in which the IRS has ruled that what appeared to be securities loans were in fact deemed sales (e.g. Samueli v. Commissioner, 132 T.C. 37 [Mar. 16, 2009], see Doc 2009-5823 or 2009 TNT 49-28).

Rehypothecation Risk

Hypothecate means to lend. Rehypothecate is to lend property that has been borrowed. Rehypothecation, or borrowing by brokerage firms to lend to clients, is more common than you might at first think. It happens for various reasons. Here is a theoretical example.

Suppose that you put $5,000 of cash in your margin account at a brokerage firm to buy 100 shares of Coca-Cola at $50 per share, and borrow $5,000 from your broker (i.e. you are buying on margin) to buy another 100 shares of Coke. Your account will own 200 shares of Coke. Your brokerage firm may just happen to have $5,000 of unused capital that it is happy to loan you on margin. But it is more likely that the brokerage firm is itself borrowing the $5,000 that it is lending to you. The brokerage firm needs collateral when it borrows the $5,000. It uses your Coke stock.

Now suppose that the brokerage firm fails. (As MF Global did in 2011, after the Jon Corzine–led firm used approximately $1 billion of customer funds to cover its own trading debts. That is, Corzine, or his firm, essentially, and unlawfully, borrowed customer funds and gambled with them, and lost).[6] If the firm has pledged your stock, that stock is gone. But the firm's creditors, possibly in the persons of the bankruptcy trustee, still have a valid claim to the $5,000 that you borrowed. And since the bankruptcy trustee has possession of your account, he can sell your other shares of Coke to cover the $5,000 that you borrowed. Pretty scary, isn't it?

That is essentially what happened to $1.6 billion in customer funds at MF Global, although eventually, many years later, most of these customer funds were returned to the customers. While that result is not the worst possible outcome, it was still extremely costly

---

[6] https://www.cftc.gov/PressRoom/PressReleases/7508-17

for many customers who experienced recovery costs, opportunity losses, stress, and other follow-on losses from not having access to their capital. Some people, including hedge fund manager James Koutoulas[7] believe Corzine belongs in jail, and that he essentially bought off the Department of Justice by raising about $49 million for Obama, and then money for the Clintons.[8]

Real World Leverage, Again

For the preceding reasons, we don't think margin borrowing is a good idea. We believe that plenty of leverage can be gained by the selection of a portfolio of securities that is, itself, levered. For example, in aggregate, the capital of US corporations is approximately half debt. Put another way, corporations (on average) are already 50% leveraged with debt.

This leverage, very broadly speaking, accounts for the roughly 6.5% average compound real return of the US stock market over the past century to century and a half. We can derive this return with some heroic assumptions, and a little arithmetic. Since 1900, US GDP growth (nominal) has averaged about 6.2%. If we reduce this by inflation of about 3%, that is real growth of about 3.2%.

It is difficult to determine the long-term average cost of corporate borrowing. We are working from interest rate series that show interest rates but not total return. Because long-term returns from bonds are determined by the coupon, we averaged the coupon rate over the period – 4.7% – subtracted inflation of about 3.2%, then estimated a loan loss of .75%. We estimated the loan loss based on Moody's publications that find that on average about 1.5% of bonds default in a year (with tremendous variation at different times in the

---

[7] https://www.newsweek.com/stalking-jon-corzine-317733. Two weeks before Obama left office, the Commodity Futures Trading Commission settled its years' long action against Corzine, fining him and banning him for life from the futures industry.

[8] See Hilary Till, The MF Global Debacle: What Were the Red Flags? (July 20, 2017). Available at SSRN: https://ssrn.com/abstract=3007759 or http://dx.doi.org/10.2139/ssrn.3007759

business cycle), and that the average recovery is about 50%. There-fore, the average loss is about .75% per year.

We thus estimate the average annual cost of borrowed cap-ital (real terms) to be the coupon, minus inflation, and minus the default losses. That is, 4.7%, less 3.2%, less .75%, for a net cost of .75% per year.

We then assume that the average corporation owns assets that, on average, grow at the long-term rate of the economy. On a real basis, that has been about 3.2%. If corporations borrowed half their capital for free (i.e. a real cost of zero), they would double the return of the economy. Using our numbers, they'd return 6.4%. We assumed that the cost of borrowed capital was .75%, and that corporations borrowed half their capital. So that would reduce return by half of .75%, or .375%, per year. So, we'd expect the real long-run average return on the aggregate US stock market to be about 6.1% per year.

In fact, it has averaged somewhat more than that since 1900. Since 1900, the average real return of the stock market in aggregate is estimated to be about 6.6%, instead of the 6.1% we estimated. How-ever, that can be explained at least in part by the rise in valuation multiple since 1900. According to Robert Shiller's data,[9] the CAPE (the cyclically adjusted price/earnings ratio) has risen since 1900 from 18.4 to 30. That increase in valuation generates a compound return of about .4% per year.

That .4%, plus our estimate of 6.1%, is extremely close to the actual 6.6% real compound growth rate of the S&P 500 reported by https://dqydj.com/sp-500-return-calculator/.

So, if you invest in the broad stock market, you're already using a fair amount of financial leverage.

---

[9] http://www.econ.yale.edu/~shiller/data/ie_data.xls

Chapter 11
Risk

Fear of Losing Money

Some people are hesitant to invest because they are worried about losing money. Indeed, it is virtually impossible to invest money and have your portfolio continually increase in value, without your portfolio ever declining from its highest point.

Experiencing the value of their assets fall is what most people mean when they say *investment risk*.

New investors, particularly younger investors, frequently keep most of their money in a bank account, savings account, or money-market fund. There may be many reasons for this, and fear is often one of them.

We do not have a magic formula to remove the fear. What we can do is explain, to the best of our ability, how we think about investment risk. The hope is that you can then make more informed decisions, and build into your outlook the fact that investments go down.

Risk Versus Uncertainty

Risk is one of those words we use every day without usually stopping to be precise about what we mean. The term *risk* is used in different ways.

175

In 1921, economist Frank Knight published his landmark, if under-appreciated, book: *Risk, Uncertainty and Profit*. In this book, Knight distinguishes between *risk* and *uncertainty*. He defines *risk* as the calculable statistical probabilities inherent in a situation in which the possible outcomes, and their probabilities, are known or knowable. Under this understanding of *risk*, in order for a situation to be subject to risk analysis, its set of possible outcomes must be knowable, along with the probabilities associated with those outcomes.

For example, betting on roulette is properly subject to risk analysis, because the possible outcomes and their probabilities can be known statistically. The same is true of betting on football, although the estimates of the probabilities involved will be less precise than those involving roulette or other casino games.

Uncertainty, in contrast, is the situation in which we find ourselves most of the time. We simply don't know all the possible outcomes. Because we don't know all the possible outcomes, we cannot calculate their probabilities, nor can we calculate accurate expected values. For example, suppose you were in Germany in 1900 investing a portfolio. Even if you had considered the possibility of war into your plans, it is exceedingly unlikely, or impossible, for you to have considered even the possibility of events like WWI, poison gas, blockade starvation, trench warfare, the Spanish Flu, the hyperinflation, or aerial bombing. Yet all of these transpired, with widespread fatal (not to mention investment) effects. God only knows what "unknown unknowns," in Donald Rumsfeld's brilliant phrase,[1] await us over the next quarter century, half century, or three-quarters of a century.

---

[1] I (Roger) remember watching Rumsfeld's press conference at which he stated, "There are known knowns; there are things we know we know. We also know there are known unknowns; that is to say we know there are some things we do not know. But there are also unknown unknowns – the ones we don't know we don't know. And if one looks throughout the history of our country and other free countries, it is the latter category that tends to be the difficult ones." Rumsfeld was ridiculed, but I thought at the time, and continue to think, that the concept of "unknown unknowns" needs to be included in any forward-looking risk assessment.

And that's precisely the point of uncertainty. We don't know, and can't really know, even the potential for many events, and yet many of those events that we don't even know are possible will occur.

History

History, however, gives us the minimum variety of events which are possible. Obviously, if something has happened before, it is possible. But merely because some event has not happened, we cannot consider it impossible.

The SEC requires that mutual funds, when citing their historical performance in advertisements, include the disclaimer "past performance does not guarantee future results." If we understand this to mean something like, "if the fund has had an extraordinarily high return in the past, do not necessarily expect that performance in the future," essentially all investment professionals and academic researchers would completely agree.

However, if we interpret past performance as finance professors tend to do, in terms of mean and standard deviation of past returns,[2] then it seems that many people behave exactly as if they believe the past *is* a guarantee of the future.

Perhaps, if we had millions of years of well-recorded history, we might be able to get comfortable in measuring the risk of investments. But we don't. We have only about a century, perhaps two, of reliable financial market data. And we have only a couple of thousand years of reasonably reliable written history. Even so, there are significant lacunae in the historical record, such as the dark period in British history after the Romans left, or the almost entirely absent historical record of the pre-Columbian New World. Lacunae in the historical record would likely not represent periods when investment returns were good.

The recorded history we do have suggests that the century of data upon which Dimson, Marsh, and Staunton (DMS) rely is perhaps not representative of all that can happen. It takes no account

---

[2] See, for example, see Dimson, Marsh, and Staunton's table reporting precisely these parameters.

of various types of disasters of nearly unbelievable proportion, many of which are well known. For example, during the fourteenth century, between a third and a half of all Europeans died in the Black Death epidemics that swept the continent. During the sixteenth century, two large empires were wiped off the face of the earth in just a few years by just a few hundred Spaniards working knowingly with the aid of local allies and unknowingly with the aid of disease. The shattering eruption of Mt. Tambora in 1815, after thousands of years of quiescence, led to two successive years of crop failure in much of Europe and what historian John Post called *The Last Great Subsistence Crisis in the Western World* in a 1977 book by that title.

On the positive side, the post-1900 data largely exclude the Industrial Revolution transition from animal power to steam power (although the transition in the developed world continued until about mid-century), the information revolution of the telegraph, and the communications revolution brought about by railroads and steamships.

For these reasons, we believe that the DMS data must be taken with a grain of salt. They are suggestive of what has happened in the past, and perhaps therefore of part of what might be possible in the future. But they certainly cannot be definitive, even though they might be the best long-term data we have. And unless you have a strong reason to believe in a different set of probable future return possibilities, history, along with a bit of theory, is the best guide we have.

Despite the limitations, DMS have done a great and valuable service for investors. To better appreciate what they have done, and what it means to you, you need to know some basic statistics.

With that in mind, we will develop some of the statistical ideas that are useful for understanding what might happen, then turn back to the long-run historical data on equity returns, and see what we can learn from it.

Using Statistics to Understand Risk

Explanation – Arithmetic and Geometric Means

The chart from DMS in Table 11.1 reports two annual return numbers for each country: a *geometric mean* and an *arithmetic mean*. The arithmetic mean is the more familiar of the two, and is what most people mean when they say *average*. Although we discussed the concept of geometric versus arithmetic means in an earlier chapter, it is pertinent to discuss again here.

Table 11.1   Geometric and Arithmetic Means by Country

Country	Geometric Mean	Arithmetic Mean	Standard Error	Standard Deviation
Australia	6.7%	8.3%	1.6%	17.7%
Austria	0.7%	4.7%	2.8%	30.0%
Belgium	2.8%	5.4%	2.2%	23.7%
Canada	5.6%	7.0%	1.6%	17.0%
Denmark	5.5%	7.4%	1.9%	20.9%
Finland	5.4%	9.3%	2.8%	30.0%
France	3.2%	5.8%	2.1%	23.1%
Germany	3.3%	8.2%	2.9%	31.7%
Ireland	4.4%	7.0%	2.1%	23.0%
Italy	2.0%	6.0%	2.7%	28.5%
Japan	4.2%	8.8%	2.7%	29.6%
Netherlands	5.0%	7.1%	2.0%	21.4%
New Zealand	6.2%	7.9%	1.8%	19.4%
Norway	4.2%	7.1%	2.5%	26.9%
Portugal	3.5%	8.5%	3.2%	34.4%
S. Africa	7.3%	9.4%	2.1%	22.1%
Spain	3.6%	5.8%	2.0%	22.0%
Sweden	5.9%	8.0%	2.0%	21.2%
Switzerland	4.5%	6.3%	1.8%	19.5%
UK	5.4%	7.2%	1.8%	19.7%
US	6.4%	8.3%	1.9%	20.1%
Europe	4.2%	6.1%	1.8%	19.8%
World Ex-US	4.3%	6.0%	1.8%	19.0%
World	5.0%	6.5%	1.6%	17.5%

Source: David Chalmers, Elroy Dimson (eds.), *Financial Market History* (University of Cambridge Press, 2016).

The arithmetic mean is what you get when you add up a bunch of numbers, and divide by the number of numbers. You can skip the mathematical formalism if you want to. We include this for those readers for whom it is easier. Mathematically, it is defined as:

$A = \dfrac{\sum\limits_{i=1}^{n} a_i}{n}$, where A is the arithmetic average, the a is the individual observation(s), and n is the number of observations. For example, if three years have returns of 4%, 11%, and 2%, the arithmetic mean is the sum of those, which is 17%, divided by 3. The arithmetic mean is 5.66%.

The geometric mean is also called the compound annual return. In this example, the geometric mean is 5.60%. The mathematical definition of the geometric mean is:

$$G = \left(\prod_{i=1}^{n}(1 + x_i)\right)^{\frac{1}{n}} - 1 = \left(\sqrt[n]{\prod_{i=1}^{n}(1 + x_i)}\right) - 1.$$

In English, we take each year's return, plus one, and multiply them together, and then take the nth root of the product, where n is the number of time periods, and subtract one. For example, the first year we get 1.04. We then multiply 1.04 by 1.11, the second year's return. That product is 1.1544. We then multiply 1.1544 by 1.02, giving us a product of 1.177488. We take the third root, because $n = 3$ in our three-year sample. The easiest way to take the third root is to use a calculator or computer and raise 1.177488 to the 1/3 power.[3] Doing so gives a result of 1.05597. To get the annual return we want, we subtract off the 1, convert to a percentage, and round, giving us 5.6%.

---

[3] If you forgot, or never learned, why this is true, here's one way to convince yourself that $\sqrt[n]{x} = x^{\frac{1}{n}}$. Suppose we raise a (positive real) number, x, to the power of n. We can write x^n. If we then take the nth root, we should end up with the same number we started with. The number we started with is x^1. To get from x^n to x^1, we merely need to find what number to multiply n by in order to get 1. That number is $\dfrac{1}{n}$ because $n \times \dfrac{1}{n} = 1$.

You may notice that the geometric mean is lower than the arithmetic mean. This will always be the case, unless there is zero variation in annual returns, in which case the two means will be equal.[4]

In the above example, the difference was small. But as the volatility (sometimes cited as the *standard deviation*, or the *variance*), of returns increases, the difference between the two means will also increase. Here is another example: 20%, 17%, –20%. The arithmetic mean is the same as the previous example, 5.66%. But the geometric mean is 3.95%.

$$G = (1.20 \times 1.17 \times 0.8)^{\frac{1}{3}} - 1 = 3.95\%.$$

So What?

This may seem somewhat theoretical. But it is important that you understand, if you are going to invest in stocks or any investment with variable returns, that the return you can expect over the long run is determined by the geometric mean, not the arithmetic mean. A geometric mean return is also called a *compound* return. Sometimes you'll see the term *compound average growth rate*, or CAGR.

That bears repeating. *Over the long run, your expected return is determined by the geometric, not arithmetic, mean.* You may find finance professionals who say the opposite, but in virtually any multiyear investing scenario, the return you care about will be the geometric mean, not the arithmetic mean.

Here's a simple example. Suppose you start with $100. In year one it doubles, so you earn an arithmetic return of 100%. At the end of year one, you have $200. In year two, your arithmetic return is negative 50%. That is, you lose half your money. You end with $100. Your arithmetic average return over the two years has been the sum of plus 100 and minus 50, divided by two, or 25%. But your geometric average return was $100/100 - 1 = 0$. Almost everyone would agree

---

[4] This fact is known as the *Arithmetic Mean—Geometric Mean Inequality* (or AM—GM or AMGM) and is considered an elementary inequality, taught early in inequality courses (of which courses American math education is sadly lacking).

that zero is the "correct" number, even though 25% is mathematically correct too. It is mathematically correct, but it is the wrong math for the situation.

When the return is not the same every year, the arithmetic mean will always be higher than the geometric mean. The difference between the arithmetic mean and the geometric mean depends on how variable the returns are.

Variance

Variance is a statistic that can be used to measure the variability of returns. (The square root of variance is called the standard deviation.) When the variance of returns is not zero, the arithmetic and geometric returns will be different.

For example, assume that you could earn 5% per year arithmetic average return, with zero variance, for 10 years. That is, you earned exactly 5% each year. One dollar invested this way will grow to $(1 + .05)^{10} = 1.629$ dollars. Because there is no variance, the arithmetic mean equals the geometric mean, and both equal the statistical *expected value*.

However, suppose that you earn the same arithmetic average of 5% per year, but this time with standard deviation (square root of the variance) of 10% per year. Now, we must compute the geometric mean. A reasonably good approximation[5] of the geometric mean is given by the formula:

$$g = \mu_a - \frac{\sigma_a^2}{2},$$

where μ_a is the arithmetic mean, and σ_a^2 is the variance (same as the standard deviation squared) of the arithmetic returns.

---

[5] There are a number of known approximations, of which this one is the simplest. It is sometimes criticized for not being accurate. We believe it is good enough, particularly considering that the data we are working with is historical sample data, and no one is justified in believing the data accurate for forward-looking purposes to more than one decimal place, if that. For a more detailed discussion, see William H. Jean and Billy P. Helms, "Geometric Mean Approximations," *Journal of Financial and Quantitative Analysis* 18, no. 3 (Sept. 1983).

Using this formula, we find that the geometric mean is approximately .045, or 4.5%. The median value (i.e. the value at the 50th percentile) is calculated by compounding the geometric mean. There are two ways to compound the return – discretely or continuously. The discrete compounding would use the following formula: $(1.045)^{10} = 1.553$, while the continuous[6] method would use the formula $e^{(.045 \times 10)} = 1.5683$.

Most stock portfolios will have a standard deviation of returns considerably higher than 10%. For example, the DMS world portfolio has historical standard deviation of 17.5%. DMS report an arithmetic mean of 7%. Applying our approximation formula to the DMS arithmetic mean and standard deviation, we calculate a geometric mean of $g = .07 - \dfrac{.175^2}{2} = .0547$, which rounds to the 5.5% reported by DMS.

Now, suppose that we wanted to use DMS's historical return and standard deviation data to project a future value. Let's say we invest $100,000 in the "DMS world" portfolio, with expected arithmetic return of 7% and standard deviation of 17.5%, and we want to calculate the "expected" value after 20 years. If we use the incorrect approach of compounding the arithmetic return, we will calculate $(1+.07)^{20} = 3.87$ times $100,000 for an "expected" value of $387,000.

Contrast this to the correct median value of $(1+.055)^{20} = 2.917$ times $100,000, or $291,700, and we see that the difference, in dollars, is large.

Another Important Implication of Volatility

As we have observed earlier and elsewhere, it is dangerous and incorrect to take any annual return number, whether the geometric mean or the arithmetic mean, and simply compound it forward for a number of years. It is essential to take into account the variability of returns as well. DMS's data provide a reasonable set of mean and standard deviation numbers, provided that we keep in mind the limited and probably biased nature of their sample.

---

[6] We include this continuous method because it appears in some finance textbooks.

The median expected future market value of the portfolio in dollars is important. But most of the time, we will also be concerned about the probable range of future dollar values that can be expected. We can use both a mathematical approach, and a computer-based simulation approach, to understand the range of probable future values implied by a starting value and a given expected return and standard deviation.

Modeling Likely Future Values

In life, and particularly in business and engineering, it is sometimes useful to build a small version of some device or system to study its properties, including whether it will work at all.

But no matter how elaborate, no matter how fancy, no matter how mathematically sophisticated a model, it is not the real world. The fact that it works in the model does not guarantee that it will work in real life. Nevertheless, models can be useful to provide you with an idea of potential range of future wealth.

Modeling Future Wealth

For most purposes, you are interested not in rates of return for their own sake, or volatility for its own sake. You are interested in how much wealth are you likely to accumulate, given certain assumptions.

The common, simple, and potentially misleading way to do this is to assume a fixed rate of return for all periods. (If you do it this way, be sure to use the geometric mean return, not the arithmetic mean.)

A better approach is to model both the expected return each period, and the volatility of those returns. Such an approach is less common and more complicated, but will hopefully be less misleading.

The two common ways to model the future value of an investment are to use a statistical approach, which we explain in the next section, or a Monte Carlo simulation. In order to make a probabilistic prediction of a range of future values, we must make some assumptions about the process that will generate those future values. This is where we make the breathtaking leap from reality to some kind of mathematical model.

The leap is breathtaking, because, as we will see, we generally reduce the full complexity of the world, which depends on the actions and interactions of billions of people, as well as natural events such as weather, earthquakes, and even meteorite strikes, down to a couple of numbers. Nevertheless, we boldly go where many have gone before, and we condense our assumptions of "what can happen in the future" into the form of a statistical distribution, usually the Normal or Gaussian distribution, characterized by a mean and a standard deviation. For our base case, we will assume no additions or withdrawals, and we assume that the annual returns[7] are drawn randomly from some distribution.[8] We will return to modeling in a later chapter.

Mathematical Approach – A Very Short Course in Statistics[9,10]

DMS's return and standard deviation numbers seem to be a reasonable guide to what has happened, although, as we discussed, their historical data must be seen only as a guide, and not a guarantee.

---

[7] More precisely, the periodic returns. In some circumstances it might be preferable to model expected monthly returns. In some specialized circumstances that apply to professional traders, hedge funds, and the like, it may even be desirable to model daily or even more frequent returns.

[8] We start to enter deeper mathematical waters here. If we are looking at the compounded returns, as long as each year's return is independent of the other years, and drawn from the same distribution (this assumption is called *iid*, for "independently and identically distributed"), as the number of observations of the return grows, the distribution of the natural logs of the returns will approach the normal distribution. This result is an instance of the *Central Limit Theorem*.

[9] We hope you are not put off by the amount of mathematical and statistical terminology, but there is no way to dumb down this material without losing important information. If you want to make your own decisions about your investments and your wealth, as opposed to trusting someone who may or may not be trustworthy or knowledgeable, you need to make the investment of time and effort to learn enough math to understand the bets you are making. If you spend 50 hours a year watching movies, TV, or videos, or you spend 50 hours a year playing video games or something similarly optional, then you can probably find the time to invest in your own human capital enough to learn this material sufficiently to follow the discussion. Just as you don't have to know chemistry to cook, as long as you know the basic tools (e.g. mean, standard deviation) and how and when to use them, you don't have to understand the math that lies behind the tools in order to use them to help you make investment decisions.

[10] I (Roger) wish here to thank Professor V "Seenu" Srinivasan, a distinguished professor at Stanford's Graduate School of Business, whose graduate course in econometrics (statistics applied specifically to economic issues) provided a rigorous basis for my understanding of these issues. Any errors are entirely mine.

Sample Mean

The assumption is that the historical returns reported by DMS (or any set of historical returns) can be fairly represented as random draws from an unchanging distribution. Given that, we understand that the mean return found by DMS is what statisticians call the *sample mean*, which is the mean of the sample. Because we are dealing with a sample, the mean we find may not equal the *true mean* or *population mean*.

We illustrate the difference between sample mean and population mean with an example. Suppose that you have a fair, six-sided die. The probability of any side coming up is equal to the probability of any other side coming up. That is, the probability of any side coming up on a single roll is 1/6. We can say that each roll of the die is a random draw from a flat distribution (i.e. each outcome is equally probable). We calculate the true mean of this distribution by summing the numbers 1 through 6 and then dividing by 6. Doing so gives 21/6 or 3½.

If we now take a real die and roll it a number of times, and write down what we get each time, we will generate a sample. For example, we roll the die ten times and get:

5	5	1	6	6	5	4	4	6	2

These rolls sum to 44. If we now divide by the number of rolls, 10, we get the sample mean, 4.4.

We know that the true mean is 3.5. What went wrong? Nothing. We have a small sample size. How unlikely is it we get a sample mean of 4.4, when the true mean is 3.5?

To answer that question, we turn to a second statistic, called the *standard error of the mean*, or just *standard error*. But before we do that, we need to introduce a statistic called the *standard deviation*.

Standard Deviation

Standard deviation is a measure of how far away a group of numbers is from the mean. You will also hear standard deviation described as a measure of how spread out a group of numbers is.

Suppose you want to state how far away each of the integers 1, 2, 3, 4, 5, and 6 is from the mean of all of them. The mean is 3½. So far, so good. But how should we measure distance? If we simply use the difference, and subtract each number from the mean, we will get the following numbers: 2½, 1½, ½, −½, −1½, −2½. If we then take the average difference, we should have what we're looking for, right? Let's try. Oops. The numbers sum to zero. That doesn't help.[11]

Maybe what we want instead is the absolute value of the difference between each number. This time we get 2½, 1½, ½, ½, 1½, 2½, which sum to 9. Dividing by six gives an average of 1½. This number is called the *mean absolute deviation.*

For several reasons, statisticians over the years have generally preferred a similar but different measure called the *standard deviation.*[12] To calculate the standard deviation of a population, we take the difference between each point and the mean, square that difference (thereby getting rid of the negative numbers), add them all together, divide by the number of data points, and then take the square root. Here's how it looks in mathematical notation:

$$\sigma = \sqrt{\frac{1}{n} \sum_{i=1}^{n} (x_i - \mu)^2}$$ where x_i is each value, and μ is the mean of the values.

The standard deviation of the possible die outcomes 1, 2, 3, 4, 5, and 6 is 1.707. This is slightly larger than the mean absolute deviation, because standard deviation weights bigger differences from the mean more heavily (due to the squaring function) than does mean absolute deviation.

---

[11] If we do it this way, the numbers will always sum to zero, because of the definition of the mean.
[12] In our simple example, a good argument can be made for mean absolute deviation. But in slightly more complex situations, such as linear regression, which is one of the mainstay tools of the empirical social sciences, standard deviation has certain mathematical properties that make it preferred. One of these is that any normal distribution can be uniquely identified by its mean and standard deviation, but not by its absolute deviation. There are people who argue that in many applications the mean absolute deviation is preferable. For our purposes, we will stick to standard deviation because it is the standard (e.g. spreadsheets calculate it, sources of investment past results almost always report a standard deviation if they report any measurement of dispersion), and we don't think it makes any practical difference, because there is so much noise in all our data anyway. Some people argue that only downside variance (called *semivariance*) matters, but semivariance is not widely used.

Population Standard Deviation Versus Sample Standard Deviation

If you were to input the numbers 1 through 6 in Excel and use it to calculate the standard deviation, you would not get 1.707. Instead, you would get 1.871. The difference reflects the fact that Excel calculates the *sample* standard deviation instead of the *population* standard deviation. The only difference between the sample standard deviation and the population standard deviation is that instead of dividing by n as you do to calculate the population standard deviation, you divide by $n-1$ to calculate the sample standard deviation.[13] When n is large enough, there is no practical difference between the sample and the population standard deviations. We include this discussion primarily so that if you try calculations in Excel, with just a few numbers, you'll understand what's going on.

Standard Error

We know that when we sample a population and calculate a mean, what we actually get is an estimate of the true mean, subject to some error: we probably don't get the true mean itself. That measurement error is referred to as the *standard error*, and is calculated by dividing the sample standard deviation by the square root of the number of observations in the sample. The standard error can be thought of as the standard deviation of the sample mean.

The Central Limit Theorem (which we do not cover here) proves that we are justified in believing that our population of sample means is distributed normally.[14] If so, the standard error is a standard deviation of the mean, and we can then use the standard normal tables to tell us where, relative to our estimate, the

---

[13] The reason for the difference is that when we calculate a sample standard deviation we actually have $n-1$ pieces of independent information. We use all n data points to calculate the sample mean. Therefore, given the mean and $n-1$ of remaining data points, we can calculate the remaining data point. If you want to see a proof, try doing a web search for "Proof that the Sample Variance is an Unbiased Estimator of the Population Variance." As of this writing, there is a good demonstration of one such proof at the website JBstatistics.com. You could also look up "Bessel's correction."

[14] Or, we hope, close enough to normal. There really is no ultimate way of knowing, since we cannot ever observe the true population.

true mean lies. For example, in a normal distribution, about 68% of the values lie within + or − 1 standard deviation of the mean. Thus, if we estimate a mean of 5%, with a standard error of 4%, we can say that there is about 68% probability that the true, population, mean lies between 1% and 9%.

We return now to our made-up dice example. We got the following rolls:

5	5	1	6	6	5	4	4	6	2

We calculated that the mean of this sample was 4.4, against a known, true mean of 3.5. Should we be surprised that we got a sample mean of 4.4? The standard error of our 4.4 estimate is the standard deviation of the sample, 1.71 (which we note is actually quite close to the theoretical standard deviation that dice should produce) divided by the square root of n. In this case, $n = 10$ so we divide by the square root of 10, which is approximately 3.16, and calculate a standard error of the mean equal to .54. So our estimate of the mean, 4.4, is 1.67 standard deviations away from the true population mean of 3.5. Consulting a table of z-scores, we find that 95% of the time, a randomly selected number will be less than 1.67 standard deviations greater than the mean.[15] That z-score of 1.67 is the same thing as saying that 5% of the time the randomly selected number will be more than 1.67 standard deviations greater than the mean. So our 4.4 sample might be a little surprising, but on average we will get a sample mean at least as great as 4.4 about 1 out of every 20 times.

Standard Error and DMS

We can now return our attention to the DMS table (Table 11.1). We look at the table, and we see that all the markets on which they report show positive estimated mean returns. Looking at the standard errors, we can see that in every case, except Austria, the sample mean return is more than two standard errors greater than zero. So,

---

[15] A z-score, also called a standard score, is a statistic that represents how many standard deviations an observed value is from the mean value of the population.

assuming the data are correct, we can be fairly certain that the true mean in each case, except Austria, was in fact positive.

We should keep in mind the fairly large standard errors when developing our expectations about likely future returns, based on our data about the past. Even if the data are completely representative of future events, they still have a great deal of variability built into them. For example, DMS's data show for the world equity real returns a geometric mean of 5.2% and a standard deviation over those 120 years 17.4%. This means that the standard error is 1.6%. So the "true" mean return could easily be one standard error lower (3.6%) or one standard error higher (6.8%) or even farther from the sampled mean.

Projecting the Likely Range of Future Values

For some purposes, such as planning retirement, it would be useful to have a quantitative understanding of how likely you are to reach your goal, given certain assumptions. To project your retirement savings, we will need to make an assumption about each year's addition to the retirement plan. We'll get to that, but we'll start with a simpler problem.

The problem we'll start with is to determine the probable range of values 40 years from now, assuming that we invest a certain sum, say $10,000, today. We know that if we invested it and earned a certain 7% arithmetic annual return, the future value would be equal to

$$10,000 \times (1.07^{40}) = 149,745.$$

However, as the preceding discussion has shown, this is the wrong question. Almost any real-world investment will have quite a bit of volatility, that is, standard deviation of annual return. Turning to the DMS data, we see that the World Basket had an average annual arithmetic return of 6.6%, and an annual standard deviation of 17.4%.

Skewness

Now we introduce another statistic called skewness. *Skewness* in a statistical distribution refers to the asymmetry of the distribution. Probably the most familiar statistical distribution is the normal, or Gaussian distribution. This distribution, when graphed, has the familiar bell-shaped curve, which has a skewness of zero.

Before we explain skewness, let's review what we mean by a *distribution*. Consider coin flips. Suppose that we flip a coin 100 times, and count the number of heads. For a single set of 100 flips, we'll get a single number. The expected number of heads out of 100 flips is 50. But we know that we won't always get exactly 50. Instead, if we conduct many trials, each trial consisting of 100 flips, we'll get a distribution. Figure 11.1 offers an example of what it may look like.

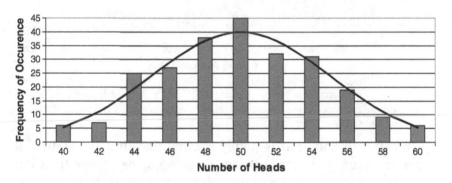

Figure 11.1   Distribution of Heads Out of 100 Flips (250 Trials)

The vertical bars show the results of our trials, while the curve shows the idealized bell-shaped curve.

Our coin flips example results in a normal distribution,[16] which has a skewness of zero. But if we conduct a similar set of trials, this time starting with $100 and compounding returns for 10 years, with each year's return drawn randomly from a distribution with mean of 0.09 and standard deviation of 0.20, and we plot the

---

[16] The binomial distribution converges to the normal distribution as n gets large. With $n = 100$ and $p = .5$, the approximation is very close.

ending value, we find that the resulting distribution is skewed (see Figure 11.2).

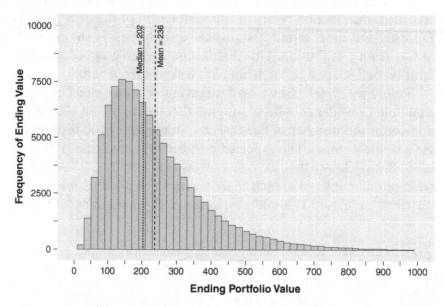

Figure 11.2 Simulated Distribution of Ending Values if $100 Is Invested for 10 Years (Annual returns distributed with Mean 9% and Standard Deviation 20%)

When a distribution is highly skewed like this, the statistical expected value (the mean) is always going to be higher than the median. The median is the value which half the time the outcome is lower than, and half the time higher than. For example, Figure 11.2 shows the result of running the simulated 10-year investment portfolio 100,000 times. Of those simulations, half the time the value ending value was just below 202, and half the time, above. The statistical expected value, however, was 236.

Percentiles

When we compound variable returns for a long time, there is a large spread of possible future values. Rather than looking at just the expected value, or even just the median value, it may be helpful to look at a spread of *percentiles*.

Percentile is a word that is easier to define by example than by a formal definition. "Using the 65th percentile as an example, the 65th percentile can be defined as the lowest score that is greater than 65% of the scores."[17]

We now apply the concept to the possible value in 40 years of $10,000 invested now, assuming that annual returns are distributed normally with a mean of 7% and a standard deviation of 17.7%.

When we perform the proper calculations, we get the following percentiles for the value of our initial $10,000 investment, in year 40.

5th Percentile	10th Percentile	20th Percentile	50th Percentile (Median)	Mean ("Expected Value")
16,208	23,705	37,256	88,321	149,745

The percentiles are interpreted as follows. Five percent of the outcomes, that is, the simulated values after 40 years, were $16,208 or below; 10% were $23,705 or below; 20% were $37,256 or below; 50% were $88,321 or below.

We notice a number of interesting facts. First, there is a significant chance of "lousy" returns even over a very long period. The 5th percentile means that, according to our assumptions, there is a 5% probability that by the end of forty years, our initial $10,000 will have grown to $16,208, or less. Similarly with the 10th and 20th percentiles.

Then we notice that there is a large difference between the median and the mean. Remember that the median is the 50th percentile. There is just as much chance that the $10,000 will grow to less than $88,321 as there is that it will grow to more than that.

The mean in this case (it will vary with the standard deviation of the distribution) is equal to nearly the 70th percentile! There is just a 3 in 10 chance of the value of the $10,000 growing by year 40 to the "expected value" of $149,745.

---

[17] David Lane, Onlinestatsbook.com.

Expected Value Revisited

The *expected value* can be expected only in the statistical sense. It is not the "most likely" value, and in fact, as before, the probability of attaining the expected value is always going to be less than 50%. It is worth belaboring this point, because there are many examples of financial professionals or other authorities who seem to overlook it.

For example, *Personal Finance for Dummies*[18] includes a table on page 155. The table shows the projected value from investing in "stocks and real estate ... . At this rate of return [9%] on $10,000 invested ... you'll have" $86,231 in 25 years, and $314,094 in 40 years. If you get out a calculator, you will see that $1.09^{25} = 8.6231$, and $1.09^{40} = 31.4094$. The author apparently simply multiplied $10,000 by these numbers. He is technically correct that, given his assumption of a 9% annual average return, the statistical expected values[19] are as he says. However, it may be misleading to focus on the expected value because, as we have noted, the expected future dollar value of the portfolio is higher than the *median* future dollar value.

Using the author's assumption of 9% annual return, and assuming that the annual volatility is DMS's number for the US stock market, 20.3%, we find that the median value in 25 years is $56,307, and in 40 years is $158,818. In fact, the "expected value" in the book is above the 70th percentile! After factoring in the effects of volatility, there is less than a 30% probability of reaching that expected value.

The key point here is that most individual investors care about dollars (rather than rates of return), and that the expected value of a skewed distribution (the kind that results when compounding) is always going to be above the median value. That means that there is less than a 50% probability of actually reaching the "expected value."

We will examine the implications of this approach to risk analysis in the coming chapters.

---

[18] Eric Tyson, *Personal Finance for Dummies* (Wiley, 2012): 155

[19] Recall that the expected value is defined as the sum of the product of each possible outcome and its corresponding probability. For example, if there is a bet that has $1/2$ probability of costing you $10 and $1/2$ probability of paying you $50, the expected value is $-\$5 + \$25 = \$20$.

Chapter 12

Assembling a Portfolio

There is no single, provably correct way to assemble a portfolio.

We will outline an approach that is based on the concepts of risk and return that are described in the finance literature and that we have developed in this book.

Some important aspects of investing success are beyond your control. If we define *success* as achieving a goal of accumulating a certain amount of wealth, some of the most important determinants of success are beyond your control.

The main aspects of your investment portfolio that you *can* control are:

1. Additions to the portfolio (savings)
2. Withdrawals from the portfolio (spending and perhaps taxes)
3. The selection of assets in your portfolio

The main aspect that you *cannot* control are the returns produced by the assets you select.[1]

These three controllable factors, together with the actual returns that the markets provide, will determine the future value of your

---

[1] Taxes are another important factor that, for the most part, are not in your control. While taxes are important, they add a very significant analytical complication. To avoid that extra complication here, we do not deal with taxes in this chapter.

portfolio. Your intellectual task as an investor is making informed decisions about the probable outcomes of actions you can control, and then taking appropriate actions. (For most people, the intellectual aspect is easier than the emotional aspect of staying with their plan when markets have fallen, and feel like they will continue to fall).

We will show you how to take the expected return, the expected volatility, and the expected correlations of the returns of several assets and, based on those numbers, calculate an expected return and expected volatility for the whole portfolio.

Forget About "Best" or "Optimal"

We must set aside trying to find the "best" or "optimal" portfolio. The best we can realistically hope for is to find a portfolio that is "good enough."

Modern culture puts a tremendous emphasis on "the best." We are inundated with lists of the *best this*, or the *best that*. When it comes to putting together a portfolio, we cannot hope to find "the best."

Here's why. Even if we could define "best," we would have virtually no chance of finding that best in advance. In theory, your portfolio could consist of just one asset, or ten or twenty, or a thousand, or any combination of the tens of thousands of possible investment assets in the world.

Just for the sake of discussion, let's hugely simplify the pool of potential investments. Let's say that the only investments we're choosing among are the 500 stocks in the S&P 500.[2] We could own any combination of these companies, in any proportions. So let's further simplify and assume that however many stocks we choose, we have to choose an equal weighting. And suppose that we somehow knew that our "optimal" portfolio should contain

---

[2] We will ignore the fact that, as of this writing, there are actually 505 different issues in the S&P 500.

exactly 250 stocks. There are over 10^{149} (a 1 followed by 149 zeroes) different possible portfolios. To find the best, we'd have to examine them all, which is not possible.[3]

So let's forget about "best" or "optimal."

Instead, we suggest making a large number of simplifying assumptions, such as considering only entire stock markets, or sectors, or indexes, until we have a manageable number. Then we suggest also making a number of (hopefully reasonable) assumptions about the expected returns, volatilities, and correlations of these assets.

Reasonable Estimates for Expected Returns – Equities

We have provided an analysis of the major asset classes, and offered our view on how to form reasonable expectations of long-run future returns. What follows is a short recap.

For equities (stocks), over the very long run (say, 50 to 100 years), the returns are driven primarily by earnings. Over shorter, but still long periods, such as 10 to 30 years, the returns are driven primarily by earnings and changes in valuation. Over shorter periods, say, fewer than 10 years, returns are driven primarily by changes in valuation (e.g. changes in the P/E ratio).

It may seem surprising, but even over periods as long as 10 years, there has been only a modest correlation between earnings growth and stock returns. And since it's hard to predict earnings growth anyway,[4] the correlation wouldn't do you much good.

---

[3] There are two main problems. The first, represented by the 10^{149} possible portfolios, is a function of the number of possible assets (assuming fixed weights, because if we allow continuously variable weights, there is literally an infinite number of possible portfolios). In computer science terms, this is the "Big-O Complexity" of the problem. If we require equal weights, the total number of possible portfolios is 2^{500}, because the number of possible portfolios given n assets is the *powerset* of n. This complexity grows extremely rapidly with the number of possible assets. There is an entire branch of engineering/applied math that seeks better ways to search such huge spaces. The second difficulty is the Markowitz optimization itself, which seeks to find the "optimal" assets and their optimal weights. The real-world issue with Markowitz optimization is that it is extremely dependent on forward-looking estimates, and extremely sensitive to errors in those estimates.

[4] Mark Bradshaw et al., "A Re-Examination of Analysts' Superiority over Time-series Forecasts of Annual Earnings," *Review of Accounting Studies* 17, no. 4 (2012).

Two Defensible Ways of Estimating Expected Returns

Over the short run, a few days to a few years, equity returns can be almost anything. That is, they are unpredictable. But over longer terms, they have in the past been more predictable. There seem to be two primary ways of forming what might be considered reasonable expectations of long-run returns. These two ways are to base expected returns on the long-run historical averages, or to also use long-run experience, and factor in the role of valuation.

"Naïve" Long-Run Historical Average

The data compiled by various researchers, such as Dimson, Marsh, and Staunton (DMS), Robert Shiller, and others, enable us to look at the historical returns for a number of national stock markets going back to about 1900.

Dimson, Marsh, and Staunton report the inflation-adjusted (so-called *real*) historical returns and volatilities shown in Table 12.1. These data are derived from the period from 1900 to 2015.

We'd like to call your attention to the range of geometric means. The lowest average return was reported for Austria, at .7%, and the highest for South Africa, at 7.3%. From a statistical point of view, we have to ask how sure are we that the observed returns represent different "true" underlying distributions.

For readers who are not familiar with this kind of statistical question, we'll try to give an intuitive explanation of what we're asking. Suppose we have two people, each of whom has flipped a coin 115 times.[5] If the coins are fair, they will come up heads on average half the time. But let's say we don't know whether the coins are fair. All we know is that person A got heads 65 times, and person B got heads 50 times.

We might suspect that person A's coin was more likely to come up heads than person B's coin. We can use statistics to calculate how likely it is (ignoring all other information, such as that "most" coins are fair) that we would observe such an outcome.

---

[5] There is nothing special about 115 flips. We used it for convenience only.

Table 12.1 Real Historical Returns and Volatilities by Country

Country	Geometric Mean	Arithmetic Mean	Standard Error	Standard Deviation
Australia	6.7%	8.3%	1.6%	17.7%
Austria	0.7%	4.7%	2.8%	30.0%
Belgium	2.8%	5.4%	2.2%	23.7%
Canada	5.6%	7.0%	1.6%	17.0%
Denmark	5.5%	7.4%	1.9%	20.9%
Finland	5.4%	9.3%	2.8%	30.0%
France	3.2%	5.8%	2.1%	23.1%
Germany	3.3%	8.2%	2.9%	31.7%
Ireland	4.4%	7.0%	2.1%	23.0%
Italy	2.0%	6.0%	2.7%	28.5%
Japan	4.2%	8.8%	2.7%	29.6%
Netherlands	5.0%	7.1%	2.0%	21.4%
New Zealand	6.2%	7.9%	1.8%	19.4%
Norway	4.2%	7.1%	2.5%	26.9%
Portugal	3.5%	8.5%	3.2%	34.4%
South Africa	7.3%	9.4%	2.1%	22.1%
Spain	3.6%	5.8%	2.0%	22.0%
Sweden	5.9%	8.0%	2.0%	21.2%
Switzerland	4.5%	6.3%	1.8%	19.5%
UK	5.4%	7.2%	1.8%	19.7%
US	6.4%	8.3%	1.9%	20.1%
Europe	4.2%	6.1%	1.8%	19.8%
World Ex-US	4.3%	6.0%	1.8%	19.0%
World	5.0%	6.5%	1.6%	17.5%

When it comes to the historical stock returns data, we are asking a similar question. We want to know whether South Africa was producing returns from a different underlying distribution than was Austria. (Again, we are ignoring other information,[6] and trying to ask only the statistical question.)

---

[6] We believe that the bias of most people would be to believe that the returns were coming from different distributions, and to explain why. For example, we might observe that Austria was destroyed twice in the period by the World Wars, while South Africa was able to supply the world with gold and other precious metals for most of that period. These and similar explanations might be correct. We are trying to ask a different question, rather than explain why the returns from South African stocks were so much higher than for Austrian stocks.

The chart in Figure 12.1 shows the distributions implied by the data for both countries.

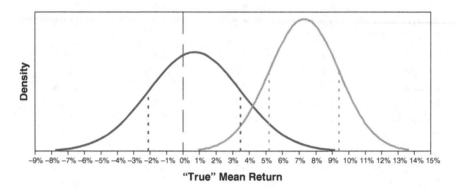

Figure 12.1   Estimated Distribution of "True" Mean Return: Austria (Left) and S. Africa Vertical Lines at Plus and Minus One Standard Deviation for Each

Each bell-shaped curve allows us to read the probability that the "true"[7] mean return for country is any particular number. The curve to the left is for Austria, and the right for South Africa. We can read, for example, that there is almost zero probability[8] that the "true" mean return for Austria was less than about −8%, and almost zero probability that the "true" mean return for Austria was greater than about 9%. Similarly, there is almost zero probability that the "true" mean return for South Africa was less than about 1%, and almost zero probability that the "true" mean return for South Africa was greater than about 13.5%.

One interesting point is where the two curves intersect. They intersect at a return of about 4.34%. According to the statistical inference,[9] there is about an 8% probability that the "true" mean

---

[7] In statistical terms, the *population* mean.

[8] We have modeled the probabilities as normal distributions. One of the properties of the normal distribution is that there is some finite, nonzero probability no matter how far, in either direction, you go from the mean. However, beyond about three standard deviations in either direction, the probabilities are very close to zero.

[9] Essentially, a statistical inference is a disciplined, informed guess about the "true" parameters of a population based on sample data. A return of 4.34% corresponds to a z-score of about 1.3 for Austria and −1.4 for S. Africa.

for South Africa was less than 4.34%, and about a 9.5% probability that the "true" mean for Austria was greater than 4.34%.

Intuitively, most people would look at the two curves and conclude that South Africa's "true" return was higher than Austria's. The statistical inference supports that conclusion. There is a very high probability, over 99%, that the "true" return for South Africa was higher.[10]

Historical

In the preceding section, we chose the two extremes. Statistically, the historical means almost certainly were drawn from different distributions. Let us assume that Dimson, Marsh, and Staunton had good data, and made no important errors in their analysis.[11]

The historical difference between the returns from the South African market and the Austrian market (based on Dimson et al.) is giant. If you could have invested $100 in each in 1900, and earned the mean returns, the Austrian investment would be worth $223 in 2015, while the South African investment would have been worth $330,000!

We dwell on this comparison to emphasize that were we to rely blindly on history, we might conclude that South Africa is almost certain to outperform Austria by a huge extent in the future.

Recent history points in the same direction, though not as strongly. In the most recent 20 years (from the end of 2000 to January 2021), the annual total return (dividends plus price change) from the Austrian[12] market has averaged 4.97% while the same return from the South African[13] market has averaged 9.36%. (Note that both of these returns are reported in nominal US dollar terms. Official US inflation has averaged about 2% over the past 20 years, so the "real" returns would be 2.97% for Austria, and 7.36% for South Africa.)

---

[10] The *t*-statistic is 20.2, with 228 degrees of freedom, and a significance level of $p<.0001$.

[11] As far as we know, there is no reason to doubt these assumptions.

[12] MSCI Austria IMI 25/50 Index, as reported on iShares.com

[13] MSCI South Africa 25/50 Index, as reported on iShares.com

Are we justified in believing that the South African market will significantly outperform the Austrian market over the long-term future because it has in the past?

Argument for Continued Outperformance

One possible justification for believing that the South African stock market will continue to significantly outperform Austria's over the long run would be if we believed that there were some permanent structural difference between the two markets that could explain the differential performance. For example, if we felt justified in believing that South Africa would enjoy a persistently higher level of economic freedom[14] than Austria, such a belief might bolster our confidence in the continued outperformance of the stock markets. Just for the record, as of 2023, Austria's economy was considered "mostly free" and South Africa's "mostly unfree."[15]

A different kind of belief-justification might rest on the concept of "out-of-sample" statistical test. It turns out that for the period 1900–1999, the South African market significantly outperformed the Austrian market. A purely statistical approach would want to "test" this "prediction" by seeing if the relationship held true in "out-of-sample" data.

The argument here might be that if we developed our "South Africa outperforms" hypothesis using the first 100 years of data, we could then test it using the next 20 years. And, as we saw, the South African outperformance does in fact continue in the next 20 years.

Argument Against Continued Outperformance

The main reason to reject the belief that the South African market will continue to outperform the Austrian market over the long run is that we do not believe that there is a compelling reason why

---

[14] See, e.g., K. Smimou and A. Karabegovic, "On the Relationship Between Economic Freedom and Equity Returns in the Emerging Markets," *Emerging Markets Review* 11, no. 2 (2010).

[15] The 2023 Index of Economic Freedom, compiled by the Heritage Institute rates Austria as the 23rd freest economy in the world (Singapore is number 1, and Austria's next-door neighbor Switzerland is 2nd) while South Africa is down at number 116.

it should. In the absence of such compelling reasons, we should believe that competition will push returns toward each other.

We might also believe that the historical data were primarily the result of contingent, chance conditions, such as the World Wars and the Cold War, that hurt Austria much more than South Africa, and local conditions such as South African exchange controls,[16] which are not likely to be repeated in the coming century.

Role of Valuation

There are two theoretical and historical reasons to believe that current valuation is likely to influence future returns. In theory, if we invest in an asset that is producing, say, a 10% annual cash distribution return, and nothing changes, the expected return from that asset will be 10%. Keeping everything else equal except the price, if we purchase the same asset at a price such that the same annual cash distribution represents a 3% return, the expected return will be 3%.

Historically, as we saw in earlier sections, returns from most asset classes, including equities, have tended to be influenced by the valuation at the beginning of the period in question.

Valuation-Based Expected Return for Equities

Over the very long run, the returns to equities are produced mainly by earnings. Over shorter runs, by price changes. In the US, which is the most heavily studied market, there has been a general, though rough, estimate of the future returns to the market, measured by the Cyclically Adjusted Price/Earnings (CAPE) ratio.

---

[16] South African exchange controls prohibit people from taking capital out of the country. This can have the effect of artificially increasing demand for stock ownership, because there are few alternatives. More importantly, for investors who cannot get their capital out of the country, it means that they do not really have the value that would be implied by the reported $US value of their holdings. I (Roger) have been told by various South Africans who left the country that, upon leaving, they lost on the order of 2/3rds and all of their wealth, due largely to the inability to legally take their wealth with them because of exchange controls. Looked at another way, the returns reported by DMS for South Africa might be at least partly illusionary, at least for investors subject to the exchange controls.

The CAPE is essentially an average of relatively recent past earnings. For simplicity, we can think of it as an estimate of the market's ability to produce earnings (i.e. the sum of the earnings of the companies that together comprise the market) at a given moment in time.

If we think of the CAPE as the P/E of the market, the reciprocal of the CAPE is the earnings yield of the market. The graph in Figure 12.2 shows the CAPE earnings yield on the horizontal axis, and the annual real (inflation-adjusted) total return of the market (dividends plus price change) over the next 10 years. The line is the (ordinary least squares) best fit.

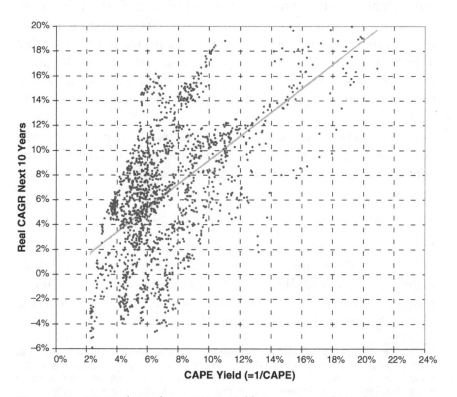

Figure 12.2   US Stock Market – CAPE Yield Versus Annual Total Return Next 10 Years Fitted Line: $y = .005 + .965_{x1}$ $R^2 = .323$
Source: Based on date available online from Robert Shiller.

The line is a poor fit. Over 10-year periods, returns have been influenced by many factors other than starting valuation. But, note that the intercept of the line (−.005) is not statistically significantly different from zero, and that the slope of the line (.965) is not statistically significantly different from one.[17]

These two statistical estimates tell us that, while we have not explained a great deal of the *variation* of returns, the historical data are completely consistent with the theory that over the long run, the returns to the stock market have been generated by earnings.

As of October, 2023, the CAPE of the S&P 500 is about 30.8. The reciprocal of 30.8 is .032, or 3.2%. As a very rough guide to the real expected annual total return on the S&P over the next 10 years, that 3.2% estimate would seem to be at least as defensible as the overall average annual real historical total return, which, in the Shiller data, is 6.9%.

As a rough guide, the earnings yield of 1/CAPE may give a better estimate for the next 10 years in most markets, as compared to the simple long-run average performance.

We have used the above straightforward linear fit of future return to CAPE yield because it is easy to understand, as can be seen in Figure 12.3 below. Arguably, we get a better fit[18] if instead we take the natural log of the CAPE, and use that as the independent variable (i.e. on the x-axis). Here's how that graph looks.

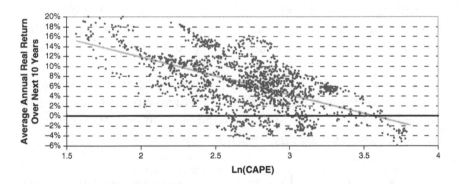

Figure 12.3 LN (CAPE) Versus Average Annual Real Return Next 10 Years (US Stocks) Regression Line: $y = .27 − .07577 \times LN(CAPE)$; $R^2 = .34$

---

[17] The *t*-statistic for the intercept is −1.65, indicating the value is not statistically significantly different from one. The standard error of the estimate of the slope is .0355, which indicates that the slope is not statistically significantly different from one.

[18] The straight linear model seems probably misspecified because the data don't "look" linear.

The fitted equation is:

$ER = .27 - .07577 \times LN(CAPE)$, where ER is the real expected annual return over the next 10 years, and LN is the natural logarithm.

Plugging the October 2023 CAPE of 30.8 into this equation results in a calculated expected return of 1.03%. This number is less than the return estimated from the linear model, probably because there has historically been some mean reversion of CAPE ratios.

Other Valuation Approaches

Determining the "correct" expected return on equities is difficult if not impossible. So it is not surprising that there are a variety of approaches, and they yield a variety of results. For example, in January 2021, Morningstar[19] published its annual "experts forecast stock and bond returns" and reported the expected long-run returns from US stocks published by Blackrock, Fidelity, Grantham Mayer Von Otterloo, JP Morgan, Morningstar, Research Affiliates, Schwab, and Vanguard. The range of expected returns was very large: from 8.8% nominal (i.e. not inflation-adjusted) to *negative* 7% real.

In our view, there are two important limitations relying on such expert views. The first limitation is that the range is so huge. So you'd have to choose one of them (and how to choose seems nonobvious), or take an average, or something. The other limitation is that, without doing a great deal of digging, it's hard to know how each firm arrives at its number.[20]

Perhaps the main takeaway, and it seems like an important one, is that all of these large firms expect returns on US stocks over a 10-year time horizon (from approximately the end of 2022) to be below the long-run average return.

---

[19] https://www.morningstar.com/portfolios/experts-forecast-stock-bond-returns-2023-edition
[20] Blackrock, for example, does disclose that its US stock return expectation is composed of a dividend yield of 1.7%, an expected earnings growth of 8.7% (but where that number comes from is not stated) and a repricing adjustment of −5.8% (and where that comes from is not stated either).

The Price/Book "Formula"

Norbert Kiemling of Star Capital has examined about 40 years of data from a number of European markets. He fitted his Price/Book value data to subsequent 10-year total returns. His fitted equation is:

$$ER = .1219 - .081LN(P/B) \qquad (1)$$

Where *ER* is expected annual return over the next 10 years, *LN* is the natural logarithm, and *P/B* is the market's price to book ratio at the time the estimate is made.

For example, we find that as of 12/31/2020, the Vanguard FTSE All-World Ex-US fund was priced at 1.8 times book. Plugging this into the previous equation, we find:

$$.0742 = .1219 - .081 \times .5878. \qquad (2)$$

So the expected return for the world excluding the US, according to the fitted equation, is 7.42%. In comparison, if we plug the S&P 500s P/B ratio, 3.9, into the equation, we find:

$$.011 = .1219 - .081 \times 1.36 \qquad (3)$$

for an expected return of just 1.1%. Kiemling's Price/Book model suggests that as of this writing, the US is very expensive compared to the rest of the world. The estimate of 1.1% is different from the 3.2% we estimated above for S&P 500 because it is a different model, (Price/Book rather than CAPE), and the model was developed using a different set of data from different markets.

Expected Return

For what it's worth, the average of our three methods for the United States based on valuation 032, .0103, and .011 average to 1.77%. That's significantly lower than the average of the Morningstar[21] "experts," which comes to about 5.2%.

---

[21] https://www.morningstar.com/articles/1018261/experts-forecast-stock-and-bond-returns-2021-edition

Our Preferred Methods

Because of the wide range of uncertainties involved, we prefer a simple method, such as the CAPE yield method illustrated previously. We like it because it is easy to understand, it has theoretical appeal, it fits the historical data, albeit with a lot of statistical noise, and it is easy to use.

Historically, the relationship between the Price/Book–value ratio of a market and future 10-year returns is highly correlated with the CAPE yield method. Low book values have been followed, with lots of statistical noise, by higher average returns.

In some cases, it is easier to observe the Price/Book ratio than the CAPE, particularly in non-US markets, and particularly in the case of many ETFs and mutual funds which report Price/Book[22] but do not report CAPE ratios.

Reasonable Estimates for Expected Volatility

Volatility is the term used to describe the nearly continuous change in traded asset prices, such as stocks and bonds. In most finance literature, volatility is represented by the standard deviation of returns.

Time Frame

Volatility measures change, and so it must be measured over time. As long-term investors, we logically should care most about long-term volatility. Helpfully, Dimson, Marsh, and Staunton have provided us with historical realized volatility for a number of markets. Table 12.2 shows their data.

The annual standard deviation of returns for the countries studied is shown in the right column. The range is from a minimum of 17.7% for Australia, to a maximum of 34.4% for Portugal. Notice that the "World" has almost the lowest volatility of all. This effect is due

---

[22] Book value is a GAAP reported number, whereas CAPE is a number that must be calculated from a series of reported earnings numbers, plus whatever "cyclical adjustments" the analyst decides to make.

Table 12.2   Historical Realized Volatility Worldwide

Country	Geometric Mean	Arithmetic Mean	Standard Error	Standard Deviation
Australia	6.7%	8.3%	1.6%	17.7%
Austria	0.7%	4.7%	2.8%	30.0%
Belgium	2.8%	5.4%	2.2%	23.7%
Canada	5.6%	7.0%	1.6%	17.0%
Denmark	5.5%	7.4%	1.9%	20.9%
Finland	5.4%	9.3%	2.8%	30.0%
France	3.2%	5.8%	2.1%	23.1%
Germany	3.3%	8.2%	2.9%	31.7%
Ireland	4.4%	7.0%	2.1%	23.0%
Italy	2.0%	6.0%	2.7%	28.5%
Japan	4.2%	8.8%	2.7%	29.6%
Netherlands	5.0%	7.1%	2.0%	21.4%
New Zealand	6.2%	7.9%	1.8%	19.4%
Norway	4.2%	7.1%	2.5%	26.9%
Portugal	3.5%	8.5%	3.2%	34.4%
South Africa	7.3%	9.4%	2.1%	22.1%
Spain	3.6%	5.8%	2.0%	22.0%
Sweden	5.9%	8.0%	2.0%	21.2%
Switzerland	4.5%	6.3%	1.8%	19.5%
UK	5.4%	7.2%	1.8%	19.7%
US	6.4%	8.3%	1.9%	20.1%
Europe	4.2%	6.1%	1.8%	19.8%
World Ex-US	4.3%	6.0%	1.8%	19.0%
World	5.0%	6.5%	1.6%	17.5%

to diversification, and it is a strong argument for spreading stock investments across more than one country.

Dimson, Marsh, and Staunton report a long-run annual standard deviation for the US stock market of 20.1%. That is consistent with the VIX measure of the volatility of S&P 500 over the last 35 years.

The VIX

VIX stands for *Volatility Index,* and is the name and ticker symbol of the Chicago Board Options Exchange's calculation of expected 30-day volatility of the S&P 500 index. Expected volatility is one of the key variables in the Black-Scholes option pricing model. At any given instant, the other variables in the Black-Scholes model can be observed directly. This means that if you have the option price, you can solve for the implied volatility. That is what the VIX does.[23]

The following chart Figure 12.4, shows the VIX (and its closely related predecessor) from 1986 until this writing.

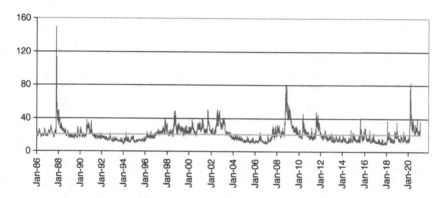

Figure 12.4   VIX Daily Value
Source: Chicago Board Options Exchange

The horizontal line is at the long-term average level, 20.3. (A VIX reading of 20.3 corresponds to an implied annual standard deviation of 20.3%).

Implied Versus Realized

The VIX measures the implied 30-day volatility of the S&P 500. That implied, or expected, volatility may be different from the actual, or realized, volatility. Looking backward, we can calculate the actual, realized volatility.

When we calculate the historical daily volatility of the S&P 500 from 1993 to 2020, and annualize it, we get a realized volatility

---

[23] The CBOE publishes a 20-page white paper describing the VIX and how it is calculated.

of 18.8%. However, when we calculate the volatility differently, using monthly data, we calculate a lower annual realized volatility for the S&P 500. Depending on the data used and the method, some people calculate historical volatility as low as about 14%.[24]

The Case for 20% Long-Run Stock Market Volatility

In the Dimson, Marsh, and Staunton data, the historical experience of most of the countries suggests that the long-run volatility of returns is around 20% per year. Of the countries in their sample that had significantly higher annual volatilities, all except Portugal and Norway were losers in the Second World War. The catastrophic effect that the defeat and destruction had on those markets may explain some of the much higher historical volatility.

We would like to have an unbiased estimate of future long-run volatility. It seems reasonable that the historical observed volatilities, which cluster around 20%, offer a reasonable basis for assuming that equity returns from various developed countries might be expected to have long-run volatilities in the neighborhood of 20%. If we treat each developed country separately, as we will see in the next section, when we combine them into a portfolio, the diversification effects will bring the overall volatility of the portfolio down below 20%.

The experience with emerging markets seems to suggest higher volatilities, and perhaps a decent guess (and that's really all it can be) is 22%, based on historical observations of the MSCI Emerging Markets Index. This assumes we treat "emerging markets" as a single asset class or market. (The volatility of individual emerging markets would be higher.)

---

[24] If returns were truly drawn randomly from an unchanging underlying distribution (*iid* in statistical terms), then the estimates of volatility would all converge to the same number. There is very strong reason to believe that the underlying volatility changes, and that would explain the differences in measured volatilities.

Expected Returns and Volatility – Bonds

The expected return on bonds is much easier to figure out than it is for equities. As we saw in chapter 3 on bonds, the yield-to-maturity of a bond is a good estimate of its future return.

As we write this, in late 2023, yields on bonds are very low. The US Treasury 10-year bond yields about 5%, almost 10 times the low that the yield reached during 2020.

The expected volatility of bonds will be a function of their duration, with longer bonds being more volatile.

The long-run historical annual standard deviation of total return (interest plus price change) on the US Treasury 10-year bond has been 7.6%, and 3% for 3-month T-Bills. Baa Corporate bonds have averaged 7.5%.[25]

When bond yields are near zero, we believe that there is a strong case for using only short-term bonds, say two years or so, because it seems that by historical standards there is no expected reward for longer-term bonds. The volatilities of short-term bonds should be low, because even if interest rates rise rapidly, the downside of short-term bonds is limited.

Expected Returns and Volatility – Cash

The expected long-run real return on cash is probably not different from zero. In the US, the long-run real return (from 1928 to 2020) has averaged .42% (i.e. 42/100ths of 1%). But over the 20 years from the turn of the century to 2020, the real rate has averaged a *negative* .60%

---

[25] Based on data from http://pages.stern.nyu.edu/~adamodar/New_Home_Page/datafile/histret-SP.html. It is a bit surprising that the Baa has marginally less historical volatility, but (a) it is not statistically different from that of the US Treasury, and (b) everything else equal, the duration of corporates would be less than that of Treasuries because the coupons on corporates were higher. It is also possible that in the sample, the average maturity of corporates was less than that of the Treasury bonds.

The distribution of real returns to cash is not quite normal.[26] The graph in Figure 12.5 illustrates.

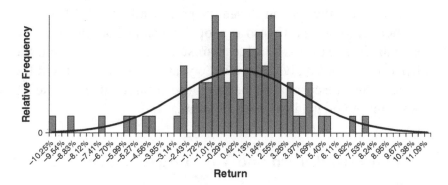

Figure 12.5   Annual Real Returns on 3-Month T-Bills Mean = .42%, SD = 3.5%, Skewness = .019, Excess Kurtosis = .628

Though the graphed bars don't look like they fit a normal distribution very well, the statistics (see footnote 26) do not allow us to reject the hypothesis that the distribution is normal.

We use the return to 3-month T-Bills as a proxy for the return to cash. The main takeaway from this review of historic T-Bill returns is that the expected real long-run return to cash is not different from zero, and it is occasionally subject to big surprises (mostly the result of unanticipated large changes in inflation).

Expected Return and Volatility – Gold

We believe the expected long-run real return to gold is zero. Robert Barro has argued that from 1836 to 2011, the average annual real

---

[26] The data are not significantly skewed. The skewness is .019. The standard error of the skewness is .25, meaning that the skewness is not significantly different from zero. The measured skewness is mostly due to the two extremes at the left side. They represent the years 1942 and 1947, both years of high unexpected inflation. The kurtosis is 3.6, or excess kurtosis of .6. The standard error of the kurtosis is .5. This corresponds to about 1.25 standard errors, meaning we cannot say with much confidence that the distribution is *leptokurtic*, meaning it has fat tails.

return to gold in the US was 1.1%, with a standard deviation of 13.1%.[27]

The volatility of gold in nominal dollars has averaged about 24.5% per year since Nixon closed the gold window in 1971.

There are two main reasons people consider holding gold in a portfolio. One reason is a hedge against currency collapse, and the other is that at least given the last 50 years since Nixon closed the gold window, the correlation between the annual returns of the US stock market and gold has been *negative*.

Expected Return and Volatility – Gold Stocks

As a class, gold stocks have not been a good investment. The historic return on gold stocks has been highly dependent on the period. Since 1983, the return on gold stocks has been limited to the dividend, which in many cases has been small or zero. As of this writing, the largest (by market capitalization) gold companies pay dividends to yield about 1 to 2%.

We believe that the evidence suggests that the long-run expected return from owning gold stocks is roughly equal to the dividend.

The historical volatility of gold stocks has been very high. Since 1983, the annual volatility of the XAU index, which is the Philadelphia Stock Exchange index of gold and silver stocks, has averaged about 38%. Since 1993, the correlation of daily returns between the XAU and S&P 500 has been about 0.2.

Expected Return and Volatility – Managed Futures

When we talk about managed futures as an asset class, we refer to a relative handful of long-established trend-following Commodity Trading Advisors (also called CTAs). While there are hundreds of

---

[27] Robert Barro and Sanjay Misra, "Gold Returns," NBER Working Paper 18759 (2013).

funds that are available to investors, there are probably fewer than 20 that have track records going back to the early 1990s or farther.[28]

When we look at the relatively short list of long-term successful CTAs, there is inevitably a degree of selection bias. Those that failed are, by definition, excluded. Nevertheless, while we don't pretend that this is a scientific sample, we believe that there is enough academic evidence, combined with our personal knowledge (see footnote 28) of two of these firms, to justify the view that rigorous, systematic trend-following in futures can produce significantly positive, long-run positive real returns that, while highly volatile, are essentially uncorrelated with the stock market returns.

Of 22 surviving funds we identified that date back to the 1980s to mid-1990s, the compound annual return has averaged 9.6%, with a range of 4.9% to 16.9%.

However, even if future returns are drawn (in a statistical sense) from the same distribution that produced these historical returns, we would expect future investor returns to be lower because a significant part of the historical return was interest earned on capital held for margin. (See chapter 7 on futures.)

We don't have exact figures on how much of the historical return was produced by interest earned on margin funds, but 3% seems like a reasonable guess, based on historical yields on 3-month Treasury bills from 1990 to 2020.

If we take the average of the historical returns, 9.6%, and subtract 3%, we are left with 6.6% return, which we can attribute to manager skill. Note that these reported returns are net of fees. The gross returns would have been higher. A typical manager may charge a 2% management fee, plus 20% of the profits.

These funds tend to have high to very high volatilities. The average annual standard deviation of the 22 funds in our sample, from their inception to the end of 2020, was almost 24%. The highest in the sample was nearly 44%. Furthermore, two of the funds, though they survived, nearly went extinct in the aftermath of the 2008 financial crisis. It is very likely that there were many

---

[28] Roger's relationship with two of these, Fort LP and Dunn Capital Management, goes back to the 1980s in the case of Fort's principals, and the 1990s in the case of Dunn.

funds that went out of business, having lost all or substantially all of their capital, and therefore disappeared from our sample.

Some of the funds, however, performed spectacularly during the financial crisis. For example, Dunn Capital's D'Best Fund returned 126% (i.e. $100 turned into $226, after fees but before taxes). Other funds cruised along as if the crisis never happened. For example, Fort's Global Diversified Classic fell about 7.5% during the crisis year of 2008, before rising to finish 2008 with a gain of 11.6%. The next year, the fund was just about flat, finishing the entire tumultuous two-year period with a gain of about 11%, and never having dropped more than about 7.5% from the year-end 2007 value. In contrast, the S&P 500 dropped by more than 50% at its worst during this two-year period.

The combination of the promise of attractive long-term returns and zero or negative correlation with the stock market are the main reason that some investors add a component of managed futures to their portfolios.

Cautions

Most of these funds have high minimums, and are not available to the typical individual investor. These funds tend to be "black boxes" in the sense that the details of their trading systems are proprietary.

If a stock portfolio suffers a severe drop, it is possible, at least in principle, for the investor to examine each stock, form an opinion as to the present value of the expected future cash flows, and make a determination as to whether the fall in market value represents a permanent loss, or is more likely a transient undervaluation.

In contrast, with a portfolio of managed futures, which will typically consist of an ever-changing portfolio of long some futures and short other futures, there is no meaningful way for an investor to determine the present value of the expected future cash flows.

Sooner or later an investor in a managed futures fund is likely to face a long, painful period of poor performance. Investors in other asset classes, such as stocks, bonds, or real estate are also likely to face such periods. But the investor in managed futures faces an intellectually (and maybe psychologically) more difficult problem, because the underlying process that produces returns is so much more difficult to comprehend in the case of managed futures.

We discussed that for equities the underlying process that produces long-run returns is earnings. One might doubt, as many investors no doubt did in bad periods such as the 1930s, the 1970s, or the crashing markets of the global financial crisis, whether stocks would ever produce higher earnings. But it is relatively easy to see how they might, and why. As long as people continue to consume goods and services, someone is going to supply those goods and services, generating at least the possibility of earnings.

Or, for bonds, even when bond prices get crushed, as they did during the global financial crisis, an investor can look at a scheduled series of coupon payments, look at the balance sheets and business prospects of the issuer, and see how the issuer might generate the promised payments.

But managed futures is different. In a sense, the managed futures investor[29] is, from an informational point of view, in a position more akin to the manager of a baseball player than to a stock investor. Even if the player has a long record of performance, if (when?) the player enters a long period of underperformance, the manager must ask himself whether the player "still has it."

Suppose a career .300 hitter (a very good hitter) enters a prolonged slump and his batting average is only .200 (very few major league players, except pitchers, have such a low average for long; either their averages increase or they are no longer in the majors). The longer the player's slump lasts, the more urgently the player's manager (or perhaps another executive of the team) faces the

---

[29] And maybe even the manager himself. I (Roger) have known Bill Dunn since the early 1990s. Most managers charge an annual management fee based on assets under management, plus a performance fee. Bill, unlike most managers, did not charge any asset-based fees, preferring instead to charge only performance fees when new highs were reached. During long drawdowns, this could (and did) become extremely painful. Dunn's D'Best Fund (and other of Dunn's funds performed similarly) reached a high in February 2003, and then entered a long drawdown that saw the fund fall, and fall, and fall (though not in a straight line) for over four years. During this period, Dunn Capital earned substantially nothing, yet still had the significant ongoing expenses of running a business. I had many conversations with Bill during those years. Bill never lost faith in his system. But I believe that near the turning point, he may have been close to throwing in the towel. In the end, Bill's patience was rewarded, as the fund came roaring back during 2008.

question of whether something permanent has changed in the player's ability to perform. The most common causes of "something permanent" are injuries, and aging, both of which are generally pretty obvious, even to fans who know only what the media reports and what they see.

But a statistical trading system, that is in most cases proprietary (and in some cases a "black box" even to the investment managers[30]), is not available for inspection by investors. And even if it were, there likely would not be any way for the investor to evaluate it, separate from its performance.

Add to that informational difficulty the fact that we know systems do "break" and funds fail, and it becomes more difficult to get comfortable with managed futures as a part of an investment portfolio.

Expected Returns and Volatility – Real Estate

History suggests that for income-producing real estate, from farmland to office buildings, the best estimate of future returns is given by the net cash-flow yield, plus inflation plus perhaps 1% annually.

The expected volatility of real estate may depend on what is meant by "real estate." The estimated volatility of returns to ownership of entire buildings is usually significantly lower than the volatility estimates for equity REITs. The reasons are probably mostly statistical, and related to the fact that buildings rarely sell, whereas shares of stock can sell every trading day. It may also be that most REITs use a significant amount of leverage, while volatility of buildings directly measured probably ignores leverage. The typical equity REIT uses leverage, and may have somewhere in the neighborhood of 30 to 40% of its capital in the form of debt.

For the individual investor, REIT volatility is probably the more relevant volatility. According to data compiled by the National Association of REITS (NAREIT), the annual volatility of returns on

---

[30] This is not to say that the managers don't know as much as can be known about their system; rather, some (not all) systems are so computationally complex that they cannot be "understood" in the way that the term is used in everyday English. Some machine learning systems are like this.

equity REITS has averaged (since about 1971) somewhere in the neighborhood of 17% to 19%.

Since 1972, based on monthly returns, the correlation between the S&P 500 and the Nareit equity index has been about .50.

Covariance Matrix

Suppose we have two asset classes, such as the S&P 500 and an equity REIT index. Suppose further that we believe the expected returns and volatilities are 5% return and 18% volatility for the S&P and 4% and 19% for the REITs. Suppose we are deciding how to allocate a portfolio between these two asset classes (and no others, and no borrowing or lending). For sake of illustration, we'll begin with a portfolio of 70% S&P and 30% REITs.

The expected return of the portfolio is simply the weighted average of the asset expected returns. In our example, it is $.7 \times .05 + .3 \times .04 = .047 = 4.7\%$.

To calculate the expected volatility (i.e. the standard deviation of returns) of the portfolio, we need to know the covariance of the two returns. This is mathematically equivalent to knowing the correlation between the returns. In the past the correlation has been about .5, so we'll use that. Here's how.

The standard deviation of the portfolio is the square root of the variance. The variance of the combined portfolio is:

$$Var(w_x X + w_y Y) = w_x^2 Var(X) + w_y^2 Var(Y)$$
$$+ 2 w_x w_y Cov(X, Y) \qquad (4)$$

Where w_x is the weight in asset X and w_y is the weight in asset Y. We can use the following equivalence:

$$\rho_{x,y} \sigma_x \sigma_y = Cov(X, Y) \qquad (5)$$

to rewrite the above as:

$$Var(w_xX + w_yY) = w_x^2Var(X) + w_y^2Var(Y)$$
$$+ 2w_xw_y\rho_{x,y}\sigma_x\sigma_y. \qquad (6)$$

$$Var(.7SP + .3RE) = .7^2 \times .18 + .3^2 \times .19 + 2 \times .7 \times .3 \times .5$$
$$\times .18 \times .19 = 2.63\%. \qquad (7)$$

Where *SP* is the S&P 500 and *RE* is the REIT index. From the variance of 2.63%, we take the square root to find the standard deviation, which is 16.2%.

We can generalize the calculation of variance (and therefore standard deviation) of a portfolio to multiple assets. For example, if there are three assets, X, Y, and Z, we get:

$$Var(w_xX + w_yY + w_zZ) = w_x^2Var(X) + w_y^2Var(Y) + w_z^2Var(Z)$$
$$+ 2w_xw_yCov(X, Y) + 2w_xw_zCov(X, Z)$$
$$+ 2w_yw_zCov(Y, Z). \qquad (8)$$

For most people, the concept of correlation is more intuitive than the concept of covariance. So for each covariance, we substitute in the expression given in equation (5) with the appropriate correlation and individual asset standard deviations. Even though we will usually be working in terms of correlations, people tend to speak of "covariance" matrices, because the correlations can be worked out from the variances and covariances.

What Covariances/Correlations to Use

There is no scientifically provable way to determine the future correlations between the returns on different asset classes. However, unlike returns or variances, which in theory can be any value, correlations are mathematically constrained to be between −1 and 1.

As with variances, covariances and correlations[31] change over time. We suggest that for long-term investors, it probably makes sense to take some kind of long-run average of the covariances/correlations, and use them in estimating the long-run volatility of a portfolio.

If we were going to use the covariances to try to find the optimal[32] portfolio, an argument could be made that we should use some kind of moving average. While we appreciate the mathematical argument[33] for the superiority of a moving average as a short-term forecast, we believe that it is neither practical nor useful for a long-term investor.

So we're looking for reasonable estimates of long-run averages.

Covariances and Portfolio Formation

As explained in detail in the Appendix, ("Some Math of Diversifications"), when asset returns are positively correlated (as has historically been the case with most asset classes, particularly including stocks) diversification can reduce risk only up to a point.

In the previous chapter, we offered some ideas regarding how to formulate reasonable expected returns and expected volatilities for certain asset classes. In this chapter, we will address the questions of (a) how to formulate expectations for correlations, and (b) how to combine those expectations regarding correlations into an expectation for overall portfolio volatility.

We are going to make some important simplifying assumptions. Among the most important simplifying assumptions are:

1. Correlation of returns is constant over time.
2. Correlation of returns between different equity asset classes (however defined) are all the same.

---

[31] As previously noted, if we know the variances and the covariances, we can calculate the correlations.

[32] In a Markowitz mean-variance sense.

[33] See, e.g. Valery Zakamulin, "A Test of Covariance-Matrix Forecasting Methods," *Journal of Portfolio Management* (Spring 2015).

3. Equity portfolios are composed of equally weighted allocations among the different equity asset classes (e.g. if we use 10 countries, each forming its own asset class, each country is weighted equally).

Stock Market Return Correlations Over Time

Historical evidence indicates that correlations are not stable over time, and though they may tend toward some average value, can move far away from that average value in a way that is probably unpredictable. For example, the returns to the US and Canadian stock markets are, on average, highly correlated. But that correlation changes over time. Figure 12.6 shows a graph illustrating the relationship from 1985 to 2020.

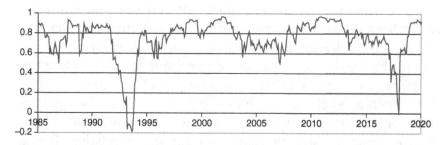

Figure 12.6 Correlation of Returns, US Versus Canada Equities, Rolling 12 Months Based on Monthly Returns

Investors seeking risk reduction (in the sense of a portfolio with lower overall volatility) would like to diversify across markets that have low correlations. Thus, it might be tempting to look at the historical record—as will be illustrated—find the markets with low historical correlation, and then assume that the correlations will continue to be low in the future.

For example, during the decade of the 1990s (from 1990 to 2000), the correlation between the return to German stocks and Swiss stocks (based on monthly returns) was about .6.

But during the next decade it averaged .84. Such fluctuations are the rule, not the exception.

Probably about the best we can practically do is make some assumption about long-run average correlation among a (relatively) large set of markets. Figure 12.7 shows historical correlations between 23 markets.

	Australia	Austria	Belgium	Canada	Switzerland	Germany	Denmark	Spain	Finland	France	United Kingdom	Greece	Hong Kong	Ireland	Israel	Italy	Japan	Netherlands	Norway	New Zealand	Portugal	Singapore	Sweden
Austria	0.6																						
Belgium	0.6	0.7																					
Canada	0.7	0.6	0.6																				
Switzerland	0.6	0.7	0.8	0.6																			
Germany	0.6	0.8	0.8	0.6	0.8																		
Denmark	0.5	0.6	0.7	0.6	0.7	0.7																	
Spain	0.6	0.6	0.7	0.6	0.7	0.7	0.6																
Finland	0.5	0.5	0.5	0.6	0.5	0.6	0.6	0.6															
France	0.6	0.7	0.8	0.7	0.8	0.9	0.7	0.8	0.6														
United Kingdom	0.7	0.7	0.8	0.7	0.7	0.7	0.7	0.7	0.6	0.8													
Greece	0.4	0.6	0.5	0.4	0.5	0.5	0.4	0.6	0.4	0.6	0.5												
Hong Kong	0.6	0.5	0.5	0.6	0.5	0.5	0.4	0.5	0.4	0.5	0.6	0.3											
Ireland	0.5	0.6	0.6	0.6	0.6	0.6	0.6	0.6	0.5	0.6	0.7	0.4	0.5										
Israel	0.4	0.4	0.4	0.5	0.4	0.4	0.4	0.4	0.4	0.4	0.5	0.3	0.3	0.3									
Italy	0.5	0.6	0.7	0.6	0.6	0.7	0.6	0.8	0.6	0.8	0.6	0.5	0.4	0.5	0.5								
Japan	0.4	0.4	0.4	0.4	0.5	0.4	0.5	0.5	0.4	0.5	0.5	0.3	0.3	0.4	0.3	0.4							
Netherlands	0.7	0.7	0.8	0.7	0.8	0.9	0.7	0.8	0.6	0.9	0.8	0.5	0.6	0.7	0.4	0.7	0.5						
Norway	0.6	0.7	0.7	0.7	0.6	0.7	0.7	0.6	0.6	0.7	0.7	0.5	0.5	0.6	0.5	0.6	0.4	0.8					
New Zealand	0.8	0.5	0.5	0.6	0.6	0.5	0.4	0.5	0.5	0.5	0.6	0.4	0.5	0.4	0.3	0.5	0.4	0.6	0.5				
Portugal	0.5	0.6	0.6	0.5	0.6	0.6	0.6	0.7	0.5	0.7	0.6	0.6	0.4	0.5	0.4	0.7	0.4	0.7	0.6	0.5			
Singapore	0.6	0.5	0.6	0.7	0.5	0.6	0.5	0.5	0.4	0.5	0.6	0.4	0.8	0.5	0.4	0.5	0.4	0.6	0.6	0.6	0.4		
Sweden	0.6	0.6	0.7	0.7	0.7	0.8	0.7	0.7	0.7	0.7	0.7	0.5	0.6	0.6	0.5	0.7	0.5	0.8	0.7	0.6	0.6	0.6	
United States	0.7	0.5	0.7	0.8	0.6	0.7	0.6	0.6	0.6	0.7	0.8	0.4	0.6	0.6	0.5	0.6	0.4	0.8	0.7	0.5	0.5	0.7	0.7

Figure 12.7   Correlation of Monthly Returns (1986–2020; some markets for shorter periods)

The unweighted average of these correlations is about 0.6. The average of the correlations between the US market and the other markets is also about 0.6. So, it may be reasonable to use 0.6 as the expected long-run average correlation between markets.

Based on the same monthly returns data from which we calculated the correlations, we calculate an average annual standard deviation of returns (equally weighted) across all the countries at about 22.5%. (The number for the US was 15.7%).

If we assume a single number for the average volatility of each market, and the average correlation between markets, and an equal weighting in a portfolio for each market, we can use the following formula to calculate an expected standard deviation for the portfolio as a whole.

The formula is that the expected standard deviation of returns of the portfolio can be given by the expression:[34]

$$\sqrt{\frac{\sigma^2}{n} + \sigma^2\rho - \frac{\sigma^2\rho}{n}} \qquad (9)$$

Where σ is the average standard deviation of a market (22.5% in this example), ρ is the average correlation (0.6 in this example) and n is the number of markets.

So, if we had a portfolio of 10 evenly weighted markets, each with expected volatility of 22.5%, and each pair of expected correlations equal to 0.6, we would calculate expected portfolio volatility of:

$$\sqrt{\frac{.225^2}{10} + .225^2 \times 0.6 - \frac{.225^2 \times 0.6}{10}} = .18 = 18\%. \qquad (10)$$

This calculated 18% is probably not significantly different from the very long-run calculation by Dimson, Marsh, and Staunton of the volatility of the world portfolio. In fact, if we were to keep all the previous assumptions the same (i.e. average standard deviation of .225 and average correlation of 0.6), and change only the number of markets from 10 to 23, and plug into the formula, we would calculate an expected portfolio volatility of 17.7%. This is within the margin of error of Dimson, Marsh, and Staunton's calculations of the historical actual volatility of the world portfolio.

One possible implication of this logic is that we might not lose much in the way of valuable diversification if, instead of spreading our equity investments across the entire world, we instead spread

---

[34] See the Appendix for a derivation of this simplified expression.

them across a subset of countries. Given our assumptions, even 10 countries would give us almost all the risk reduction potentially available from diversifying equities across countries.

A further implication is that, if valuations in some countries are significantly lower than in others, we probably don't lose much risk reduction (if any) from excluding the highest valuations in favor of the lower ones.

Calculating Expected Returns and Volatilities for a Multi-Asset Portfolio

Let us assume that we have identified a reasonable number of asset classes that we want to include in a portfolio, and we have for each asset class a reasonable expected return and expected volatility (i.e. variance). Also, let us assume that we have a reasonable assumption about the expected correlation for each pair of returns.

Normally, in a standard academic finance presentation, the next step would be to describe the efficient frontier and how to calculate it. This step, for which Harry Markowitz received the Nobel Prize, we skip.

We skip it because in our judgment, the portfolio optimization process is one of those tools that can be dangerous for a nonexpert. Even Markowitz himself is said not to have used it in his portfolio.[35] The problem is not in the math. The problem is a sort of "garbage in, garbage out" problem. The optimization math will tend to overweight assets in which our estimate of the expected future returns is too high. In some sense, we can think of the optimization algorithm as sniffing out precisely those assets whose returns we overestimate, and/or whose volatilities we underestimate.[36]

---

[35] Financial writer Jason Zweig writes about what Markowitz, and several other well-known financial economists, have said about their own personal portfolios at https://jasonzweig.com/what-harry-markowitz-meant/

[36] See, e.g. Victor DeMiguel, Lorenzo Garlappi, and Raman Uppal, "Optimal Versus Naïve Diversification: How Inefficient is the 1/N Portfolio Strategy?" *Review of Financial Studies* 22, no. 5 (2009).

Instead of computing an optimal portfolio, we're going to describe how to compute the expected return and expected variance of a portfolio of several assets.

Calculating the Return and Variance of a Portfolio

The following math may look intimidating. We begin by showing the highly symbolic form, because for those people who know how to read it, it is short, concise, and complete. For those whose math is a bit rusty, we will explain it and show you how to calculate it, for example, using Excel.

Return

If we know the expected return on each asset in a portfolio, the expected return of the entire portfolio is the linear weighted average of the expected return of each asset. In symbols:

$$R(P) = \sum_{i=1}^{N} w_i R_i \tag{11}$$

Where $R(P)$ is the expected return on the portfolio, N is the number of assets, w_i is the weight of the ith asset, and R_i is the expected return on the ith asset.

For example, suppose we have three assets whose expected returns are 2%, 4%, and 7%, and whose weights are 50%, 30%, and 20% respectively. The expected return on the portfolio would be 3.6%, calculated thus:

$$0.036 = (0.5 \times .02) + (0.3 \times .04) + (0.2 \times .07). \tag{12}$$

Variance (Volatility)

To calculate the variance of a portfolio, we need to know the weight of each asset, the variance of each asset, and the full set of correlations between each asset (this latter is usually called the covariance matrix). If we know those, the variance is:

$$Var(P) = \sum_{i=1}^{N} w_i^2 \sigma_i^2 + \sum_{i=1}^{N} \sum_{j=1}^{N} w_i w_j \rho_{ij} \sigma_i \sigma_j. \quad (13)$$

Remember that the covariance matrix (or the correlation matrix) is symmetrical. That is, the correlation between, say, Spain and the UK is always equal to the correlation between the UK and Spain (because they are the same thing). The formulation written in equation (13) will count each of those separately. The answer will come out correctly. But it is often shown in the following simplified form, in which case each pair is only counted once, and then the sum is doubled.

We've already seen examples, one of which we repeat here:

$$Var(w_x X + w_y Y) = w_x^2 Var(X) + w_y^2 Var(Y) + 2w_x w_y \rho_{x,y} \sigma_x \sigma_y. \quad (14)$$

$$Var(.7SP + .3RE) = .7^2 \times .18 + .3^2 \times .19 + 2 \times .7 \times .3 \times .5$$

$$\times .18 \times .19 = 2.63\%. \quad (15)$$

Example with Six Assets

Suppose we have six asset classes, and we have the following expected returns and annual standard deviations of returns:

	Weight	Expected Annual Return	Annual Standard Deviation
World Equities Ex-US	60%	6%	19%
US Equities	10%	3%	20%
Real Estate	10%	4%	20%
Gold	5%	0%	25%
Gold Stocks	5%	2%	38%
Cash	10%	0%	3%

We also need the table of correlations. Suppose it is as follows:

	World Equities Ex-US	US Equities	Real Estate	Gold	Gold Stocks	Cash
World Equities Ex-US	1	0.8	0.5	0	0	0
US Equities	0.8	1	0.5	0	0	0
Real Estate	0.5	0.5	1	0.5	0	0
Gold	0	0	0.5	1	0.8	0
Gold Stocks	0	0	0	0.8	1	0
Cash	0	0	0	0	0	1

When we plug all the data into the formulas, we find that the expected return from this portfolio is 4.4%, and the standard deviation is 14.59%. (These numbers are for illustration purposes only. In the next chapter, partly for simplicity, we use Dimson, Marsh, and Staunton's historical actual numbers for the world portfolio.)

Matrix Algebra[37]

In order to keep this section short, we are going to assume that you know some linear algebra. If you never had the opportunity to learn it, or forgot it, please feel free to skip this section, though you should still be able to apply the technique described.

As we saw previously, for example in equation (6), the formula for variance with just two assets is simple. But as the number of assets grows, the formula quickly gets unwieldy. The number of terms in the variance formula is:

$$T = \frac{n^2 + n}{2} \tag{16}$$

---

[37] This section is a highly condensed version of part of Tom Arnold's "Advanced Portfolio Theory: Why Understanding the Math Matters," Journal of Financial Education (Fall/Winter 2002).

where T is the number of terms, and n is the number of assets. So, for three assets, there would be 6 terms, for four assets 10 terms, for five assets 15 terms, and so on.[38]

Matrix algebra can simplify the problem of calculating the variance as the number of assets grows.

Expected Returns

We know that the expected return from a portfolio is the weighted average of the expected returns of the assets in the portfolio. We will illustrate with three assets. We have a vector of returns, R, and another vector of weights, W. We can consider each of these a 3×1 matrix. For example:

$$R = \begin{bmatrix} r_1 \\ r_2 \\ r_3 \end{bmatrix}, \quad W = \begin{bmatrix} w_1 \\ w_2 \\ w_3 \end{bmatrix}.$$

To use matrix algebra, we transpose R, which becomes R^T and multiply $R^T W$, which gives us a 1×1 matrix, i.e., a scalar, the expected return on the portfolio. So, we'd have:

$$R^T W = [r_1 \ r_2 \ r_3] \begin{bmatrix} w_1 \\ w_2 \\ w_3 \end{bmatrix} = r_1 w_1 + r_2 w_2 + r_3 w_3.$$

To do this in Excel you have to know the trick. (Excel updates frequently, so you may not be able to follow these instructions word-for-word. Nevertheless, we hope they provide you with the framework you need to work with whatever version of Excel you have.) Excel has a function called TRANSPOSE, and a function called MMULT. To implement these functions, instead of hitting the ENTER key after you finish typing the formula, you must hit CTRL+SHIFT+ENTER.

For example, suppose that the weights we used above are in column A, rows 1 through 6, and the individual returns are in column B, rows 1 through 6. Using any empty cell on the sheet, say cell C1,

---

[38] The sequence is the so-called Triangular Numbers.

you'd type "=MMULT(TRANSPOSE(A1:A6),B1:B6)" (without quotation marks) and then hold down CTRL and SHIFT while pressing ENTER.

Variance

For the variance calculation,[39] we do a little prework before multiplying our matrices. We multiply each weight times its corresponding standard deviation. If we use three assets, it would look like:

$$WS = \begin{bmatrix} w_1\sigma_1 \\ w_2\sigma_2 \\ w_3\sigma_3 \end{bmatrix};$$

We will also need the transpose of this, WS^T.

$$WS^T = \begin{bmatrix} w_1\sigma_1 & w_2\sigma_2 & w_3\sigma_3 \end{bmatrix}$$

And we'll need the correlation matrix, C. It will be a symmetric 3×3 matrix, with 1s on the diagonal. For example:

$$C = \begin{bmatrix} 1 & \rho_{1,2,} & \rho_{1,3} \\ \rho_{1,2} & 1 & \rho_{2,3} \\ \rho_{1,3} & \rho_{2,3} & 1 \end{bmatrix}$$

We then multiply them as: $WS^T \cdot C \cdot WS$

$$\begin{bmatrix} w_1\sigma_1 & w_2\sigma_2 & w_3\sigma_3 \end{bmatrix} \begin{bmatrix} 1 & \rho_{1,2,} & \rho_{1,3} \\ \rho_{1,2} & 1 & \rho_{2,3} \\ \rho_{1,3} & \rho_{2,3} & 1 \end{bmatrix} \begin{bmatrix} w_1\sigma_1 \\ w_2\sigma_2 \\ w_3\sigma_3 \end{bmatrix}.$$

---

[39] We show this calculation differently than Tom Arnold. Arnold shows how to do it using the covariance matrix; we show it using the correlation matrix. Recall that $COV_{a,b} = \rho_{a,b}\sigma_a\sigma_b$. The two methods are slightly different routes to the same end.

The result will be a scalar, the variance of the portfolio. To do this in excel, we use MMULT twice. MMULT will multiply two matrices at a time only. So we will use:

"=MMULT(MMULT(Transpose(WS),C),WS)" without the quotation marks.

Remember to use CTRL+SHIFT+ENTER.
Here is an example of how this might look in Excel:

	Weight	Expected Annual Return	Annual Standard Deviation	WS
World Equities Ex-US	60%	6%	19%	0.1140
US Equities	10%	3%	20%	0.0200
Real Estate	10%	4%	20%	0.0200
Gold	5%	0%	25%	0.0125
Gold Stocks	5%	2%	38%	0.0190
Cash	10%	0%	3%	0.0030

Let us assume that the 6×1 matrix (i.e. the column) labeled "WS" is Excel column E, and let us assume that the cells in the column, in Excel language, are E2:E7.

Now we need the correlation matrix, "C." We only care for now about the numbers. That matrix is:

1	0.8	0.5	0	0	0
0.8	1	0.5	0	0	0
0.5	0.5	1	0.5	0	0
0	0	0.5	1	0.8	0
0	0	0	0.8	1	0
0	0	0	0	0	1

Let us assume that it occupies the Excel cells H2:M7.

To calculate the answer, we would select an empty cell, and type into that cell ranges that correspond to WS and C. The formula is:

"=MMULT(MMULT(Transpose(WS),C),WS)"

And with the cell references added, it is

"=MMULT(MMULT(Transpose(E2:E7),H2:M7),E2:E7)".

The result should be a single number, .02128 in this case, which is the variance. Then take the square root to arrive at the standard deviation, .1459, or 14.59%.

Chapter 13
Portfolio Simulations

Simulating a Variety of Portfolios Based on Cash and the World Equity Market

This section demonstrates one way of simulating potential future values of an investment strategy.

In this section, we will simulate several portfolios assuming two assets: the "risk" asset is the world equity market, as estimated by Dimson, Marsh, and Staunton, and the "riskless" asset is short-term US T-Bills. We will use expected real returns based on long-run historical data. The real annual arithmetic[1] return for the world portfolio has been 6.6% from 1900 to 2019, according to DMS, with an annual standard deviation of 17.4%.

The long-run historical returns to US T-Bills have been slightly positive in real terms, but slightly negative in real terms during the twenty-first century. We will use an expected real return of 0% for T-Bills, with an annual standard deviation of returns of 3%. We will assume that the return to T-Bills has a zero correlation with the return from the World Equity portfolio.

---

[1] In a simulation of the long-run returns on a portfolio in which each year's return is drawn randomly, the drawings should be from a distribution whose mean is the *arithmetic* mean of the expected returns. This is because we are drawing one-year returns one at a time. Over a one-year period, the arithmetic annual return and the geometric annual return are the same. For a more detailed discussion (about 2,800 words), see Michael Kitces's 2017 article, at https://www.kitces.com/blog/volatility-drag-variance-drain-mean-arithmetic-vs-geometric-average-investment-returns/.

These assumptions make it easy for us to define a set of portfolios which allocate 100% completely among these two asset classes. We will define, and simulate, 11 such portfolios, running from 100% cash to 100% equities.

In order to keep the analysis from getting grotesquely complicated, we will make some simplifying (though unrealistic) assumptions. We will assume a young adult, age 25, who earns $100,000 per year (in real terms, and it never changes), who works for 40 years, to age 65, then retires for 20 years. (Sixty years is approximately the life expectancy of a 25 year old.)

For simplicity, this entire analysis will ignore taxes. We will assume that the young adult saves 20% of his or her pre-tax income each year, and invests it tax-free each year in the set portfolio, then retires and then continues to spend the same amount that he or she was spending each year before retiring.

We will illustrate the portfolios shown in Table 13.1.

The 11 portfolios progress from 100% in T-Bills to 100% in World Equities. In everyday "risk" language, it is common to speak of Portfolio 1, which is 100% in cash, as "low risk" or even "riskless," while Portfolio 11 would be considered "aggressive."[2]

This language is correct if we view *risk* strictly as expected portfolio volatility. In Table 13.1, the expected annual standard deviation of returns of Portfolio 1 is 3%, while the expected annual standard deviation of returns of Portfolio 11 is 17.4%.

However, if we conceive of *risk* as the probability of not achieving our long-term goals, we might rank the portfolios differently.

In the simulations that follow,[3] we have assumed that starting at age 25, our hypothetical earner/saver/investor begins saving $20,000[4] per year and continues to save the same amount each year

---

[2] Charles Schwab and Co., for example, in *A Guide to Risk Profiles and Potential Portfolio Returns*, refers to a spectrum of risk that runs from *conservative* to *aggressive-growth*.

[3] We ran them in the programming language *R*. We are not programmers. We have done our best, but we do not guarantee any aspect of the simulations, from methodology, to coding, to assumptions.

[4] We ignore inflation to simplify the analysis. Inflation risk is real, and we do not mean to suggest that it should be ignored in the real world.

Table 13.1   Simulated Portfolio Characteristics

			Expected Annual Return	Expected Annual Standard Deviation of Return
		World Equity Portfolio	6.6%	17.4%
		T-Bills	0.0%	3.0%

Portfolio Number	*Percent In World Equities*	*Percent in T-Bills*	*Portfolio Expected Annual Return*	*Portfolio Expected Annual Standard Deviation of Return*
1	0%	100%	0.00%	3.00%
2	10%	90%	0.66%	3.21%
3	20%	80%	1.32%	4.23%
4	30%	70%	1.98%	5.63%
5	40%	60%	2.64%	7.19%
6	50%	50%	3.30%	8.83%
7	60%	40%	3.96%	10.51%
8	70%	30%	4.62%	12.21%
9	80%	20%	5.28%	13.93%
10	90%	10%	5.94%	15.66%
11	100%	0%	6.60%	17.40%

until age 65. Upon retiring at age 65, our hypothetical person continues to spend the same amount, $80,000, that he or she spent every year while working. The only difference between the analyses (other than small random statistical fluctuations) is that we vary the percentage of the portfolio allocated to T-Bills and to World Equities.

Portfolio 0

Portfolio 0 is 0% in Equities and 100% in T-Bills. The graph is read as follows. The horizontal or x-axis shows years. At the end of year 0, the investor has saved $20,000, and invested it. The total value of the investment portfolio is shown on the vertical or y-axis.

The y-axis is scaled to the logarithm, base 10, of the value. For example, notice that the distance between 10,000 and 100,000 is equal to the distance between 100,000 and 1,000,000. Logarithmic scaling is useful when graphing compound growth.

The different shades represent different percentiles of projected future portfolio values. In 10% of the simulations, the value of the portfolio is at or below the 10th percentile line. In 20% of the simulations, the value of the portfolio is at or below the 20th percentile, and so on.

In this graph, because the investment is 100% in T-Bills and the expected volatility is low, the lines are all fairly close together.

The main lesson from the graph in Figure 13.1 is that, even saving 20% of your (constant) income for 40 years, and investing it in T-Bills at an expected zero real return, will not allow you to live for

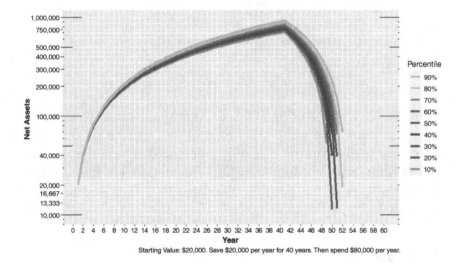

Starting Value: $20,000. Save $20,000 per year for 40 years. Then spend $80,000 per year.

Figure 13.1   Monte Carlo Simulation of Portfolio Values (Portfolio 0)
Annual Returns Drawn *iid* from Normal Distribution, $\mu = 0\%$ and $\sigma = 3\%$ (10,000 Simulation Runs)

more than about 12 years once you stop saving and start spending your investment portfolio, if you keep spending at the same rate as you did before you retired.

Portfolio 1, shown in Figure 13.2, assumes that 10% of your portfolio is invested in the World Equity market, and the remaining 90% in T-Bills. You are still almost guaranteed to run out of money.

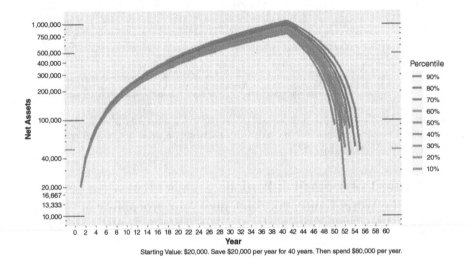

Starting Value: $20,000. Save $20,000 per year for 40 years. Then spend $80,000 per year.

Figure 13.2   Monte Carlo Simulation of Portfolio Values (Portfolio 1) Annual Returns Drawn *iid* from Normal Distribution, $\mu = 0.66\%$ and $\sigma = 3.21\%$ (10,000 Simulation Runs)

As we will see from the following graphs, given our assumptions of constant income and constant real spending (that is, you are assumed to spend the same amount each year while you are working as you do after you retire), 20% in equities, as shown in Portfolio 2 (Figure 13.3 as follows), begins to give you a glimmer of hope of not running out of money. Still, it's barely a glimmer.

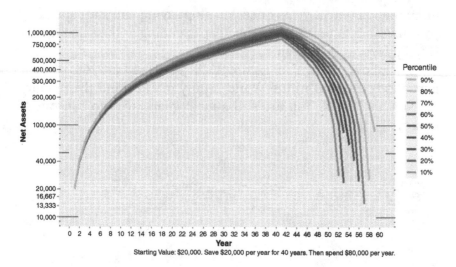

Figure 13.3   Monte Carlo Simulation of Portfolio Values (Portfolio 2)
Annual Returns Drawn *iid* from Normal Distribution, $\mu = 1.32\%$ and $\sigma = 4.23\%$
(10,000 Simulation Runs)

Figure 13.4, a graph of Portfolio 3, shows that when you have 30% in the World Equity portfolio, now your probability of running out of money drops from almost certain down to "only" about 70%.

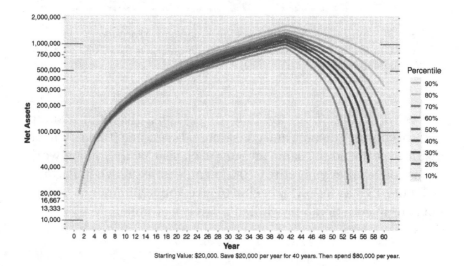

Figure 13.4   Monte Carlo Simulation of Portfolio Values (Portfolio 3)
Annual Returns Drawn *iid* from Normal Distribution, $\mu = 1.98\%$ and $\sigma = 5.63\%$
(10,000 Simulation Runs)

We can read this by observing that the curve representing the 70th percentile, the third curve from the top, still has about $160,000 by year 60. Of course, if you live a couple of years past that, you'll then run out of money.

Portfolio 4 (Figure 13.5) has a 40% allocation to World Equities, and 60% in T-Bills. This portfolio shows about a 60% chance of making it to year 60 without running out of money. But that still means about a 40% probability that you will run out.

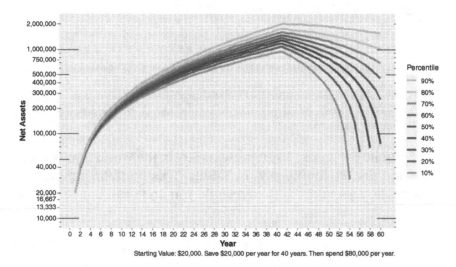

Figure 13.5   Monte Carlo Simulation of Portfolio Values (Portfolio 4) Annual Returns Drawn *iid* from Normal Distribution, $\mu = 2.64\%$ and $\sigma = 7.19\%$ (10,000 Simulation Runs)

Portfolio 5 (Figure 13.6) represents 50% invested in the World Equity portfolio, and 50% in T-Bills. This simulation shows that your results now only have to be at the 30th percentile in order not to run out of money. In other words, there's a 70% or so chance that you'll have enough money through year 60.

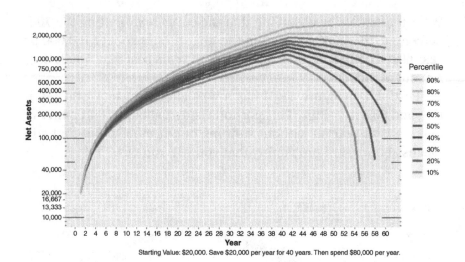

Figure 13.6   Monte Carlo Simulation of Portfolio Values (Portfolio 5)
Annual Returns Drawn *iid* from Normal Distribution, μ = 3.3% and σ = 8.83%
(10,000 Simulation Runs)

Portfolio 6 (Figure 13.7) represents 60% in the World Equity Portfolio and the remaining 40% in T-Bills. This portfolio simulation
shows that even at the 20th percentile you don't run out of money

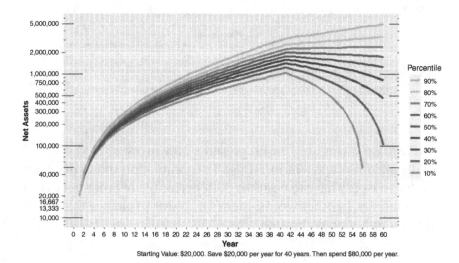

Figure 13.7   Monte Carlo Simulation of Portfolio Values (Portfolio 6)
Annual Returns Drawn *iid* from Normal Distribution, μ = 3.96% and σ = 10.51%
(10,000 Simulation Runs)

by year 60, but that 20th percentile looks poised to run out a year or two later. A 20% probability of running out equates to an 80% probability of not running out.

Portfolio 7 (Figure 13.8) allocates 70% of the portfolio to the World Equity market. A 70% allocation to equities is considered by Morningstar to be "aggressive."[5] And yet even with the 70% allocation to equities there is somewhere between a 10% and 20% probability of running out of money.

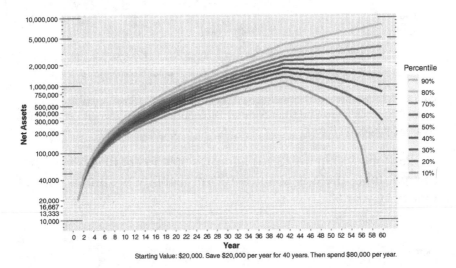

Starting Value: $20,000. Save $20,000 per year for 40 years. Then spend $80,000 per year.

Figure 13.8   Monte Carlo Simulation of Portfolio Values (Portfolio 7) Annual Returns Drawn *iid* from Normal Distribution, $\mu = 4.62\%$ and $\sigma = 12.21\%$ (10,000 Simulation Runs)

Portfolio 8 (Figure 13.9 as follows) allocates 80% to the World Equity portfolio. With this portfolio, there is still roughly a 10% probability of running out of money, but the 20th percentile (i.e. there's an 80% probability you'll do this well or better) ends year 60 with you still having about $500,000.

[5] http://morningstardirect.morningstar.com/clientcomm/Morningstar_Categories_US_April_2016.pdf, p. 9.

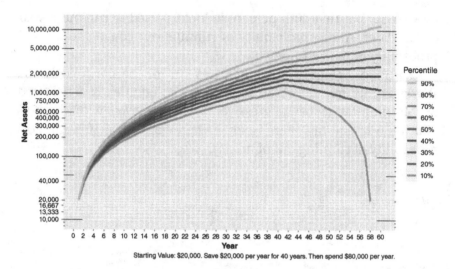

Figure 13.9   Monte Carlo Simulation of Portfolio Values (Portfolio 8)
Annual Returns Drawn *iid* from Normal Distribution, $\mu = 5.28\%$ and $\sigma = 13.93\%$
(10,000 Simulation Runs)

Portfolio 9 (Figure 13.10) allocates 90% to equities. Even with this portfolio, there is about a 10% probability of running out of money by year 60.

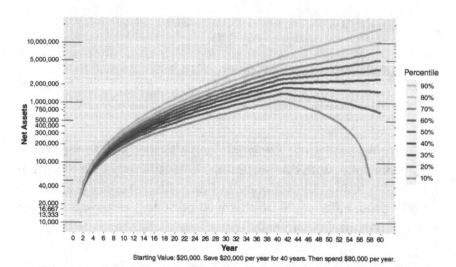

Figure 13.10   Monte Carlo Simulation of Portfolio Values (Portfolio 9)
Annual Returns Drawn *iid* from Normal Distribution, $\mu = 5.94\%$ and $\sigma = 15.66\%$
(10,000 Simulation Runs)

Portfolio 10 (Figure 13.11) allocates 100% to equities. A look at the graph suggests that on the downside, Portfolio 10 doesn't do much better than Portfolio 9, but doesn't do worse either. However, at the top several percentiles graphed, Portfolio 10 does better.

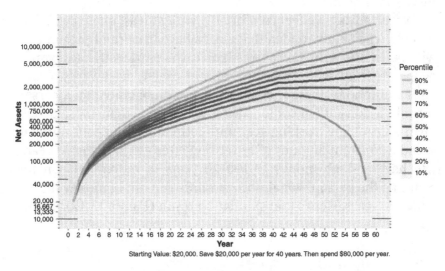

Starting Value: $20,000. Save $20,000 per year for 40 years. Then spend $80,000 per year.

Figure 13.11   Monte Carlo Simulation of Portfolio Values (Portfolio 10) Annual Returns Drawn *iid* from Normal Distribution, $\mu = 6.6\%$ and $\sigma = 17.4\%$ (10,000 Simulation Runs)

Implications

The foregoing simulations are based on a simple set of assumptions. You might argue that they are oversimplified. For example, we have assumed (unrealistically) that the person's income, in real terms, is constant through his or her working life. Most people can expect that their real income, while they are working, will tend to grow, at least for a while, as they gain experience, skill, and perhaps seniority.

We have also assumed that a person elects a single investment allocation and never changes it over 60 years. This is unrealistic.

We have ignored taxes.

We have assumed away inflation.

We have assumed that a person spends the same amount, in real terms, every year.

We have assumed that the volatility and expected return of a given portfolio is constant over 60 years.

And no doubt there are other unrealistic assumptions built into these simulations.

Nevertheless, we feel comfortable with at least one conclusion, namely: The standard idea that stocks have been (and presumably will be in the future) riskier than cash, particularly for young people, is from this perspective almost exactly backwards. Given our assumptions, there is essentially zero probability that a person earning a constant income, saving 20% (more than most people save) every single working year until retirement, and continuing to spend a constant amount after retiring after working for 40 years, will have enough money to last 20 years of retirement. On the contrary, the person will almost certainly run out of money in well under 20 years. Here's that simulation result (Figure 13.12) again:

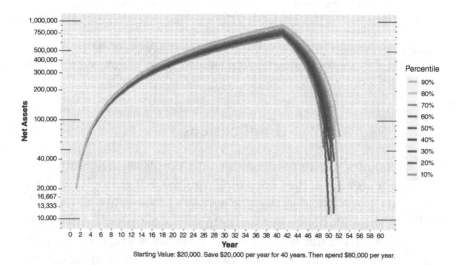

Starting Value: $20,000. Save $20,000 per year for 40 years. Then spend $80,000 per year.

Figure 13.12   Monte Carlo Simulation of Portfolio Values (Portfolio 0) Annual Returns Drawn *iid* from Normal Distribution, $\mu = 0\%$ and $\sigma = 3\%$ (10,000 Simulation Runs)

And in contrast, the same person doing everything the same, except investing much more into equities (90%), has an almost 90% probability of having enough money to last at least 20 years of retirement, and a better than even probability of not only having enough, but continuing to see his net worth grow even after retirement. Here's that simulation result (Figure 13.13) again:

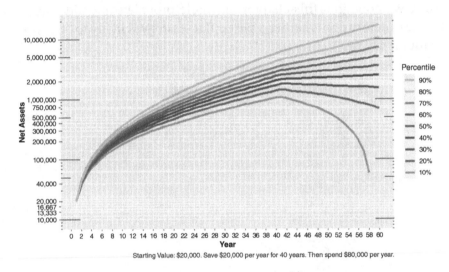

Starting Value: $20,000. Save $20,000 per year for 40 years. Then spend $80,000 per year.

Figure 13.13   Monte Carlo Simulation of Portfolio Values (Portfolio 9) Annual Returns Drawn *iid* from Normal Distribution, $\mu = 5.94\%$ and $\sigma = 15.66\%$ (10,000 Simulation Runs)

For a young person, the strategy seems clear. Allocate most or all of your portfolio (possibly after setting aside an emergency fund, conventionally 3–6 months of living expenses) to equities, and continue to add to it every year (or add to it automatically every time you get paid), and leave this in place year after year.

Later, as you approach retirement age, you might see where you are. If your investments have done well (in simulation terms, if you have ended up in one of the upper percentiles), you might find that you can greatly reduce your risk of running out of money by reducing your allocation to equities.

Conclusion

This chapter (indeed, the entire book) is not intended as investment advice. Rather, it is an attempt to illustrate one way to try to make sense of a set of assumptions about saving, investing, and spending. Many readers may be surprised by the perspective on risk that these simulations suggest. There is no "one size fits all" in investing. We hope that this chapter may help provide some ideas about how to determine whether a particular strategy is likely to "fit" your situation.

Chapter 14
Professional Advice

Our primary goal in this book is to outline a well-informed, logical approach to personal finance. We realize that to actually understand what you're doing (and not simply rely on some rules of thumb that might or might not be appropriate) requires a certain investment of time and energy. Some people might not have the time or energy to devote to learning the material and approach we discuss in this book.

Even if you know and understand such an approach, however, it does not follow that that you cannot, or should not, also seek the advice of professionals. Professional advice can and should play an important role for many people.

There is no one-size-fits-all answer to whether or not you should seek professional advice. It's your decision. As we try to do with personal finance knowledge, we hope to give you important background information to allow you to make informed decisions about whether or not to seek the advice of a personal finance professional.

In some circles, professional financial advisors are seen in a negative light. Warren Buffett, for example, has made comments that may be interpreted as against professional advisors. Buffett has – on more than one occasion – recommended the Vanguard S&P 500 Index Fund, with the implication being that there is no role for a professional advisor.

Interestingly, however, Vanguard (which almost certainly knows a whole lot more about individual investors than does Buffett),

247

believes advisors can add a great deal of value in the real world to actual individual investors. Vanguard even quantifies the value-added. They estimate it can be 3% per year.[1]

Personal Financial Planners

The US Bureau of Labor Statistics reported[2] that as of May 2018, there were 200,260 people employed in the United States as personal financial planners. According to the Bureau, this category includes people who "Advise clients on financial plans using knowledge of tax and investment strategies, securities, insurance, pension plans, and real estate. Duties include assessing clients' assets, liabilities, cash flow, insurance coverage, tax status, and financial objectives."

Of these 200,000 people, the Bureau reports that about a quarter are involved in portfolio investing in assets such as stocks, bonds, mutual funds, and commodities. The others are primarily involved with credit and/or insurance.

The remainder of this chapter provides a high-level overview of the research regarding the benefits and costs of employing personal financial professionals for individual investors.

Who Should Consider Professional Advice

Just as not everyone needs the services of a lawyer or a doctor at all times in their lives, not everyone needs the services of a financial planner. The evidence suggests that the people who benefit the most from the services of a financial planner tend to be more financially literate, wealthier, and older.

---

[1] Vanguard Research, 2019, "Putting a Value on Your Alpha: Quantifying Vanguard Advisor's Alpha," https://advisors.vanguard.com/insights/article/putting-a-value-on-your-value-quantifying-advisors-alpha#:~:text=This%20research%20paper%20delves%20into,trying%20to%20outperform%20the%20market

[2] Bureau of Labor Statistics, "Occupational Employment and Wages," (May 2018), https://www.bls.gov/oes/2018/may/oes132052.htm

Financial Literacy

Financial literacy is a term widely used, but there is no general consensus about a particular definition. Sandra J. Huston, a professor of personal financial planning at Texas Tech, suggests that financial literacy is a function of knowledge about and skill in the following four areas:

1. *Money*, including time value, purchasing power, and basic accounting
2. *Borrowing*, including credit cards, consumer loans and mortgages
3. *Investing*, including savings accounts, stocks, bonds, and mutual funds
4. *Risk management*, including insurance[3]

If you are not sure whether you would be considered financially literate, FINRA provides a short quiz to help you make the assessment.

FINRA's Quiz

FINRA, which stands for Financial Industry Regulatory Authority, offers a six-question financial literacy quiz.[4] Here are the questions (answers at the end of the chapter):

1. Suppose you have $100 in a savings account earning 2 percent interest a year. After five years, how much would you have?
   (a) More than $102
   (b) Exactly $102
   (c) Less than $102
   (d) Don't know
2. Imagine that the interest rate on your savings account is 1 percent a year and inflation is 2 percent a year. After one year, would

---

[3] Sandra J. Huston, "Measuring Financial Literacy," *Journal of Consumer Affairs* 44 (2010).
[4] https://www.usfinancialcapability.org/quiz.php

the money in the account buy more than it does today, exactly the same or less than today?
   (a) More
   (b) Same
   (c) Less
   (d) Don't know
3. If interest rates rise, what will typically happen to bond prices?
   (a) Rise
   (b) Fall
   (c) Stay the same
   (d) No relationship
4. True or false: A 15-year mortgage typically requires higher monthly payments than a 30-year mortgage but the total interest over the life of the loan will be less.
   (a) True
   (b) False
   (c) Don't know
5. True or false: Buying a single company's stock usually provides a safer return than a stock mutual fund.
   (a) True
   (b) False
   (c) Don't know
6. BONUS QUESTION: Suppose you owe $1,000 on a loan and the interest rate you are charged is 20% per year compounded annually. If you didn't pay anything off, at this interest rate, how many years would it take for the amount you owe to double?
   (a) Less than 2
   (b) 2 to 4
   (c) 5 to 9
   (d) 10 or more
   (e) Don't know

As of the beginning of 2021, FINRA reported that the average of the people who took the quiz was 3 correct, 1.3 wrong, and 1.6 don't know. (One hopes that the failure of the responses to add up to six represents merely a programming glitch.)

Interpreting the FINRA Quiz

By the standards of this book, FINRA doesn't seem to demand much knowledge to qualify as "financially literate." However, it appears[5] to us that what these questions are getting at is much deeper than it might seem at first. The first question probes whether the quiz-taker has a conception of compound interest, while the second question touches on a somewhat sophisticated combination of analyses of both the effects of compound growth, and change in the purchasing power of money. The question is simple, but the understanding tested is not.

Consider question two. If you understand the question, you understand how interest allows your assets to grow, and how even though you have more dollars at the end of a year, that greater number of dollars may buy less than the smaller number you started with. If you understand the question (as opposed to get it right by guessing), you do have a certain level of sophisticated understanding.

Question three is a question of fact. Once you know the fact that, everything else equal, bond prices fall when interest rates rise, you know it.

Question four is again a test of knowledge of a certain set of facts pertaining to mortgages. If you've never had a mortgage, you might have no reason to know.

Question five is, somewhat clumsily, getting at the idea of diversification.

In contrast, question six, while considered a "bonus" question, really only tests a specific piece of knowledge regarding how to solve the present value equation,

$$FV = PV \times (1 + r)^t,$$

---

[5] See, e.g. Annamaria Lusardi and Olivia Mitchell, "The Economic Importance of Financial Literacy," *Journal of Economic Literature* (2014).

for t. Unless this is the kind of thing you do on a regular basis, you'd probably have to look it up. The solution is

$$t = \frac{\ln\left(\frac{FV}{PV}\right)}{\ln(1 + r)},$$

where ln is the natural logarithm. In the specific case of doubling at an interest rate, r, of 20%, we plug in as follows:

$$t = \frac{\ln(2)}{\ln(1.2)} = \frac{.693}{.182} \approx 3.8.$$

You could also apply the "rule of 72" which gives an approximate doubling time in years as the quotient when you divide 72 by the interest rate. In this example, $72/20 = 3.6$.

Numeracy

You don't need much mathematical sophistication to apply the rule of 72. All you need is to know the rule, and have access to a calculator. In fact, one reason the "rule of 72" uses 72 as the numerator is that 72 has more integer factors (2, 3, 4, 6, 8, 9, 12, 18, 24, and 36) than any other candidate number, meaning that if you practice a little, you can make a good mental estimate of the doubling time for a wide range of interest rates.

Aside on the Rule of 72

This aside is completely optional. To understand why the Rule of 72 works does require a certain level of mathematical sophistication. If we want to know how long it will take in years, t, for an asset to double in value if the asset grows at r percent per year, we solve the present value equation, as we did previously. When we solve it, we get the result:

$$t = \frac{\ln(2)}{\ln(1 + r)} = \frac{.693}{\ln(1 + r)}.$$

We then observe that, for relatively small values of r, (e.g. common rates of return), $ln(1+r) \approx r$, where the symbol $\approx$ means *approximately equals*. So, for example, if $r = .1$, we find that $ln(1.1) = .095$. This formula for t then simplifies to:

$$t = \frac{.693}{r}.$$

We then multiply the numerator and the denominator by 100, to get rid of the decimals. This gives a numerator of 69.3, and a denominator of $100r$. But since r is usually expressed as a percentage, (which is 100 times the decimal expression of the same number, e.g. 3% is the same as .03), we get an approximation formula for t:

$$t = \frac{69.3}{R}$$

where R is r times 100, or put differently, R is just the number part of the percent return. The rule is expressed as a Rule of 72, not 69.3, because 72 has so many integer factors, and is much easier to divide mentally than is 69.3. We have known people who could use the Rule of 72 to compute a doubling time in less time than it takes to read this sentence, but who couldn't explain a logarithm, and might not even know what one is or why you'd ever want to use one.

Financial Literacy and Professional Advice

There is considerable evidence that people with *greater* financial literacy benefit more from professional advice than those with less. J. Michael Collins, a professor at the University of Wisconsin, studied the issue and says the following.

> Data from the 2009 FINRA Financial Capability Survey indicate that advice more often serves as a complement to, rather than a substitute for, financial capability.[6]

---

[6] J. Michael Collins, "Financial Advice: A Substitute for Financial Literacy?" *Financial Services Review* (Winter 2012).

Consistent with this finding is another finding that investors with a *high* level of financial literacy are *more* willing to pay for professional advice than those with lower levels of financial literacy.[7]

How Professionals Add Value

There are many ways in which financial advisors may add value, and the specifics will probably vary from advisor to advisor and from client to client. But there are some generalizations that can be made, based on studies of large numbers of people.

In the aftermath of the global financial crisis, Mitchell Marsden and colleagues conducted a scientific survey of 2,191 retirement savers. They report,

> The study's major finding is that working with an advisor is related to several important financial planning activities, including goal setting, calculation of retirement needs, retirement account diversification, use of supplemental retirement accounts, accumulation of emergency funds, positive behavioral responses to the recent economic crisis, and retirement confidence.[8]

Vanguard[9] lists seven major areas in which it finds that advisors add value to clients. These are:

1. Suitable asset allocation
2. Cost control
3. Portfolio rebalancing
4. Behavioral coaching
5. Asset location
6. Withdrawal strategy
7. Total return versus income investing

[7] Y. Chauhan and D. K. Dey, "Does Financial Literacy Affect the Value of Financial Advice?" *Journal of Behavioral and Experimental Finance* (March 2020).
[8] Mitchell Marsden, Cathleen Zick, Robert Mayer, "The Value of Seeking Financial Advice," *Journal of Family and Economic Issues*, May, 2011.
[9] Vanguard, "Putting a Value on Your Alpha."

Of these, the most significant in dollar terms is probably *behavioral coaching*. Behavioral coaching is a fancy name for what many of us may call hand-holding. During market downturns, crashes, panics, bear markets, or whatever you want to call it when asset values are falling and people are losing money, history has shown that it can be very helpful for many people to have an advisor to talk to. Many advisors will openly admit that their job is not so much to "beat the market" as it is to keep clients from "beating themselves."

How Much Value Financial Planners Add

Vanguard's findings are consist with those of a number of other researchers who have published studies indicating that financial planners add value, net of the cost of retaining them.

For example, W. V. Harlow and associates surveyed over 4,000 working households. They state, "We find that an advisor adds more than 15 percentage points of income replacement in retirement."[10]

Benjamin Cummings, in his PhD dissertation, found that

> individuals with a financial advisor are more likely to experience greater wealth accumulation (or retention) over time. Using a financial advisor is significant and positively related to subsequent net worth, especially on net worth values more than a decade after using professional financial advice.[11]

Professors Shan Lei and Rui Yao found that "households that reported using financial planners demonstrated better portfolio performance than those that did not."[12] Using a sample of 3,494 responses to the Fed's 2013 Survey of Consumer Finances, they estimated the investors using the services of financial planners earned a higher risk-adjusted returns compared to self-directed investors.

---

[10] W. V. Harlow, Keith Brown, and Stephen Janks, "The Use and Value of Financial Advice for Retirement Planning," *Journal of Retirement* (Winter, 2020).

[11] Benjamin F. Cummings, Three Essays on the Use and Value of Financial Advice, PhD Dissertation, Texas Tech (2013): 142.

[12] Shan Lei and Rui Yao, "Use of Financial Planners and Portfolio Performance," *Journal of Financial Counseling and Planning* (2016): 27. DOI:10.1891/1052-3073.27.1.92

Planner Value Added – "Gamma"

At the beginning of this chapter, we referred to Warren Buffett and his advocacy of index funds. Buffett's main point is that it is hard to consistently select stocks that will beat the market. Beating the market by stock selection is often referred to as "alpha." You may recognize that *alpha* (α) from the discussion of Capital Asset Pricing Model (chapter 9), in which the expected return from a stock was sum of a "risk-free" rate, plus the risk-adjusted market rate of return, in which the risk-adjustment factor is called *beta* (β). Thus, in the simple Capital Asset Pricing Model of the world, there are only two sources of return: the risk-free rate and beta times the market return. Any excess return is alpha.

But in the world of actual individual investors, realized real-world returns are significantly influenced by behavior. The concept of *gamma*[13] attempts to add a factor for behavior, and many other real-world elements, into the discussion of actual, realized returns. The term *gamma*, being the Greek letter immediately following *beta* in the alphabet, is attempting to make clear that financial planners are not primarily intended to add alpha.

Canadian researchers Claude Montemarquette and Nathalie Vienott-Briot have published several studies of the benefits and costs of financial planners. They have used long-term data to estimate the value that financial planning has added, in the real world, to investors in their data set. Some of their key findings are that investors with financial advisors, as compared to those without, have on average significantly greater wealth, the wealth gap grows over time, and the data strongly suggest that the growth in wealth is caused by the presence of a financial advisor.[14]

They report that "for directly comparable individuals, those who had a financial advisor for at least four to six years will have almost

---

[13] In the jargon-filled world of academic finance, the Greek letter gamma (γ) does show up in a number of places, including some more complicated versions of the Capital Asset Pricing Model, and in the world of options pricing, in which γ is often used as shorthand for the second derivative of the option price with respect to change in the price of the underlying asset.

[14] Claude Montemarquette and Nathalie Vienott-Briot, "The Gamma Factor and the Value of Financial Advice," Scientific Series 2016s-35, CIRANO, Montreal, 2016.

58% more financial assets than those who did not."[15] Furthermore, the advantage grows over time. After 15 years, those with an advisor had "2.73 times the asset value of the equivalent non-advised household."

It is possible that what they and others are observing is a selection effect. That is, it is possible that rather than financial advisors actually adding value, the observation that people with advisors have greater assets than similar people without advisors is simply a reflection of wealthier people being more likely to hire advisors.

But Montemarquette and Vienott-Briot believe that they have controlled for this selection effect, and that they are measuring real value-added from financial advisors. One approach they took was to look at what happened to comparable investors who all started with an advisor, but some dropped their advisors. They found that subsequent to dropping an advisor, those investors on average fared worse than those who kept an advisor.

Their conclusion is clear: "Financial advice matters, and the results are robust."[16]

Factors to Consider When Selecting an Advisor

If you are selecting a financial advisor, perhaps your first consideration should be to make sure you are clear on what you expect your advisor to do for you. There are probably infinite ways of framing this question, but we're going to suggest one way, based on what we call the Extended Real-World Capital Asset Pricing Model.

As you recall, in the original Capital Asset Pricing Model, there are two sources of return: risk-free return, α (alpha), and the amount of non-diversifiable risk you take, β (beta). In the extended real-world model, we add a third term: γ (gamma), the success you have in doing what you should do, such as saving and investing

---

[15] Montemarquette and Vienott-Briot, "The Gamma Factor": 23.
[16] Montemarquette and Vienott-Briot, "The Gamma Factor": 41.

appropriate amounts, being tax-efficient, and avoiding behavioral errors. Confusingly, what we call gamma is sometimes called "advisor's alpha." But whatever you call it, it is the value that an advisor can add *without* "beating the market" and *without* loading you up with extra risk.

Alpha

While there are advisors who have long, successful track records of adding *alpha* (people like Buffett), identifying them is outside the scope of this book.

Beta

Based on our reading of the literature, and discussions with dozens or hundreds of advisors, we believe that an important way that advisors add value is in helping clients take risk, *beta*, efficiently. As we discussed in chapter 9, there is plenty of risk that investors can take on that they cannot expect to be paid for. That risk is called *diversifiable* risk. A good advisor will not eliminate risk; however, a good advisor should help you take the least amount of risk compatible with a good chance of achieving your goals.

Gamma

As discussed earlier, gamma covers a diffuse set of behaviors, from selecting and maintaining appropriate asset allocation, to tax planning, estate planning, insurance, and hand-holding during bad market times. A good advisor should be able to help you capture gamma.

In terms of the Extended Real-World Capital Asset Pricing Model, we believe it is a reasonable goal to forget about alpha. Instead, you may want to seek an advisor who will help you achieve an appropriate beta, and capture a significant amount of gamma.

Advisor Characteristics

We believe that the most important factors to consider in selecting a professional advisor are:

1. Integrity
2. Incentives
3. Skill
4. Personality

Integrity

A professional advisor should be someone you trust, and someone who deserves that trust. An advisor's integrity cannot usually be observed directly in a short time, so you will need to rely on additional indicators. Among the most valuable of these may be referrals from people you trust who know the advisor well.

You may also want to do a background check, which can run the gamut from an internet search all the way up to retaining a professional background checker. There are several official sites that are easy to check.

FINRA maintains a website called Brokercheck, at brokercheck .finra.org. If a broker is registered, a record, even if the record is blank, should be available here.

The US Securities and Exchange Commission maintains a database of individuals who have been named as defendants or respondents in SEC actions. As of this writing, you can find a search bar at https://www.sec.gov/litigations/sec-action-look-up.

The SEC also maintains an investment adviser disclosure website. As of this writing, the URL is https://adviserinfo.sec.gov.

Some commentators stress that your advisor should be a fiduciary. We would merely note that being a fiduciary does not equate to integrity.

Incentives

Most people understand that, all other things held constant, at the margin[17] people respond to incentives. For example, everything else equal, you are more likely to work at a job if you get paid than if you don't.

Financial advisors are people, and therefore they respond to incentives. In our experience dealing professionally with hundreds of advisors, most care a lot about their clients, and really want to do the right thing for them. Most advisors also care about their reputations. Most also care about getting paid, and how they get paid is one of the incentives to which they respond.

For several decades, there has been a general trend away from commission-based stock brokerage toward *fee-only* financial planning. According to some in the financial planning world, fee-only is better for clients because it involves fewer conflicts of interest than commissions. One difficulty is that there is no universally recognized definition of fee-only.

We believe that rather than focusing on a name, such as fee-only, it may be more informative to understand exactly how an advisor is compensated. That compensation may be straightforward, such as a quarterly fee based on the market value of assets under management.

The key is not necessarily how the advisor gets paid. The key is understanding how closely, or not, the advisor's incentives are aligned with your goals. The alignment can rarely or never be perfect. That's one reason that integrity is important.

Skill

In reading the literature in preparation for writing this section, we were surprised how few mentions there are about advisor skill. There are many commentators who stress the importance of a variety of credentials. However, we were not able to find

---

[17] "At the margin" is economist-speak that means, in general terms, there's some effect but it's not the only effect.

any published research supporting the claim that any particular credential was associated with advisor skill. Nevertheless, it seems reasonable that, everything else equal, people with credentials may have at least as much knowledge and skill, as compared to those without.

There is a virtual alphabet soup of credentials, almost too many to count. But there are probably three that are widely considered most valuable. These three are the Certified Financial Planner (CFP), Chartered Financial Analyst (CFA), and Certified Public Accountant (CPA).

Each of these takes years to acquire, and include a great deal of knowledge. Everything else equal, it is a positive sign if an advisor has one of these credentials.

In addition to the knowledge and skills of planning and investing, a good advisor is able to communicate with clients. While it may be hard for you to evaluate an advisor's skill in technical areas, you should be able to evaluate how well a prospective advisor can explain to you what they think you need to know.

Personality

The evidence suggests that the benefits of having a professional financial advisor are greatest when a client stays with an advisor over long periods of time. That is more likely to happen if there is a good fit between the client and advisor, which will depend on many factors. Some of these factors are philosophy, communication style, preferences along the analytical-intuitive spectrum, and interpersonal chemistry.

By *philosophy*, we mean an approach to the process of financial planning and investment. Each advisor will have an approach. If you believe that the alpha, beta, and gamma ways of thinking make sense, find out how a prospective advisor thinks about each of these three elements of value added, and whether that fits with your thinking.

Communication styles can be highly personal. Everything else equal, you'll probably have a better experience with someone with whom you feel comfortable communicating. For most people, an advisor who is a good listener will be a big plus, as will an advisor who is able to communicate the right information at the right level of abstraction for you.

Some people are more intuitive, others more analytical. Financial planners tend to be more analytical on average.[18] People who tend toward an analytical style might want an advisor who revels in technical detail, while others might prefer that the advisor deal with the technical stuff and not burden the client with it.

Finally, everything else equal, it may make sense to choose an advisor you like, because the evidence shows that advisors add the most value when the relationship is long term.

---

[18] John Nofsinger and Abhishek Varma, "How Analytical is Your Financial Advisor?" *Financial Services Review* 16 (2007).

Checklist

A professional relationship is complicated, and cannot be reduced to a set of boxes to check. Nevertheless, some readers may find it helpful to have a checklist to remind them of areas to investigate and/or discuss with potential financial advisors.

Integrity
- ☐ Do you have a referral from a person you trust?
- ☐ Does the advisor have any violations?
- ☐ Is there anything that makes you nervous about the advisor?
- ☐ Can the advisor put you in touch with long-time clients and/or professional associates?
- ☐ Do you know the advisor's reputation in the professional and/or client community?
- ☐ If the advisor is affiliated with a firm, what is that firm's reputation?

Incentives
- ☐ How closely are the advisor's incentives aligned with your goals?
- ☐ How does the advisor get paid?
- ☐ Does the advisor have a policy of fully disclosing compensation?

Skills
- ☐ How long has the advisor been in business?
- ☐ If the advisor is willing to share his/her own results with you, how have they been?
- ☐ How long does the typical client stay with the advisor?
- ☐ Are there any special skills the advisor wants you to know about?

Personal
- ☐ Can the advisor articulate a philosophy that you are comfortable with?
- ☐ Do you feel the advisor does a good job communicating with you?
- ☐ Can the advisor communicate with you at the level of technical detail you desire?
- ☐ What is your overall feeling about the advisor?

Chapter 15

From Theory to Practice

T his book does not constitute professional advice. In this chapter, we seek to help you think about the practical side of investing using the concepts we have discussed.

In our simplified example of a young investor, we discussed how investing in 100% equities could give the investor the least risk of running out of money. We believe the conclusion generalizes to many situations, but all investors should consider the specifics of their own situations.

So, what next steps might you take from here?

When investing, at a minimum you probably want to include an allocation to equities. Whether you include other asset classes (other than cash) is up to you. Within equities, you probably want to ensure that your portfolio is diversified both within a country and among countries. Although the expected returns used in our simulations did not include consideration of valuations of equities (expected returns were based on the extremely long-run average, by which we mean the average for about 100 years, for the entire world market), you may want to tilt your portfolio to better value (lower P/B and lower P/E ratios). One way to do that, would be to weight cheaper markets more heavily than expensive ones.

Investing through mutual funds or exchange-traded funds (ETFs) allows you to diversify more than you might be able to on your own, and if you use them, low-cost funds may be more cost-effective than feasible alternatives. Both types of funds allow you to invest in a variety of sectors and geographies, though you might be disappointed in the relative lack of low-cost, value-oriented funds outside the United States.

A great deal of evidence shows that the vast majority of mutual funds and ETFs have not been able to consistently deliver returns (net of expenses) greater than the market by selecting stocks. For example, in the United States, the S&P 500 index, and funds that track it, have delivered higher returns over long periods of time than the great majority of actively managed "stock selecting" funds.

Nevertheless, some people are tempted to look at a fund's returns for the past few years, and invest in the fund with the highest past returns. It's tempting, but it doesn't work.

The phenomenon of buying funds that have generated high returns recently is called "chasing returns," and although it's a tempting strategy, it is not advisable. Evaluating a fund based solely on its short-term returns ignores the huge weight of evidence that such a strategy does not usually produce above-market returns. As we discussed in chapter 9, in the short term, prices tend to follow a random walk with drift. So in the short term, prices are essentially unpredictable.

Instead of trying to choose particular funds that have recently outperformed the market, the weight of historical evidence suggests that you might outperform "the market" by investing in portfolios that have low (by historical standards and/or relative to the market) price-to-book and price-to-earnings ratios.

To identify ETFs that might be a good investment, we think it makes sense to select funds that are relatively cheap in terms of P/B and P/E ratios, as well as ETFs that are diversified in terms of sector and geography. For example, as of August 2023, such a fund is Vanguard's VEU Fund, which has a price-to-book ratio of 1.6 and a price-to-earnings ratio of 11.7. Given that at the same time the S&P 500 had a P/E ratio of around 25, the fund's P/E ratio is relatively low.

A simple way to get equity exposure and diversification is to invest in an ETF such as the Vanguard Total World Fund (VTWAX). This fund is a market cap-weighted fund which invests in the entire world (emerging markets, Europe, America, Asia, and the Middle East), as the name implies. But compare this fund, which as of this writing, a P/E ratio of 16.6 and a P/B of 2.4, to the Vanguard Total World Fund Ex-US (VFWAX). The ex-US fund is invested in the entire world except for the United States. As measured by P/E ratio and P/B ratio, it's cheaper, with respective ratios of 16.6 and 2.4. The primary difference among the funds is their asset allocation: the Total World Fund has 60.7% invested in the United States.

As of August 2023, the P/E ratio of the S&P 500 is around 25, while its P/B ratio is about 4.29. Because the US markets are more expensive relative to the rest of the world, the fund that excludes the United States offers better value – but that does not mean such a fund will necessarily deliver better returns over the long run. Based on historical patterns, however, the odds are good that the Ex-US returns will be higher than the US returns over a medium to long run.

In addition to considering the P/B and P/E ratios of funds, you may want to consider the fees that they charge. As of May 2021, the Vanguard Total World Fund charged fees of .10%, or 10 basis points, whereas the Vanguard Total World Fund Ex-US charged fees of .11%, or 11 basis points.

Once you've identified one or more diversified funds that you are comfortable with, a simple way (we're not saying it's the best way) to invest in a portfolio that is 90% equities and 10% cash would be to allocate 90% of your investable funds to a world index fund, and 10% to a short-term money market fund. That's about the simplest way to do it. There's no limit to the amount of complexity if you decide you want more.

Appendix
Some Math of Diversification

I n the case of betting on the outcome of a coin flip, we saw that by breaking the total amount bet into smaller and smaller amounts, and betting the smaller amount on an increasingly larger number of bets, we could reduce the spread of outcomes around the expected value. For example, when we made a single bet of $1,000, with a payoff of $2,100 for heads and $0 for tails, we calculated an expected value of $50, with a large variance, or standard deviation. Standard deviation is the square root of variance. For most actual uses, standard deviation is more useful, but some of the math is easier to follow if we look at the variance also.

Variance

Variance is a measure of the "spread" of outcomes of random events or sets of random events. In the language of statistics, *variance* is defined as $\sigma^2 = \frac{\sum_i^n (x_i - \mu)^2}{n}$ where μ is the mean or *expected* value, x_i's are the individual outcomes, and n is the number of trials. The symbol σ^2 (pronounced "sigma squared") is the common mathematical/statistical way to denote variance.

In the case of a coin flip, if we assign, say, 1 to the outcome "heads" and 0 to the outcome "tails," we can calculate that the variance is .25. Here's how: When the coin comes up heads, the quantity inside the parentheses in the formula is $(1 - .5)$, which equals 0.5, and when the coin comes up tails, it is $(0 - .5)$ which is -0.5. Either way, when squared, the number is 0.25, which is the variance. The standard deviation is the square root of the variance. In this case the standard deviation is 0.5. Notice that the mean or expected outcome is $0.5 \times 1 + 0.5 \times 0 = 0.5$. It is *not* generally the case that the mean and standard deviation are the same.

Standard Deviation

The *standard deviation* is defined as the square root of the variance, so in this case the standard deviation is the square root of 0.25, which is 0.5.

A coin flip is a special case of a *binomial random variable*. Two outcomes are possible: heads (which we say is valued at 1) and tails, valued at zero. Because only two outcomes are possible, if the probability of heads is p, the probability of tails (i.e. not heads) is $1 - p$.[1] In the case of a fair coin, we define the probability of heads, and tails, as both equal to 0.5.[2]

---

[1] This assumes that the coin must come up either heads or tails, with no other possibility. Because the coin is assumed to be either heads or tails, and nothing else, this *outcome space* is said to be *mutually exclusive and collectively exhaustive*. In the real world, coins may, rarely, land and remain on edge.

[2] Without going too deeply into the philosophy of probability, we can say that the coin is fair if as the number of flips approaches infinity, the probability of heads (or tails) approaches .5. In real life, using standard modern US quarters, Stanford's Persi Diaconis has argued on theoretical and limited empirical grounds that coins tossed by hand and caught come up the same way they started about 51% of the time. There is intuition to explain this. Suppose a coin starts off with heads facing up. If we assume that at all times it will be either heads or tails up while in flight, it will alternate as follows: H T H T H T. . . . The number of heads will always be either one greater than, or equal to, the number of tails. Similarly, if it starts off tails up, tails will enjoy this slight edge. Modern computer languages (e.g. C, R, Python) implement psuedorandom number generators that are "good enough" for the kind of simulations we show in this chapter. There are warnings about using standard pseudorandom number generators for cryptography and security measures.

The standard deviation of a binomial random variable is equal to $\sqrt{np(1-p)}$. And in the special case of a coin flip (or simulated coin flip in which p is 0.5), the formula simplifies to $\sqrt{.25n} = .5\sqrt{n} = \frac{\sqrt{n}}{2}$.

We can check how this formula compares to the calculation we made above for the standard deviation of a coin flip. In our case, $n = 1$, so the calculated standard deviation is, as expected, 0.5.

The standard deviation we have calculated is for a "unit," because the payoff was 1 or 0. If instead we said the payoff for heads was 10, the standard deviation would be 5, if the payoff were 100, the standard deviation would be 50, and so on.

If we just make a single bet, and make it bigger, the "risk" as measured by the standard deviation of outcome scales up linearly. That is, a 10 times bigger bet has a 10 times bigger standard deviation.

But what if instead of a single $100 bet, we made 100 bets of $1 each?

The standard deviation of a single $100 bet (by which we mean it pays $100 for heads and 0 for tails) is $50. To calculate the standard deviation of 100 bets, however, we use the formula $\sqrt{np(1-p)}$ which in this case works out to $\sqrt{100 \times .5 \times .5}$ or the square root of 25, which is 5.

Examples Using Bet of Coin Flip with Positive Expected Value

Suppose we have $1,000 available to bet on the outcome of a coin flip, with a payoff of $2,100 for heads and 0 for tails. The expected value of this bet is $0.5 \times \$2,100 + 0.5 \times 0$, minus the $1,000 we bet. That works out to $\$1,050 - \$1,000 = \$50$. Suppose we also have the ability to split the bet into a bunch of smaller bets that are identical in every way. For example, some of the possible ways we could bet the $1,000 are illustrated in Table A.1.

Table A.1   Expected Values of Bets

Number of Bets	Cost per Bet	Payoff per Bet for Heads	Total Expected Value for the Bets
1	$1,000	$1050 − $1000 = $50	$50
10	$100	$105 − $100 = $5	$50
00	$10	$10.50 − $10 = $.50	$50
1,000	$1	$1.05 − $1 = $.05	$50

The expected value of the total payoff doesn't change; however, the distribution of probable payouts does change. That is, what we commonly talk about as the riskiness of the bet does change. In each case we are betting a total of $1,000. We can use our formula to calculate the standard deviation, in dollars, of the outcomes as shown in Table A.2.

Table A.2   Standard Deviation of Bet Outcomes

Number of Bets	Cost per Bet	Standard Deviation Calculation	Standard Deviation of Outcomes
1	$1,000	$1000 × .5 × $\sqrt{1}$	$500
10	$100	$100 × .5 × $\sqrt{10}$	$158.11
100	$10	$10 × .5 × $\sqrt{100}$	$50
10,00	$1	$1 × .5 × $\sqrt{1000}$	$15.81

In all cases, the expected value of the bet or group of bets is $50. But as we divide the total amount we bet into a larger number of smaller bets, the less variation there is around the expected value of $50.

In theory, we can make the standard deviation as small as desired by breaking the total $1,000 into progressively more identical smaller bets. Here is how it looks mathematically:

$$\sigma = \frac{\$1000}{n} \times .5 \times \sqrt{n},$$

where σ is the standard deviation, in dollars, and n is the number of bets into which we divide the $1,000. We see that the limit as n approaches infinity is 0. This math means that, if we were able to find an arbitrarily large number of investments, each of which had the same expected return and risk, except that the payoff from each was completely independent of the payoffs from each of the others, then we could divide our total investment among them and bring the risk down arbitrarily close to zero.

Independent Events – The Key to Reducing Risk

If only investing were that simple. The mathematical key to eliminating risk in the previous example is that we assumed that we can divide our bet (or investment) into infinitely many, infinitely small bets. The assumption we sneaked in, that does not generally hold in the world of investments, is that the flips of the coin were all *independent*. Independent means that the outcome of any given coin flip is uncorrelated with the outcome of any other flip.

In the real world, independent investment returns are hard to come by.[3] That is, history shows that over time the returns from most investments are positively correlated with each other. We'll unpack what that means statistically in a moment. But before we do that, an intuitive explanation is in order. In the example with coin flips, we assumed that the outcome of each coin flip was independent of the outcome of other coin flips. For coin flips, that is a pretty good assumption.

But in the investing world, there are certain factors, such as interest rates, inflation, and perhaps the level of economic activity or uncertainty, that tend to affect all investments the same way at the same time. For these and perhaps other reasons, investment returns from different investments are not generally independent of each other.

That makes the math more complicated, and limits the amount that diversification can reduce risk. You can simply take on faith the claim that diversification can reduce, but not eliminate, investing risk. For most people, that's probably enough. But if you want to understand the math better, read on. (Note that even if we get the math 100% correct, which we hope to do, there is virtually no chance

---

[3] Gambling activities do provide the opportunity for large numbers of small, independent bets. However, the expected returns are negative, and therefore a large number of small, identical, independent bets is almost guaranteed to created losses. This is the flip side of what generates income for the "house."

that the math maps directly to the world. That is, we are building a model, and the model is an imperfect representation of the world. We hope the differences between the model and the real world are not too great.)

Random Variables

Earlier in the appendix, we discussed the variance and standard deviation of a single random variable. When each of us learned statistics, it took a while to understand the meaning of the term *random variable*. So we'll try to explain it here. In familiar school math, including algebra and calculus, the term *variable* usually refers to a quantity in an equation. The variable can take different values, but only one value at a time.

For example, if we have an equation $y = 5x + 2$, we can plug in any value we choose for x, and we find the value of y associated with that value of x. If $x = 1$, $y = 7$; if $x = 0$, $y = 2$, and so on.

But when we are doing statistics, and we say that X is a *random variable* (by convention, random variables are usually designated by upper case letters), we mean something quite different. This material is often taught quickly, and skimmed over. So at the risk of boring you, we will take a bit of time to try to explain it.

In fact, X is not actually a variable, and it is not actually random. Let's unpack that. A formal definition of random variable is:

A *random variable* is a real-valued function of the experimental outcome.[4]

Recall that a function maps a *domain* to a *range*. For any value in the domain, there is exactly one value in the range.

[4] Dimitri Bertsekas and John Tsitsiklis, *Introduction to Probability*, 2nd ed. (Athena Scientific, 2008: 72.

In the context of random variables, the domain is called the *sample space*. The random variable is actually a function that tells us how to find the unique real number for every possible event in the sample space. For example, consider the roll of a single standard six-sided die. The most common random variable (i.e. function) associated with rolling a die is simply to read the number that faces up when the die comes to rest. But we could instead define the random variable that assigns 1 to even numbers and 0 to odd numbers. The die itself is not the random variable. The random variable is the function that tells us what number(s) to associate with the experimental outcome.

When we conduct the experiment (e.g. flip the coin) or observe the "experiment" (e.g. we see what the total return on the investment was for the past month), we get an actual number. This number is called a *realization* of the random variable.

Additional Examples of Random Variables

1. Suppose the "experiment" is a roll of two dice, and we are interested in the sum of the faces that come up. That function, summing the two faces, is the random variable.
2. If the experiment is a coin flip, that by itself is not a random variable. If we assign 1 to heads and 0 to tails, that is a random variable.
3. If the experiment is to measure the temperature, the random variable is the assignment of a numerical measure of degrees to the result (e.g. we measure that the temperature is 70 degrees Fahrenheit. Depending on how accurately we define the random variable, it could be a discrete variable (it might jump in minimum increments of, say, 1/10th of a degree) or a continuous variable (able to take any real number value).
4. If the experiment is to observe the returns from an investment, we might define the random variable as the total return (i.e. the sum of any income plus or minus any capital gain) over a given period. For example, we might define the random variable as the total return from the S&P 500 for a calendar year.

Random variables can be either *discrete* or *continuous*. The coin flip is an example of a *discrete* process, in which X can take only certain numbers. Other examples of discrete random variables would include the number of people who attend a baseball game, the number of cars sold in a year, or your income for a year. Continuous random variables can take any real number (perhaps any real number between some limits, such as greater than or equal to zero). Examples of continuous variables are the quantity of gasoline sold in a week, the temperature, or the lapse of time. We will make a note of whether a variable is discrete or continuous if it matters and/or it is not obvious.

The *random* part of the term *random variable* refers to the fact that the actual value of the variable is not known until the "experiment" is performed. Or, in the case of investment returns, until after the investment period has finished.

Before the experiment is conducted, or the measurement observed, we say that the random variable is characterized by a probability distribution. Sometimes we can know that distribution with high accuracy; at other times we are guessing at the distribution.

In the case of an ideal fair coin flip, with the random variable defined as 1 for heads and 0 for tails, the probability distribution is known, with probability of .5 for heads and .5 for tails. However, the probability distribution is known exactly only because we defined the situation. That is, we define an ideal fair coin flip precisely by its having an equal probability of coming up heads or tails every flip.

Binomial Distribution

The probabilities associated with coin flipping are described by a *binomial distribution*. If we flip a coin once, there is one way to get heads, out of two possible outcomes. If we flip a coin twice, there are four possible outcomes:

HH, HT, TH, TT

Suppose we want to know the probability of getting exactly two heads. We can look and see that we can get two heads exactly one way out of four possible outcomes. So the probability of getting exactly two heads is ¼ or .25.

If we flip a coin three times, there are eight possible outcomes:

HHH, HHT, HTT, TTT, TTH, THH, HTH, THT

We can ask various questions, and by counting we can find the probabilities we are interested in. For example, the probability of getting exactly two tails is 3/8, because there are three ways it can happen.

You can see that this method of counting the probabilities will get messy very fast, because every time we add a coin flip, the number of possible outcomes doubles. In the eighteenth century, French mathematician Abraham de Moivre found that as the number of coin flips (or n for any binomial, whether coin flips or anything else) gets large, the binomial distribution approaches the normal distribution. The normal distribution is the famous "bell curve," and many random phenomena can be accurately approximated by a normal distribution.

Normal Distribution

If a random variable is normally distributed, and you know the mean and the standard deviation, you can calculate the probabilities associated with the random variable. For example, adult female (or male) heights in the United States are a common textbook example of a normally distributed variable. And away from the extremes, the normal distribution is a close approximation.

Adult female heights in the United States were distributed with mean 63.7 inches, and standard deviation 2.66 inches when reported in 2014.[5] With a normally distributed variable, we know that roughly 68% of the observations are within one standard

---

[5] National Health and Nutrition Examination Survey, Series 3, #39, p. 14, in *Anthropometric Reference Data for Children and Adults: United States, 2011–2014* (US Dept. of Health and Human Services, CDC, August, 2016).

SOME MATH OF DIVERSIFICATION

deviation of the mean. For women's heights, then, 68% are between 61 inches and 66.3 inches.

The normal distribution is useful because many variables are distributed approximately normally, and because it is very commonly used, and therefore implemented in many software packages.

Covariance

Up until now, we've been talking about situations with a single random variable. Now we're going to talk about more than one random variable, where the random variables are not independent. For example, one random variable may be the monthly return on Microsoft stock, and another the monthly return on Coca-Cola stock. Because common factors affect both variables at the same time, the variables are not independent.

If we have two random variables, X and Y, the *covariance* of X and Y is defined as:

$$Cov(X, Y) = \sigma_{XY} = \frac{\sum_{i}^{n}(x_i - \mu_x)(y_i - \mu_y)}{n} \tag{1}$$

An equivalent way of writing (1) is as follows:

$$Cov(X, Y) = \sigma_{XY} = E((X - \mu_x)(Y - \mu_y)) \tag{2}$$

where the E operator is the expectations operator. We can expand:

$$Cov(X, Y) = \sigma_{XY} = E(XY - X\mu_y - Y\mu_x + \mu_x\mu_y) \tag{3}$$

$$Cov(X, Y) = \sigma_{XY} = E(XY) - \mu_x E(Y) - \mu_y E(X) + E(\mu_x\mu_y) \tag{4}$$

We now note that the expectation of a single variable is simply its mean, and the expectation of a mean is itself.

$$Cov(X, Y) = \sigma_{XY} = E(XY) - \mu_x\mu_y - \mu_y\mu_x + \mu_x\mu_y \tag{5}$$

Which simplifies to:

$$Cov(X, Y) = \sigma_{XY} = E(XY) - \mu_x\mu_y \qquad (6)$$

Variance is simply a special case of covariance in which $X = Y$.

Sum of Variances

We may often want to know the variance of a portfolio that consists of more than one asset. Suppose that the returns on one asset are represented by the random variable X, and for a second asset by the random variable Y. We want to know the variance of the total portfolio. We want the variance of $X+Y$ or $Var(X+Y)$.

By the definition of variance, we get:

$$Var(X + Y) = E((X + Y)^2) - [E(X + Y)]^2 \qquad (7)$$

Expanding the squares yields:

$$Var(X + Y) = E(X^2 + 2XY + Y^2) - (\mu_x + \mu_y)^2 \qquad (8)$$

$$Var(X + Y) = E(X^2 + 2XY + Y^2) - (\mu_x^2 + 2\mu_x\mu_y + \mu_y^2) \qquad (9)$$

$$Var(X + Y) = E(X^2) + 2E(XY) + E(Y^2) - (\mu_x^2 + 2\mu_x\mu_y + \mu_y^2) \qquad (10)$$

Now we rearrange:

$$Var(X + Y) = [E(X^2) - \mu_x^2] + [E(Y^2) - \mu_y^2] + 2[E(XY) - \mu_x\mu_y] \qquad (11)$$

Notice that the right side now has three expressions in square brackets which we recognize.

$$Var(X + Y) = Var(X) + Var(Y) + 2Cov(X, Y) \qquad (12)$$

Equation (12) generalizes to multiple random variables. For example, with three random variables:

$$Var(X + Y + Z) = Var(X) + Var(Y) + Var(Z) + 2Cov(X, Y)$$
$$+ 2Cov(X, Z) + 2Cov(Y, Z) \qquad (12a)$$

Binomial Expansion

We note that if there are n random variables, the number of variance terms is n. There is one covariance term for every pair of variables. Because Cov(X,Y) is the same as *Cov(X,Y)*, we are actually interested in counting the number of distinct pairs, disregarding order, and then doubling it. If we have n items, there are n *choose 2* pairs (disregarding order). We note that n *choose 2* can be written:

$$\frac{n(n-1)}{2} \tag{12b}$$

We will use this fact later. But first, let's look at what happens when the random variables have weights.

Weights

In an investing context, we will often have weights associated with each asset. For example, suppose our portfolio consisted of $100 of Microsoft stock and $100 of Coca-Cola stock. We could weight each at 100, but it is more common to assign the weights as percentages of the total, so that the total weights in a portfolio add up to 1.

We can handle the weights as follows. Suppose we have weight a on random variable X and weight b on random variable Y. We can find the covariance, Cov(aX, bY) from the definition:

$$Cov(aX, bY) = E((aX - E(aX))(bY - E(bY))) \tag{13}$$

Recall that the expectation operator in this case means the arithmetic mean. So we can factor out the coefficients a and b.

$$Cov(aX, bY) = E(a(X - E(X))b(Y - E(Y))) \tag{14}$$

And again take the coefficients outside the overall E operator:

$$Cov(aX, bY) = ab[E((X - E(X))(Y - E(Y)))] \tag{15}$$

Inside the square brackets is the definition of covariance. So this leaves us with:

$$Cov(aX, bY) = abCov(X, Y). \tag{16}$$

And because variance is a special case of covariance,

$$Var(aX) = Cov(aX, aX) = aaCov(X, X) = a^2Var(X) \tag{17}$$

Variance of a Portfolio

Let us consider a portfolio of three assets. We are trying to determine the variance of returns, when each asset has weight w and returns are given by a random variable X, Y, or Z, respectively. So we want to know the variance of the portfolio given by:

$$Var(w_xX + w_yY + w_zZ) \tag{18}$$

Applying equations 12a and (17), we find:

$$Var(w_xX + w_yY + w_zZ) = w_x^2Var(X) + w_y^2Var(Y) + w_z^2Var(Z)$$
$$+2w_xw_yCov(X, Y) + 2w_xw_zCov(X, Z)$$
$$+2w_yw_zCov(Y, Z) \tag{19}$$

Correlation Coefficient

Covariances can be difficult to interpret, because they have units. We can normalize a covariance by dividing it by the product of the standard deviations of the two random variables. This yields a normalized statistic that always takes a value between negative 1 and 1, and is formally called the *population Pearson Correlation Coefficient*. It is conventionally referred to by the Greek letter rho, ρ. So we can write:

$$\rho_{x,y} = \frac{Cov(X, Y)}{\sigma_x\sigma_y}. \tag{20}$$

The same statistic, when based on a sample instead of a population, is called the *sample Pearson Correlation Coefficient*, and is conventionally designated by a lower case "r." When our number of observations of the random variable is large, there is usually no practical difference between ρ and r.

Note that we can isolate the covariance term in (20), yielding:

$$\rho_{x,y}\sigma_x\sigma_y = Cov(X, Y) \qquad (21)$$

This is useful because comparing correlation coefficients among assets allows us to do an apples-to-apples comparison much more easily than if we used the raw covariances. Or, looked at another way, if we want to ask "what if" questions, most people find it more intuitive to ask what if, for example, the correlation between two assets is, say, .5, instead of making a harder to understand assumption about covariances.

Demonstration That If Assets Are Correlated, Risk Can Never Be Eliminated

We saw that if our assets are uncorrelated, we can (in theory) eliminate the risk by making the variance as small as desired by dividing the total amount invested among a very large (in the limit, an infinite number of infinitely small) number of investments.

But if the returns are correlated, we can never eliminate the risk, no matter how much we diversify.

Let us begin by considering a portfolio of three assets. For simplicity, we will assume that each one has the same variance, and the covariances (correlations) among all pairs of assets is also equal. We will weight each one equally. Recall that variance is conventionally written σ^2. We could then write:

$$Var(wX + wY + wZ) = w_x^2\sigma_x^2 + w_y^2\sigma_y^2 + w_z^2\sigma_z^2 + 2w_xw_y\rho_{x,y}\sigma_x\sigma_y$$

$$+2w_xw_z\rho_{x,z}\sigma_x\sigma_z + 2w_yw_z\rho_{y,z}\sigma_y\sigma_z \qquad (22)$$

We're getting there. Recall that all the weights are equal, all the variances are equal, and the correlations are equal. So (22) simplifies to:

$$Var(wX + wY + wZ) = 3w^2\sigma^2 + 6\rho\sigma^2 \qquad (23)$$

Now consider what it would look like if we had n assets, all with equal weights, all with equal variances, and with all correlations equal. Each weight would be $1/n$ (because if we have, say five assets, each weight is 1/5 of the total).

As the model in (23) suggests, we'd have two terms: the variances and the correlation/covariances. We could write:

$$n\left[\left(\frac{1}{n}\right)^2 \sigma^2\right] + 2[nC2]\left[\left(\frac{1}{n}\right)^2 \sigma^2 \rho\right] \qquad (24)$$

where $nC2$ is the function *n choose 2*. So we rewrite:

$$n\left[\left(\frac{1}{n}\right)^2 \sigma^2\right] + 2\left[\frac{n(n-1)}{2}\right]\left[\left(\frac{1}{n}\right)^2 \sigma^2 \rho\right] \qquad (25)$$

which simplifies to:

$$\frac{\sigma^2}{n} + (n^2 - n)\left[\frac{\sigma^2 \rho}{n^2}\right] = \frac{\sigma^2}{n} + \sigma^2 \rho - \frac{\sigma^2 \rho}{n} \qquad (26)$$

Now take the limit as n goes to infinity of the right-hand version of equation (26), yielding:

$$\sigma^2 \rho \qquad (27)$$

We are left with a simple expression that shows we'll always have some variance remaining, even if we had an infinite number of infinitely small investments, as long as ρ is positive.

How Much Diversification Is Enough?

If diversification helps us reduce risk, which it usually will (in theory as long as the asset being added isn't perfectly correlated with any asset we already own), we might wonder how much diversification is enough. Is it less risky to own 500 stocks than to own 30?

The perhaps surprising answer is: not necessarily. In theory, as we have just demonstrated at length, if everything else is equal, then more diversification results in reduced risk. But in the real world, everything else is rarely, if ever, equal. The Dow Jones Industrial Average ("DJI") is an index with 30 stocks, while the S&P 500 is an index with 500 stocks. In the period between 2007 and May 2019, the more diversified S&P 500 was slightly more volatile over that period, with the annualized standard deviation of daily returns of the S&P 500 at 19.6%, compared to the DJI at 18.7%.

Over the years, a number of practitioners and academicians have looked at the question of how much diversification is enough. Answers have ranged from three (Warren Buffett: "I would rather pick three businesses from those we own than own a diversified group of 50."[6]) to 120,[7] to arguably 250 or more.[8]

In 23 US large-cap stocks sampled from 2006 to 2019, the average annual standard deviation was 21%, with a range of 30.1% (Mastercard) to a low of 14.3% (McDonald's). The average correlation between pairs of these stocks was .46, with a maximum of .8 (between Loews and Home Depot) and a minimum of .33 (between Mastercard and PepsiCo). Using the standard deviations for each stock, and the correlations, we estimated that an evenly weighted portfolio consisting of those 23 stocks over the time period would have had an annual standard deviation of 14.8%, thanks to the effects of diversification. When we backtested the actual portfolio using portfoliovisualizer.com, we found that the portfolio had an actual realized annual standard deviation of 13.5%, practically identical to that of the Dow Jones Industrial Average over the period. The two numbers, 14.8% and 13.5%, are different probably because the volatilities and correlations were not constant during the period.

However, our theoretical estimate and the actual number are pretty close to each other, and particularly when we are concerned

---

[6] "1996 Berkshire Hathaway Annual Meeting," video, buffett.cnbc.com, https://buffett.cnbc.com/video/1996/05/06/afternoon-session---1996-berkshire-hathaway-annual-meeting.html

[7] Meir Statman, "How Much Diversification Is Enough?" Santa Clara University, 2002, https://papers.ssrn.com/sol3/papers.cfm?abstract_id=365241

[8] Vitali Alexeev and Francis Tapon, "Equity Portfolio Diversification: How Many Stocks Are Enough? Evidence from Five Developed Markets" (November 28, 2012). FIRN Research Paper. Available at SSRN: https://ssrn.com/abstract=2182295 or http://dx.doi.org/10.2139/ssrn.2182295. The paper is quite technical and detailed, and does not give a single unambiguous answer.

about looking forward, it is probably meaningless to make decisions on the basis of differences as small as that between these two numbers, simply because there is so much noise in the historical data, and guesswork in the forward-looking data.

We will return to the question of how many stocks are required for a diversified portfolio. But before we do, we will look at the issue of weighting stocks in a portfolio.

Equal Weighting Versus Market Capitalization Weighting

Most of the common stock market indexes, such as the S&P 500 and the MSCI indexes, are weighted by market capitalization. That means, for example, that of the 500 stocks in the S&P 500, the largest, as of summer 2023, is Apple (AAPL), with a market cap of $2.75 trillion and a weighting of about 7.37%, and the 500th largest is Fortrea. (If you check the math, you'll notice that the ratio of the market caps is not the same as the ratio of the weights in the index. That is because S&P uses a number they call the "free float" market cap, which excludes stock held by insiders and certain other stockholders who are considered "permanent" holders.)

The argument for promulgating a market-cap based index is that such an index is investable (at least in theory) by even the largest institutions. By definition, there is always enough stock available in the market to make it possible for an institution to be able to purchase shares in the proportion that they are represented in the index. That is because the representation adjusts automatically, and no index investor has to buy or sell when index components change their relative valuation. This "no action required" characteristic is theoretically quite important.

For example, if one day Microsoft is 4% of the index and Exxon is 3%, but then oil stocks surge and Exxon rises to 4% of the index, no one who was invested in the index needs to take any action to remain invested in the index.

These are two important reasons that large institutional investors might correctly judge that they should use a market-cap weighted index.

But these reasons probably do not apply to individual investors.

Reasons to Prefer Equal Weighting

Theory

The main reason to diversify a stock portfolio is to avoid taking risk that we do not reasonably expect to be compensated for taking. We explained the basic theory with the coin flipping example.

Using similar reasoning, derived from statistics, we can show that given certain assumptions, equal weighting is superior to unequal weighting. Let us take the simplest case, and assume we have only two stocks. Suppose that we have no special insight, but believe that the returns on each can be fairly estimated to be distributed normally with mean .06 and standard deviation .22. And let us assume that the correlation between the returns will be .6.

Recall that the variance of the portfolio will be given by:

$$Var(w_x X + w_y Y) = w_x^2 Var(X) + w_y^2 Var(Y) + 2w_x w_y Cov(X, Y)$$

We will derive the conditions for the optimal weighting for a two-asset portfolio. We will designate the assets as X and Y. The total weighting of the portfolio must equal 1, so the weight of asset 1 can be called w and the weight of asset 2 is therefore $1 - w$.

$$Weight_1 = w$$

$$Weight_2 = 1 - w$$

We want to find the weights that result in the minimum variance, given the variance of return of each asset and the covariance of the returns. We recall that the variance of the portfolio is given by:

$$Var(wX + (1 - w)Y) = w^2 Var(X) + (1 - w)^2 Var(Y)$$

$$+ 2w(1 - w) Cov(X, Y)$$

Let's simplify our notation a bit, by calling the left side P (for portfolio), and expanding out the parentheses on the right side.

$$Var(P) = w^2Var(X) + Var(Y) - 2wVar(Y) + w^2Var(Y)$$
$$+ 2wCov(X,Y) - 2w^2Cov(X,Y)$$

As you will recall from calculus, we can use the derivative to find the minimum of a quadratic function such as this one. Now we take the derivative with respect to w:

$$\frac{\partial Var(P)}{\partial w} = 2wVar(X) - 2Var(Y) + 2wVar(Y)$$
$$+ 2Cov(X,Y) - 4wCov(X,Y)$$

We set the derivative equal to zero, and move the w terms to the left and the others to the right:

$$2w[Var(X) + Var(Y) - 2Cov(X,Y)] = 2[Var(Y) - Cov(X,Y)]$$

Solving for w:

$$w = \frac{Var(Y) - Cov(X,Y)}{Var(X) + Var(Y) - 2Cov(X,Y)}$$

We now substitute in $\rho\sigma_x\sigma_y$ for Cov(X,Y) and σ^2 for the variances, to get:

$$w = \frac{\sigma_y^2 - \rho\sigma_x\sigma_y}{\sigma_x^2 + \sigma_y^2 - 2\rho\sigma_x\sigma_y}$$

That's not so simple. But if we really don't have any strong reason to believe that the variances of the two assets are different, then the equation simplifies a great deal. It becomes:

$$w = \frac{\sigma^2 - \rho\sigma\sigma}{\sigma^2 + \sigma^2 - 2\rho\sigma\sigma}$$

which simplifies to:

$$w = \frac{\sigma^2(1-\rho)}{2\sigma^2(1-\rho)}$$

which, when we cancel everything, leaves us with $\frac{1}{2}$, that is, equal weighting.

So, we have shown that if the variances of return of each asset is the same, equal weighting is optimal.

Because a quadratic function has only one global extreme,[9] and because we showed that if the variances are equal, that extreme (i.e. the minimum portfolio variance) occurs when weights are equal, then if weights are not equal, the portfolio variance must not be at a minimum.

But suppose we selected unequal weights for the assets, and asserted that these unequal weights yielded the portfolio with minimum variance. Then, because we have already proven that if the variances are equal the portfolio-variance-minimizing weights will be equal, it must be the case that the individual asset variances are not equal.

That is, if we select unequal weighting, we are making regarding our beliefs about the relative values of the variances and/or the values of the correlation of returns.

Sometimes we might be comfortable, and feel justified, expecting that the returns of one asset (or asset class) will have a significantly different variance in the future.

Market-Capitalization Weighting

Market-capitalization weighting of an index results in very unequal weightings. As of this writing, Apple is highest weight, at 6.5%, in the S&P 500, while the bottom 100 stocks combined account for only about 2.5% of the index.

However, perhaps because of the large range of market capitalizations of the S&P 500 stocks (as of early 2024, Apple is close to $2.8 trillion, all the way down to Macy's, which had a market capitalization just 1/1000th of Apple's when Macy's was removed from the S&P 500 in 2020), the S&P 500 is dominated by the large stocks, which have tended to have lower volatility than the smaller stocks in the index.

---

[9] In general, a polynomial of degree n will have at most $n-1$ global extrema. A polynomial of even degree must have at least one global extreme, therefore, a quadratic must have exactly one.

Over the past 15 years, the market capitalization weighted S&P 500 has had a lower volatility than the equally weighted version of the same index. However, the return of the equally weighted index has been higher over most periods during the last quarter century or so that the equally weighted index has been calculated.

These facts are open to more than one interpretation. An interpretation consistent with the Capital Asset Pricing Model is that the equally weighted index should have a higher return because it has a higher volatility. Another interpretation to explain the higher return is that the average size of the companies in the equally weighted index is much smaller than in the market capitalization weighted index. This second point, put another way, is that the S&P 500 is really pretty much a mega-cap index, like the Dow Jones Industrial Average. The top 10% (i.e. the biggest 50) of the companies in the S&P 500 represent over 50% of the value of the index.

Market-Cap Weighting and Statistical Bias

Market-cap weighting is suboptimal if each stock's price is not an unbiased estimate of its true value. This statement requires a bit of unpacking.

The assumption of the Efficient Market Hypothesis is that at any moment in time, the market price of stock reflects all available information about that stock.[10] If this assumption holds, the price of a stock is said to be a statistically unbiased estimate of its true value.

However, if there are times that the market price of a stock differs from its "true" or unbiased price, then market capitalization weighting will systematically overweight overvalued stocks and underweight undervalued stocks. A highly simplified example helps to explain.

Instead of companies, where we never know the true parameters, let's posit that we have a portfolio consisting of 10 assets. Each

---

[10] Eugene Fama identified three forms of the hypothesis: weak, semi-strong, and strong. The weak form says only that there is no information in past prices. That is, so-called "charting" doesn't work. The semi-strong form says that all public information, past prices, and fundamental information, are already reflected in the price. And the strong form says that all information, including nonpublic information, is already reflected in the price.

asset is defined as a statistical process that produces returns from a given normal distribution with mean 10% and variance 20%. Each asset has the same distribution. Also assume that every covariance is equal.

We have already shown that the minimum variance portfolio will be equally weighted. So the minimum variance results when weights are equal. And by assumption, expected returns and variances are all equal. Therefore if the market misprices any of these assets, a capitalization weighted index will buy too much of the overpriced asset and not enough of the underpriced asset.

Diversification Within an Asset Class and Between Asset Classes

Within an Asset Class

From the point of view of diversification within the asset class, there are two kinds of asset classes: the *unified* and the dispersed. A unified asset class is one in which there is either only one real asset, or all the varieties of the asset class are so highly correlated with each other that for investment purposes the covariance matrix among them all is not significantly different from a matrix of 1s. An example of a unified asset class is gold.

Unified Asset Classes

Gold

There are several reasonable approaches to adding exposure to gold to a portfolio. Among these are ownership of bullion, ownership of coins, or a variety of "paper" gold products such as the ETF with ticker symbol GLD. The correlation of returns between these different forms of gold is not significantly different from 1. So in statistical terms, there is no reason to diversify. Note, however, that there might be institutional reasons that an investor might want to own, for example, some gold coins as well as some "paper" gold. Coins might be considered more useful in an emergency, while the paper gold is more easily traded during normal times, and does not need to be stored or insured.

Treasury Bills and Money Market Instruments

Because all issues of T-Bills are short term, and because they are all issued by the US government, the returns on different bills are highly correlated with each other. Even the correlation between the one-month and the one-year bill return is over .985. Other money market instruments may have slightly lower correlations, but the reason, if there is one, to include non-Treasuries is return-related, not risk-related. Almost everyone agrees that adding non-treasury money market instruments to a money market portfolio will increase the risk, even if such increased risk does not show up in statistical measures of volatility or covariance.

The high correlations of returns on money market instruments means that an investor may decide to invest directly in T-Bills, rather than a diversified portfolio such as that offered by a money market fund, with no increase in (statistical) risk. Depending on the amounts involved, it may even generate higher after-fee returns for an investor to hold T-Bills directly compared to holding money market fund shares.

Sovereign Government Own-Fiat-Money Bonds

By sovereign government own-fiat-money bonds, we mean bonds issued by a government in a currency that it can print. In 2019, the biggest such issuers were the United States, Japan, and the United Kingdom. The European Union countries that are members of the Euro do not qualify, because the individual governments cannot, on their own, create Euros to pay off their bonds, as Greece's ongoing debt crisis has made clear.

But for the countries that can print their own currency, the only difference between bonds is maturity.

Dispersed Asset Classes

Bonds

Bond volatility will vary based on maturity and perceived credit. Longer-term bonds, everything else equal, are more volatile than short-term bonds. Nevertheless, the major diversifiable risk of a bond portfolio is credit risk. As all government bonds have, presumably, the same credit risk, there is no credit risk reason to diversify the holdings of government bonds.

With corporate bonds, or other bonds that have non-government credit risk, diversification can continue to reduce risk even up to the point of holding hundreds of bonds. That's because corporate defaults and downgrades are relatively rare, but when they occur, they can have dramatic negative influence on the price of the bonds.

Theoretical Example of Diversifying Bond Default Risk

One key difference between the risk of owning stocks and the risk of owning bonds is that with high-grade bonds (not speculative or junk bonds), the best that can happen is that the bond pays everything it is supposed to pay. Let us consider an example of a one-year bond that pays 4%. For simplicity, we will assume that the bond either pays off in full (i.e. $104) or pays nothing. And, let us assume that there is a 1% probability of default.

We can model investment in a single such bond as the flip of an unfair coin. In this case, there is a 99% probability that the flip pays off $104, and a 1% probability that it pays zero.[11] The expected value is .99 × $104, which is $102.96.

If you own a single such bond, obviously there is a 99% probability that you will receive $104, and a 1% probability that you will receive nothing. We will now apply essentially the same analysis

---

[11] This would seem to be a reasonable simplification. Moody's reports that the average annual credit loss on bonds it rated has been about .9% since 1983. Moody's Investor Service Data Report, *Annual Default Study: Corporate Default and Recovery Rates, 1920–2017*, Feb. 15, 2018.

that we did with coin flips. We assume that many identical bonds are available, and the probability of default on each is 1%, but all are independent of each other. (In the real world, this isn't true, as all bonds tend to be affected by the macroeconomic situation. But for this analysis, it simplifies without significantly distorting our findings.)

We can use the binomial probability density function to calculate the probability that x number of the bonds we own, out of a portfolio with n identical bonds, each with a probability p of defaulting, will default. The function is:

$$f(x) = (nCx)p^x(1 - p)^{(n-x)}$$

where nCx is the function n *choose* x, also known as the *binomial coefficient*. For example, if we own a portfolio of 10 bonds ($n = 10$), each with a 1% probability of default ($p = .01$), we can calculate that there is a 90.44% probability that none of the bonds ($x = 0$) will default, a 9.14% probability that exactly one bond will default, a .4% probability that two bonds will default, and about 1 in 10,000 probability that 3 bonds will default. If we add those up, the probability is .999998 that our portfolio will have at most 3 defaults. If we divided our investment into 10 equal portions, we are nearly guaranteed that our loss will be, at most, about 30% (i.e. 3 out of 10).

We can reduce the risk further by diversifying the portfolio further. If instead of dividing our investment equally among 10 bonds, we divide equally among 100 bonds, we can apply the binomial probability function to calculate that we have a .999929 probability of experiencing 6 or fewer defaults. Thus, we are nearly guaranteed that the maximum loss will not be more than about 6%. (It would actually be less than 6%, because the 94% of bonds that paid off would all pay their 4% interest. But we're only trying here to illustrate the benefit of bond diversification.)

More diversification is possible. Suppose we were able to divide the investment among 1,000 identical bonds. In this case, we have a .999994 probability of having 26 or fewer of the bonds default. Even if 26 of the 1,000 bonds defaulted, the remaining 974 paying in full would be enough to ensure that the return was positive.

Asymmetrical Risk

With investment grade bonds (as compared to stocks or, perhaps, junk bonds), the best that can happen is you get what you were supposed to get; that is, the best that can happen is you get your money back plus a bit of interest. Essentially all the risk you take is on the downside. This is an example of asymmetrical risk, and it works against you in bonds.

The answer is to hold a very diversified portfolio of bonds. That is what bond mutual funds do. For example, as of summer 2023, the Vanguard Intermediate Term Investment Grade bond fund owns over 1,800 different bonds.[12]

We conclude that if a bond portfolio contains only sovereign government (i.e. a government borrowing in a currency that it can print) there is probably no risk reduction benefit from diversifying.

However, any other portfolio that has issuer-specific risk should be very highly diversified. A thousand bonds is not too many. Of course, it takes a lot of money to assemble a portfolio of 1,000 bonds without driving transactions costs high. A so-called "round lot" of bonds may be as low as $100,000, but this is strictly a retail size trade. A 2015 study published by FINRA[13] found that the lowest transactions costs for bond trades were associated with trades of $25 million. Not many individual investors can have a diversified portfolio of bonds and hold that much in a single issue.

Stocks

Across How Many Stock Markets Should You Diversify?

If the stock markets of different countries represent different asset classes within the broader category of stocks, it raises the question of how much benefit, if any, might result from diversifying equity investments across more than one country.

---

[12] At the end of 2020, this Vanguard fund had over $37 billion of assets. As we will discuss, this is large enough to benefit from both low transactions costs and very wide diversification.

[13] https://www.finra.org/sites/default/files/OCE_researchnote_liquidity_2015_12.pdf

Of course, if we had a working crystal ball, we would look at future returns, and make our investment decisions on that basis. Lacking such foresight, however, it might make sense to diversify.

History suggests that the stock markets of many different countries actually do represent different subclasses within the broader class of equities. I reviewed the monthly returns from 20 different countries[14] from a period covering 1975 to 2018 for 14 of the countries, and as short as the period 1991 to 2018 for Ireland. Table A.3 shows the annualized standard deviation of returns for each country.

Table A.3   Annualized Standard Deviation of Returns by Country

Country	Annual Standard Deviation
Austria	23.6%
Australia	23.7%
Belgium	19.6%
Canada	19.3%
Denmark	19.2%
Finland	27.8%
France	22.0%
Germany	20.7%
Hong Kong	28.6%
Ireland	23.4%
Italy	25.1%
Japan	20.1%
Netherlands	19.1%
New Zealand	21.4%
Norway	26.0%
Singapore	25.8%
Spain	23.1%
Sweden	23.3%
Switzerland	17.2%
UK	20.4%

[14] The countries are Austria, Australia, Belgium, Canada, Denmark, Finland, France, Germany, Hong Kong, Ireland, Italy, Japan, the Netherlands, New Zealand, Norway, Singapore, Spain, Sweden, Switzerland, United Kingdom. The return data is from Eugene Fama and Ken French, who maintain online data at https://mba.tuck.dartmouth.edu/pages/faculty/ken.french/Data_Library/f-f_bench_factor.html.

In hindsight, Switzerland was the country with the lowest standard deviation of returns in the sample. It turns out that an equally weighted portfolio of all 20 countries would have had a slightly lower standard deviation: 16.99%. We do not believe the difference from 17.2% is significant in either a statistical or a practical sense.

But do we need all 20 countries to have a reasonable expectation of having "enough" diversification? Let's look at the historical correlation matrix of returns, and then consider how simulated portfolios, based on historical actual returns, would have done. (See Table A.4.)

The highest correlation, between Germany and the Netherlands, is .81, and the smallest, .34, is between Japan and Australia.

It is important to note that this table is backward-looking, and there is little reason to believe that any of these past correlations is an accurate prediction of future correlations. (There is a significant amount of published empirical research showing that correlations tend to vary quite a bit over time.) The average of all these correlations (excluding the own-correlations, which are by definition one) is .56.

If we use the average standard deviation, .225, and the average correlation coefficient, which we're rounding to .56, we can apply the formula we developed in equation (26) previously:

$$\frac{\sigma^2}{n} + \sigma^2\rho - \frac{\sigma^2\rho}{n}$$

to estimate what the standard deviation (the variance, and we'll then take the square root to get a standard deviation) of an equal weighted portfolio would be. An n of all 20 markets yields a theoretical portfolio standard deviation of 17.2%. This is pretty close to the actual 17%.

The theoretical portfolio standard deviation if we use only 10 of the countries, evenly weighted, is 17.5%. This is very close to the average portfolio standard deviation we get when we randomly select 10 of the countries and form a historical hypothetical portfolio.

Table A.4 Matrix of Correlated Returns, by Country

	Austria	Australia	Belgium	Canada	Denmark	Finland	France	Germany	Hong Kong	Ireland	Italy	Japan	Netherlands	N Zealand	Norway	Singapore	Spain	Sweden	Switzerland	UK
Austria	1.00																			
Australia	0.55	1.00																		
Belgium	0.67	0.48	1.00																	
Canada	0.54	0.67	0.50	1.00																
Denmark	0.66	0.58	0.74	0.62	1.00															
Finland	0.45	0.57	0.49	0.58	0.55	1.00														
France	0.65	0.52	0.73	0.56	0.73	0.62	1.00													
Germany	0.71	0.49	0.73	0.54	0.75	0.62	0.74	1.00												
Hong Kong	0.48	0.52	0.41	0.50	0.47	0.45	0.42	0.46	1.00											
Ireland	0.62	0.58	0.66	0.56	0.67	0.53	0.66	0.65	0.43	1.00										
Italy	0.60	0.42	0.56	0.47	0.66	0.60	0.63	0.59	0.37	0.56	1.00									
Japan	0.34	0.39	0.42	0.37	0.42	0.41	0.46	0.41	0.35	0.41	0.41	1.00								
Netherlands	0.69	0.56	0.78	0.64	0.77	0.62	0.74	0.81	0.54	0.70	0.59	0.46	1.00							
New Zealand	0.51	0.73	0.46	0.55	0.46	0.45	0.49	0.49	0.49	0.47	0.44	0.43	0.56	1.00						
Norway	0.63	0.57	0.61	0.63	0.69	0.58	0.59	0.58	0.47	0.61	0.45	0.34	0.65	0.54	1.00					
Singapore	0.53	0.57	0.46	0.57	0.54	0.47	0.45	0.47	0.68	0.46	0.37	0.39	0.56	0.59	0.51	1.00				
Spain	0.62	0.48	0.58	0.49	0.68	0.59	0.62	0.61	0.38	0.63	0.61	0.43	0.62	0.53	0.48	0.40	1.00			
Sweden	0.56	0.56	0.57	0.56	0.71	0.71	0.59	0.66	0.48	0.61	0.54	0.44	0.68	0.58	0.59	0.51	0.59	1.00		
Switzerland	0.65	0.53	0.71	0.54	0.69	0.51	0.69	0.75	0.47	0.63	0.51	0.47	0.78	0.53	0.57	0.49	0.53	0.60	1.00	
UK	0.64	0.59	0.63	0.66	0.72	0.61	0.65	0.60	0.53	0.71	0.52	0.43	0.72	0.56	0.58	0.59	0.52	0.56	0.66	1.00

(Note that there are 20 choose 10, or 20 C10 written in math terms, which is 184,756 possible such portfolios; hence we just sampled some at random.)

If instead of the actual historical average .56 correlation we used a rounded guess of .5, we would expect the equal weighted 20 country portfolio to have a standard deviation of 16.3%. The difference between 16.3% and 17.2% is statistically significant (we estimate), but probably not practically significant.

How Stable Are the Parameters?

It is a well-established historical fact that, empirically, some of the key parameters in which we are interested, including return, standard deviation, and correlations between assets vary over time. Figure A.1 shows rolling three-year standard deviations for the 20 countries.

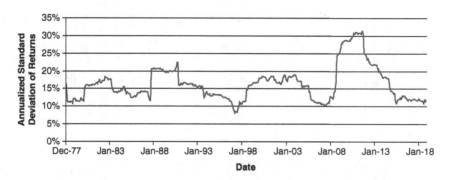

Figure A.1   Rolling 3-Year Annualized Standard Deviation of Returns Equally Weighted 20-Country Portfolio

It is widely known that returns vary greatly over time, with some three-year periods (for example) showing excellent returns, and other three-year periods showing very poor returns.

The correlations between pairs of returns are also not stable over time. If we arbitrarily divide the total period at which we are looking – 1975 to 2018 – in half, we find that the average correlation between pairs of countries was about .41 in the first half of the data, and about .69 in the second half. Note that the second half of the data includes the period 2007 to 2010, during which stock markets around the world plunged together, with very high correlations during those years. The average correlation between markets, in our sample of 20 countries, was .85 during those four years.

Conclusions: How Many Countries?

If we assume that, broadly speaking, the future will be like the past, we can expect that the long-run average correlation between the returns of pairs of countries' stock markets will be in the neighborhood of .5. We can also assume that the standard deviation of the average countries' stock market returns will be in the neighborhood of 22.5%. If this continues to be so, there is significant reduction in expected portfolio volatility until we have about 10 countries. Ten would be the "magic number" even if there were 30, 40, or 50 countries, as long as the expected correlations were similar. Beyond 10 countries, as both theory and the past 45 years of data show, additional countries reduce the expected portfolio volatility by a very small amount. However, if there were zero cost to adding countries, it would be worth it to do so for the very small expected extra reduction in volatility.

The question then becomes, what is the expected cost of adding a country? We will address that question separately.

Statistical Normality

Many statistical processes are based on the assumption of a normal distribution. A normal distribution has several statistical properties which can be summarized in terms of its *moments*:[15]

1st: Mean – a measure of the "average"
2nd: Variance – a measure of the dispersion of the data

---

[15] The moments are numbered according to the power to which the difference between each observation and the mean is raised in computing the moment. For example, the variance, the second moment, is calculated as $\frac{1}{N}\sum_{i=1}^{N}(\mu - x_i)^2$. The exponent, the 2, corresponds to the variance being referred to as the 2nd moment.

3rd: Skewness – a measure of the symmetry, or lack thereof, of the data

4th: Kurtosis – a measure of the "fatness" of the tails relative to a normal distribution

Our equally weighted 20 country portfolio of monthly returns is not normally distributed. We can determine this in several ways. Perhaps the most intuitive of these is the *skewness*. The data are skewed left. That is, the left (negative) tail of the distribution is bigger than the right tail. In the real world, this means that big losses occurred more frequently than would be expected if the data were normally distributed. In Figure A.2, we have graphed a histogram of the monthly returns, along with a fitted curve, and a normal curve with the same mean and standard deviation as our data.

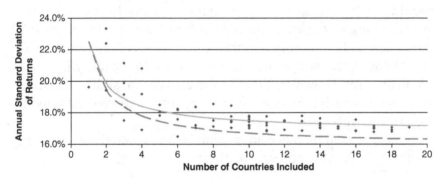

Figure A.2   Standard Deviation of Portfolio Versus Number of Countries Included Solid Line Is Theoretical w/rho = .56; Dashed rho = .5; Points Are Randomly Selected Portfolios

The closer the two curves are two each other, the closer the actual data is to normal. The skewness is not very obvious in the graph, but if you look closely you can see that the gray line is higher on the left side than the right, and the left tail (losses) extends farther out.

We can calculate the skewness, and when we do, we find that for this data set it is –.69. A skewness of zero would mean no skewness, and a negative number means left skew. Is the –.69 skewness significant? We can refer to the standard error of the skewness. (Recall that a standard error of a statistic is like the standard deviation of the sample statistic.) An estimate of the standard error of skewness is given by the formula[16] $\sqrt{\frac{6}{n}}$ where n is the number of data points (i.e. the number of monthly return observations in our data set.) In our data set, we have 528 monthly observations, so the approximate standard error is .107. The skewness is $-.69$, which is more than two standard errors away from zero, so we can be pretty certain that our data is skewed to a statistically significant degree. (Recall, however, that statistical significance is not necessarily the same as real-world significance.)

The kurtosis of this data is 3.26 (sometimes reported as "excess" kurtosis of .26). This statistic too has a standard error. It can be estimated[17] as $\sqrt{\frac{24}{n}}$, and in this case that works out to .21. The excess kurtosis, then, is just a bit more than one standard error away from zero, and we can conclude that the excess kurtosis is not significantly different from zero.

What have we learned? We suspect our data is close to normal, but that it's not quite normal, with the occasional nasty surprise. But we already knew about the nasty surprises. They are called market crashes, and anyone who knows a little history, or has lived through markets for long enough, knows about them.

What is interesting is that the real-world data are "close enough" to normally distributed that for our purposes, modeling the probability bands for future wealth given certain assumptions, we can use the assumption of normality.

---

[16] This estimator is a simplification of $\sqrt{\frac{6n(n-1)}{(n-2)(n+1)(n+3)}}$. The limit of this expression, as $n \to \infty$ is $\sqrt{\frac{6}{n}}$. For a fuller discussion, see, e.g. Bradley Harding et al., "Standard Errors: A Review and Evaluation of Standard Error Estimators Using Monte Carlo Simulations," *Quantitative Methods for Psychology* 10, no. 2 (2014).

[17] This estimator is the limit as $n \to \infty$ of $SEK = 2(SES)\sqrt{\frac{n^2-1}{(n-3)(n+5)}}$ where "SEK" is the standard error of kurtosis and "SES" is the standard error of skewness.

How Many Stocks Within a Country?

Based on historical evidence, it seems that individual stock returns are not distributed close to normally. Hendrik Bessembinder[18] has examined the cumulative returns from over 26,000 US companies between 1926 and 2019, and found that the majority, 57.8%, "reduced rather than increased shareholder wealth."

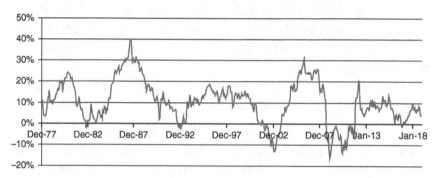

Figure A.3   Rolling 3-Year Returns
Equally Weighted 20 Country Portfolio

To generate the graph in Figure A.3, we sorted the 26,168 companies in Bessembinder's sample by wealth generated. Then, from left to right we graphed them. Note that the gray curve is below zero, that is, the companies destroyed wealth, until we get to the 57.8th percentile. Figure A.3 shows the middle of the distribution. Figure A.4 shows the entire distribution.

At the far left are a relatively small number of catastrophic wealth-destroying companies (the worst was Worldcom, which Bessembinder reports destroyed about $100 billion of shareholder wealth). At the far right are a relatively small number of companies which generated most of the net wealth creation.

Of the $47 trillion of total net (after subtracting out the losses), the top 100 companies accounted for $25.4 trillion, or over half the total. These top 100 companies are mostly household names, such as Apple, Microsoft, Exxon, Walmart, and Disney.

---

[18] Hendrik Bessembinder, "Wealth Creation in the US Public Stock Markets 1926–2019," *Journal of Investing* (April 2021).

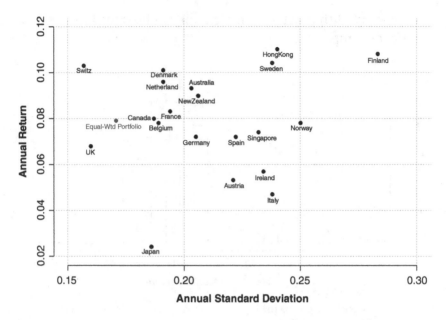

Figure A.4   Return, Standard Deviation of Returns for the Period 1991–2018

One implication of Bessembinder's data is that a portfolio that, for whatever reason, doesn't own some of the few stocks that create the most value will underperform the entire market.

Median Expected Return

A second implication of the data is that, historically, the expected return of the median company (i.e. the company at the 50th percentile) has been *negative*.

When we arrange the data by cumulative wealth creation, we find that we need to include 95% (yes!) of the companies before the cumulative wealth creation becomes positive. That is, if it were not for the top 5% (by count) of companies, the entire wealth creation of the entire US stock market would have been a net zero. But in actuality, it was positive $47 trillion. And, as Bessembinder shows, the vast majority of that net wealth creation can be traced to a relative handful of companies.

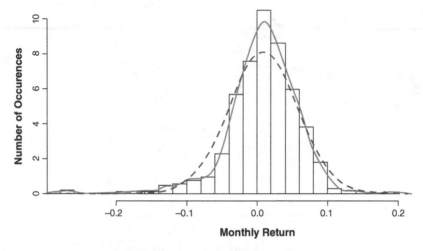

Figure A.5   Monthly Returns for Equal Weighted Portfolios 20 Countries
Dotted Line Shows Normal Distribution
Data Source: Fama/French

One potential lesson from the Bessembinder analysis is that, in a market where by count most of the companies are small, a truly random selection of companies will have to include more companies to get a "representative" portfolio than it would if all companies had the same expected return and risk.

Everything else equal, in a market like the US market with thousands of companies, the naïve diversification rule, shown in the following equation, probably results in too few companies.

We showed earlier that, if variances and covariances among assets can be assumed to be the same, we obtain most of the diversification benefit available with a relatively small number of assets.

Everything else equal, when variance is very high, we need more stocks to obtain a portfolio with reasonable variance. We can obtain a theoretical estimate of the minimum possible variance, based on certain assumptions, using the equation developed earlier, repeated here:

$$\frac{\sigma^2}{n} + \sigma^2\rho - \frac{\sigma^2\rho}{n}$$

In the US, when we include all the small companies, the annual standard deviation of the average stock may be very high. Bessembinder reports average annual standard deviation of about 62.5% (and the variance is therefore .39), and if we assume average correlation between pairs of stocks is .5, then as the number of such stocks in the portfolio approaches infinity, the variance of the portfolio approaches $.5 \times .39 \approx .195$. This result isn't too far off the actual historical experience of the overall US market.

Given these same assumptions, we can calculate theoretical portfolio standard deviations for a finite number of stocks (see Table A.5).

Table A.5   Theoretical Portfolio Standard Deviation

Number of Stocks	Theoretical Portfolio Standard Deviation
1	39.1%
2	29.3%
3	26.0%
4	24.4%
5	23.4%
6	22.8%
7	22.3%
8	22.0%
9	21.7%
10	21.5%
11	21.3%
12	21.2%
13	21.0%
14	20.9%
15	20.8%
16	20.8%
17	20.7%
18	20.6%
19	20.6%
20	20.5%
21	20.5%
22	20.4%
23	20.4%
24	20.3%
25	20.3%
26	20.3%
27	20.3%
28	20.2%
29	20.2%
30	20.2%

However, we know that a crucial assumption does not hold. Even if the "typical" US stock has a standard deviation of 62.5%, the typical large stock has a much lower standard deviation.

This is probably the reason that a large-cap portfolio, such as the Dow Jones Industrial Average, with 30 stocks, is as well diversified as the much larger S&P 500. But a small-cap portfolio will probably need many, many more stocks to achieve the same level of diversification.

The Effect of Errors in Parameter Estimation

Compound returns result in skewed distributions, even if the annual returns are normally distributed.

The expected geometric return (CAGR, compound return) can be approximated as the expected arithmetic return, minus half the variance of return. In symbols (as noted in the text):

$$\mu_g = \mu_a - \frac{\sigma_a^2}{2} \tag{28}$$

So, for example, if we have a stock with expected annual return of 6%, with a standard deviation of return of .4, the expected geometric return is actually negative.

$$\mu_g = .06 - \frac{.4^2}{2} = .06 - \frac{.16}{2} = .06 - .08 = -.02$$

Error in Estimation

It would be natural to think, for example, that if we estimate the expected arithmetic return of a stock as .06, but it really should be .04, that at worst we should expect to earn less, but it would still be profitable. But the effect of skewness can turn what we expect to be a gain into a loss. Here's an example. Suppose that a stock has a standard deviation of return of 30% (many stocks do). Suppose further that I estimate the arithmetic annual return to be 6%.

The expected geometric return is then going to be .06 − .045 = 1.5%. Not great, perhaps, but at least positive. But if the actual (which is not observable) expected arithmetic return is 4%, then the expected geometric return is negative half a percent.

For high-volatility stocks, the effect is even more pronounced. Consider, for example, Tesla. As of 2023, Tesla stock has a historical volatility (annualized standard deviation of return) of about 50%. (The "implied volatility" on Tesla options is also close to 50%).

By solving equation (1) for μ_a we can calculate the minimum expected arithmetic return necessary for the expected compound return to be just zero.

$$\mu_g + \frac{\sigma_a^2}{2} = \mu_a. \tag{29}$$

It comes to a stunning 12.5%!

Another Point of View

To develop some intuition about why higher volatility lowers expected compound returns, let's look again at coin flips and bets. Suppose that you start with $100, and you are going to bet it on a series of coin flips. But instead of dividing your investment into a bunch of coin flips, this time you are going to invest the entire amount into the first coin flip, then take the resulting proceeds and invest those into another coin flip. Suppose that each coin flip represents the return on a stock for a year, and that we're going to invest in that stock for 10 years. If the coin comes up heads, the return is 30%, and if it comes up tails, negative 10%.[19] The arithmetic expected return is a positive 10%.

For example, on the first bet, we invest $100. If the coin comes up heads, we get $130, and if it comes up tails, we get $90. Either way, we take the proceeds and reinvest them again. On each flip,

---

[19] William Bernstein uses this example, which he attributes to "Uncle Fred," in *The Intelligent Asset Allocator*.

the return will be either plus 30% or minus 10%. We can calculate the standard deviation[20] of each such bet as:

$$\sigma = \sqrt{\frac{(.3 - .1)^2 + (-.1 - .1)^2}{2}} = .2$$

We see that the expected arithmetic mean return is 10%, and standard deviation is 20%. Using our estimation formula, we calculate an expected compound return of 8%, which is pretty close to the expected compound return calculated by multiplying .9 and 1.3. That equals 1.17, the square root of which is 1.0817, for a compound return of 8.17%.

Bernstein uses this example as a metaphor for investing in the stock market. In a way, the example is reasonable, because the mean and standard deviation of the bet are similar to the historical mean and standard deviation of the stock market.

However, there are (at least) two fundamental, and psychologically very real and very important differences between this coin flip model and the real stock market. One difference is that with the coin flip, we believe that we have a full understanding[21] of the process that generates the return. In other words, we believe very strongly that the coin will continue to come up heads, on average, half the time. With the stock market, we know that there's probably more we don't know than we do know. We have very limited historical data on stock market returns. We have only a rough economic model of how and why they produce returns. In short, we cannot be nearly as confident that stocks will continue to perform in the future, broadly speaking, as they have in the past.

---

[20] Note that if you attempt to calculate the standard deviation using some standard deviation calculators, such as the "stdev" function in Excel or the "sd" function in R, you will get a different answer, namely .2828. The difference arises because above we calculated the population standard deviation, and most software assumes that you want the sample standard deviation. Recall that they differ by 1 in the denominator. When the denominator is large, the effect is small. But here, where the denominator is 2, it makes a big difference.

[21] It doesn't matter whether we understand the physics of a coin flip. We believe, on the basis of a tremendous amount of evidence, and little or no reason to doubt, that fair coins come up heads half the time on average; we believe that coins have no memory, etc. In short, we are justified in believing that we know everything worth knowing about the distribution of outcomes produced by coin flipping.

Second, in the coin flip example, the worst that can happen is that in any one year we lose 10%. But real markets can, and often do, produce losses in a single year much greater than 10%.

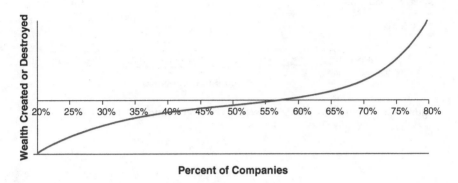

Figure A.6   Cumulative Distribution of Wealth Creation
Data source: Bessembinder, 1926–2019

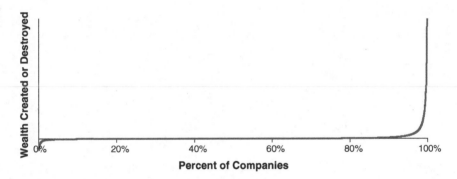

Figure A.7   Cumulative Distribution of Wealth Creation
Data source: Bessembinder, 1926–2019

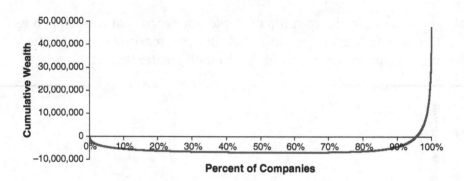

Figure A.8   Cumulative Wealth Creation of US Companies, 1926–2019

Index

Page numbers followed by *f* and *t* refer to figures and tables, respectively.

Three Free Offers for Readers

This book focuses almost exclusively on investing. Equally important for most investors are the issues of taxes, and inflation.

Inflation

We have a book that explains the history, the theory, the likely future of inflation, and contains a chapter on how to invest in the face of inflation.

For a free copy of the chapter on investing in the fact of inflation, please send us an email to Inflation@SterlingFoundations.com. Please provide full contact information, including phone number and mailing address, and please reference "Inflation Chapter Offer in Investor's Dilemma."

You can also purchase the book directly from us for 50% off by referencing this offer.

Taxes

The difference between good and ordinary tax planning can equal or exceed the difference between good and ordinary investment results.

We work with high net worth individuals, and their advisors, to develop and implement a variety of conservative, proven and effective tax planning techniques. Email us at TaxPlanning@ SterlingFoundations.com to schedule a free, no obligation consultation.

Blog

We publish a weekly blog on a variety of topics of interest to investors, and advisors to investors. To subscribe for free, go to blog.sterlingfoundations.com.

We reserve the right to limit this offer for any reason.